BUILD IT

SMART

300 EASY-TO-BUILD HOME PLANS

INCLUDES HOME BUILDING REFERENCE GUIDE
FIND A BUILDER • MORTGAGE TIPS • PLANNING IDEAS

BUILD IT SMART

Published by Home Planners, LLC
Wholly Owned by Hanley-Wood, LLC
One Thomas Circle, NW, Suite 600
Washington, DC 20005

DISTRIBUTION CENTER
29333 Lorie Lane
Wixom, Michigan 48393

Group Vice President, General Manager, Andrew Schultz
Vice President, Publishing, Jennifer Pearce
Executive Editor, Linda Bellamy
Managing Editor, Jason D. Vaughan
Editor, Nate Ewell
Associate Editor, Simon Hyoun
Senior Plans Merchandiser, Morenci C. Clark
Plans Merchandiser, Nicole Phipps
Proofreader/Copywriter, Dyana Weis
Graphic Artist, Joong Min
Plan Data Team Leader, Ryan Emge
Production Manager, Brenda McClary

Vice President, Retail Sales, Scott Hill
National Sales Manager, Bruce Holmes
Director, Plan Products, Matt Higgins

For direct sales, contact Retail Vision at (800) 381-1288 ext 6053

BIG DESIGNS, INC.
President, Creative Director, Anthony D'Elia
Vice President, Business Manager, Megan D'Elia
Vice President, Design Director, Chris Bonavita
Editorial Director, John Roach
Assistant Editor, Tricia Starkey
Senior Art Director, Stephen Reinfurt
Production Director, David Barbella
Photo Editor, Christine DiVuolo
Art Director, Jessica Hagenbuch
Graphic Designer, Mary Ellen Mulshine
Graphic Designer, Lindsey O'Neill-Myers
Graphic Designer, Jacque Young
Assistant Photo Editor, Brian Wilson
Assistant Production Manager, Rich Fuentes

PHOTO CREDITS

Facing Page Top: Photo by Exposures Unlimited, Ron & Donna Kolb.
Facing Page Bottom: ©1994 Donald A. Gardner, Inc., Photography courtesy of Donald A. Gardner Architects, Inc.
Front Cover Center: ©1993 Donald A. Gardner Architects, Inc., Photography Courtesy
of Donald A. Gardner Architects, Inc. Design HPK0400219. See page 223.
Front Cover Right: Photo by Sam Gray.
Back Cover Center: Photo by Dave Dawson. Design HPK0400006. See page 10.
Back Cover Right: Photo courtesy of William E. Poole Designs Inc., Courtesy of the Islands of Beaufort,
Beaufort, S.C. Design HPK0400021. See page 25.

10 9 8 7 6 5 4 3 2 1

Printed in the United States of America

Library of Congress Control Number: 2004106199

ISBN: 1-931131-30-9

11

BUILD IT SMART

21

contents

reference

ordering information

Welcome Home

Your new home is within reach

Building a new home is one of the most exciting and rewarding projects you can embark on. It's an opportunity to reinvent the place you call home, and to capture the hopes and dreams of you and your family along the way.

In *Build it Smart*, we've made it as easy as possible to realize those dreams. This extensive collection of home plans focuses on efficient designs that provide the most value for your money. With an emphasis on quality living spaces—and not on extravagant rooflines or additional space that will never be used—these designs will deliver exactly what you want from

your new home, without the unnecessary extras that will only add to your mortgage. In addition, they are designed with an eye towards energy efficiency, promising cost savings down the road.

The home-building process can also be a challenging and mysterious one, which is why we've included a 16-page home-builder's reference guide in the back of this book. This comprehensive outline helps lead you through the home-building process, from finding a plan that works for you to selecting your builder. We've also included a number of money-saving tips and expert advice

to insure that the construction of your home goes smoothly.

In short, this book offers everything you need to begin your home-building journey. Not only is it a valuable resource to help you select a plan, with blueprints available for every home, but it offers priceless advice to help you *Build it Smart*. ■

ABOVE: A charming front porch with three dormers above welcome you home to this three-bedroom cottage. Find floor plans and more information for design HPK0400019 on page 23.

plan# HPK0400001

Style: Traditional
First Floor: 1,563 sq. ft.
Second Floor: 772 sq. ft.
Total: 2,335 sq. ft.
Bedrooms: 3
Bathrooms: 2½
Width: 45' - 0"
Depth: 55' - 8"
Foundation: Crawlspace

SEARCH ONLINE @ EPLANS.COM

Graceful, elegant living takes place in this charming cottage, which showcases a stone-and-stucco facade. Inside, the formal dining room features a columned entrance and a tray ceiling; nearby, the kitchen boasts a central island and a bay window. The expansive gathering room includes a fireplace and opens to the covered rear veranda, which extends to a side deck. The master suite, also with a tray ceiling, offers a walk-in closet and lavish private bath. Upstairs, two family bedrooms—both with walk-in closets—share a full bath and the captain's quarters, which opens to a deck.

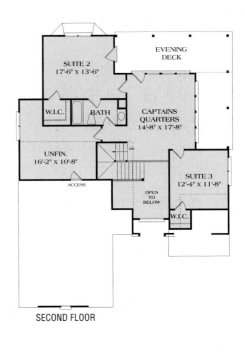

SECOND FLOOR

FIRST FLOOR

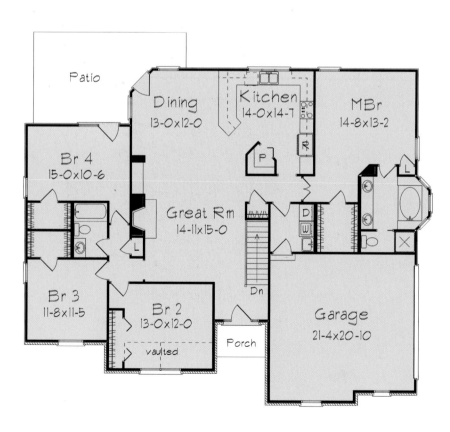

plan⊕# HPK0400002

Style: Traditional
Square Footage: 1,882
Bedrooms: 4
Bathrooms: 2
Width: 58' - 0"
Depth: 47' - 6"
Foundation: Basement

SEARCH ONLINE @ EPLANS.COM

An elegant brick facade and arch-topped windows give this home plenty of curb appeal. Its compact shape and side-loading garage make it perfect for a corner lot. Inside, the great room is enhanced by a fireplace and opens to the rear patio via the dining room. The deluxe master bath is distinguished by the large tub and double-sink vanity, and spacious closets are found in all four bedrooms. The delightful kitchen easily serves the dining area and great room.

plan# HPK0400003

Style: Traditional
First Floor: 716 sq. ft.
Second Floor: 784 sq. ft.
Total: 1,500 sq. ft.
Bedrooms: 3
Bathrooms: 2½
Width: 36' - 0"
Depth: 44' - 0"
Foundation: Crawlspace

SEARCH ONLINE @ EPLANS.COM

A traditional neighborhood look is accented by stone and decorative arches on this stylish new design. Simplicity is the hallmark of this plan, giving the interior great flow and openness. The foyer, with a coat closet, leads directly into the two-story great room with abundant natural light and a warming fireplace. The island kitchen and dining area are to the left and enjoy rear-porch access. Upstairs, a vaulted master suite with a private bath joins two additional bedrooms to complete the plan.

SECOND FLOOR

FIRST FLOOR

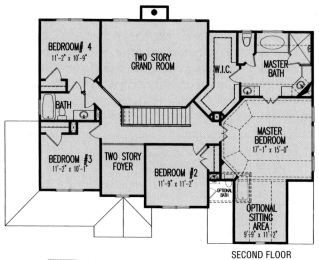

SECOND FLOOR

plan# HPK0400004

Style: Country Cottage
First Floor: 1,417 sq. ft.
Second Floor: 1,169 sq. ft.
Total: 2,586 sq. ft.
Bonus Space: 119 sq. ft.
Bedrooms: 4
Bathrooms: 2½
Width: 52' - 0"
Depth: 43' - 6"
Foundation: Slab, Basement

SEARCH ONLINE @ EPLANS.COM

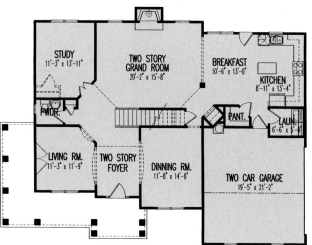

FIRST FLOOR

A wraparound covered porch welcomes you to this efficient two-story home. Inside, the formal rooms open directly off the foyer, and the two-story grand room is toward the rear. A private study is available for home office space. The U-shaped kitchen features a work island and an adjacent breakfast area. Upstairs, three family bedrooms share a full bath and an overlook to the grand room. The deluxe master suite offers a large private bath, huge walk-in closet, and an optional sitting area.

plan# HPK0400005

Style: Neoclassic
First Floor: 1,524 sq. ft.
Second Floor: 558 sq. ft.
Total: 2,082 sq. ft.
Bonus Space: 267 sq. ft.
Bedrooms: 3
Bathrooms: 2½
Width: 60' - 0"
Depth: 50' - 4"
Foundation: Basement

SEARCH ONLINE @ EPLANS.COM

An interesting roofline and multitextured exterior provide a rich, solid look to this extraordinary home. From the foyer, your view will go directly to the cozy fireplace and stylish French doors of the great room. A grand entry into the formal dining room, coupled with the volume ceiling, pulls these two rooms together for a spacious feeling. Natural light floods the breakfast area making this a bright and cheery place to start your day. Split stairs lead to the second floor where a balcony overlooking the foyer directs you to two secluded bedrooms or to a computer area with a desk and bookshelves.

SECOND FLOOR

FIRST FLOOR

Quote One®

Cost to build? See page 333
to order complete cost estimate
to build this house in your area!

SECOND FLOOR

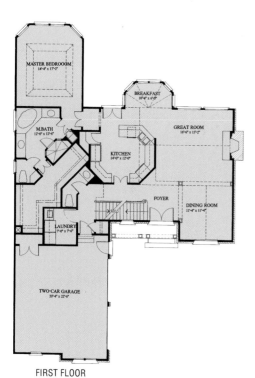

FIRST FLOOR

plan # HPK0400006

Style: Traditional
First Floor: 1,580 sq. ft.
Second Floor: 595 sq. ft.
Total: 2,175 sq. ft.
Bedrooms: 3
Bathrooms: 2½
Width: 50' - 2"
Depth: 70' - 11"
Foundation: Walkout Basement

SEARCH ONLINE @ EPLANS.COM

This home is a true Southern original.
Inside, the spacious foyer leads directly to a large
vaulted great room with its handsome fireplace. The
dining room, just off the foyer, features a dramatic
vaulted ceiling. The spacious kitchen offers both storage and large work areas opening up to the breakfast
room. At the rear of the home, you will find the master suite with its garden tub, His and Hers vanities, and
an oversize closet. The second floor provides two
additional bedrooms with a shared bath and a balcony
overlook to the foyer below.

plan# HPK0400007

Style: Country Cottage
Square Footage: 1,979
Bedrooms: 3
Bathrooms: 2
Width: 67' - 2"
Depth: 44' - 2"
Foundation: Basement

SEARCH ONLINE @ EPLANS.COM

Many fine features mark this one-story country cottage, not least of which are the handsome columns in the front entry and the spacious rear deck. Inside, built-in media centers in the master suite and great room are convenient and attractive. The master suite also boasts a walk-in closet and lavish, amenity-filled bath. The great room, with a corner fireplace, is separated from the kitchen by a curved counter and from the formal dining area by a single column. A handy laundry opens both to the kitchen and the two-car garage.

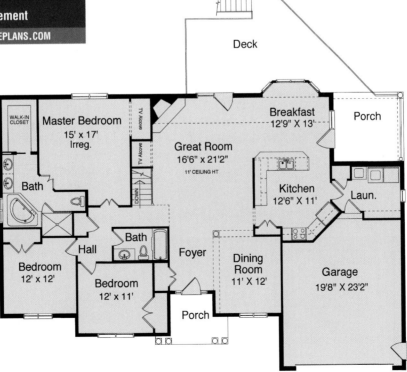

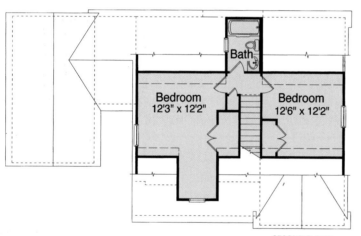

SECOND FLOOR

plan# HPK0400008

Style: Cape Cod
First Floor: 873 sq. ft.
Second Floor: 481 sq. ft.
Total: 1,354 sq. ft.
Bedrooms: 3
Bathrooms: 2
Width: 51' - 6"
Depth: 31' - 8"
Foundation: Basement

SEARCH ONLINE @ EPLANS.COM

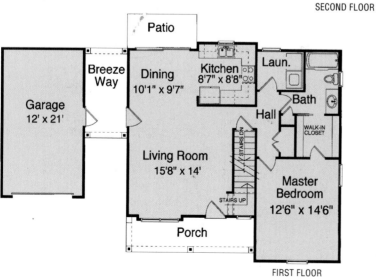

FIRST FLOOR

A siding exterior with a covered porch, gabled roof, and breezeway combine to create a fashionable home. Perfect for full-time family living or as a summer cottage, this 1½-story design offers an open living room and dining area, U-shaped kitchen, separate laundry room, and first-floor master suite. A large sliding glass door provides access from the dining area to the rear yard, offering a favorable indoor/outdoor relationship. Two bedrooms and a full bath are available on the second floor.

plan # HPK0400009

Style: Country Cottage
Square Footage: 1,748
Bonus Space: 303 sq. ft.
Bedrooms: 3
Bathrooms: 2
Width: 55' - 0"
Depth: 55' - 0"
Foundation: Crawlspace, Basement

SEARCH ONLINE @ EPLANS.COM

With down-home style and Revival detailing, this home is sure to be the talk of the neighborhood. Inside, an elongated foyer leads to a vaulted family room, complete with decorative columns and a centerpiece fireplace. Separated for privacy, the master bedroom delights with a tray ceiling, window seat, and a walk-in wardrobe with a separate linen closet. The master bath features a whirlpool tub and walk-in shower. Two family bedrooms are located on the right side of the plan and share a full hall bath. An optional fourth bedroom and bath are available upstairs.

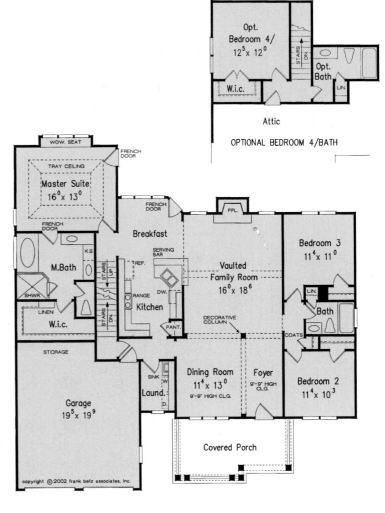

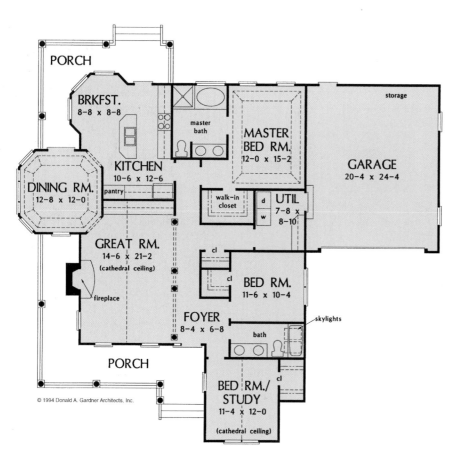

© 1994 Donald A. Gardner Architects, Inc.

plan # HPK0400010

Style: Farmhouse
Square Footage: 1,737
Bedrooms: 3
Bathrooms: 2
Width: 65' - 10"
Depth: 59' - 8"

SEARCH ONLINE @ EPLANS.COM

Inviting porches are just the beginning of this lovely country home. To the left of the foyer, a columned entry supplies a classic touch to a spacious great room that features a cathedral ceiling, built-in bookshelves, and a fireplace that invites you to share its warmth. An octagonal dining room with a tray ceiling provides a perfect setting for formal occasions. The adjacent kitchen is designed to easily serve both formal and informal areas. It includes an island cooktop and a built-in pantry, with the sunny breakfast area just a step away. The master suite, separated from two family bedrooms by the walk-in closet and utility room, offers privacy and comfort.

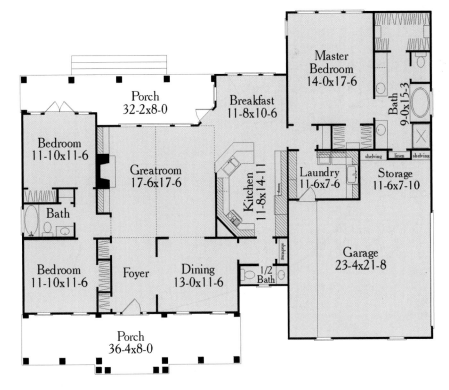

plan# HPK0400011

Style: Traditional
Square Footage: 2,046
Bedrooms: 3
Bathrooms: 2½
Width: 68' - 2"
Depth: 57' - 4"
Foundation: Crawlspace, Slab, Basement

SEARCH ONLINE @ EPLANS.COM

A six-panel door with an arched transom makes an impressive entry. Upon entering the foyer, the formal dining room resides to the right. The great room comes complete with a cozy fireplace and built-ins. On the far left of the home, two bedrooms share a full bath and a linen closet. The kitchen and breakfast room provide ample space for the family to enjoy meals together. The rear porch is also accessible from a rear bedroom and from an angled door between the great room and breakfast room. In the master bedroom, two walk-in closets provide plenty of space, and two separate vanities make dressing less crowded.

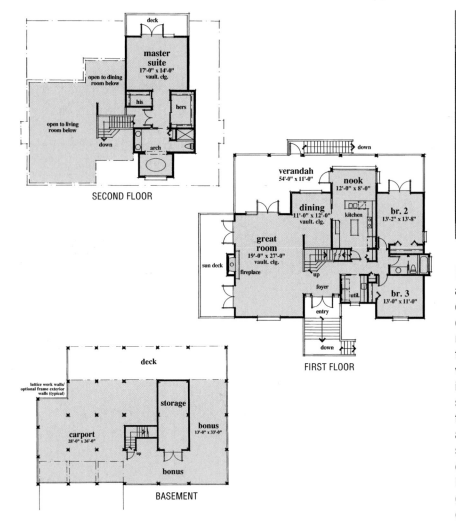

SECOND FLOOR

master suite
17'-0" x 14'-0"
vault. clg.

his

hers

open to dining room below

open to living room below

down

arch

deck

FIRST FLOOR

verandah
54'-0" x 11'-0"

nook
12'-0" x 8'-0"

dining
11'-0" x 12'-0"
vault. clg.

kitchen

br. 2
13'-2" x 13'-8"

great room
19'-0" x 27'-0"
vault. clg.

sun deck

fireplace

up

foyer

util.

br. 3
13'-0" x 11'-0"

entry

down

BASEMENT

deck

lattice work walls/
optional frame exterior
walls (typical)

storage

bonus
13'-0" x 33'-0"

carport
28'-0" x 26'-0"

up

bonus

plan # HPK0400012

Style: Floridian
First Floor: 1,736 sq. ft.
Second Floor: 640 sq. ft.
Total: 2,376 sq. ft.
Bonus Space: 840 sq. ft.
Bedrooms: 3
Bathrooms: 2
Width: 54' - 0"
Depth: 44' - 0"
Foundation: Slab

SEARCH ONLINE @ EPLANS.COM

Lattice door panels, shutters, a balustrade and a metal roof add character to this delightful coastal home. Double doors flanking a fireplace open to the side sundeck from the spacious great room. Access to the rear veranda is also provided from this room. An adjacent dining room provides views of the rear grounds and space for formal and informal entertaining. The glassed-in nook shares space with the L-shaped kitchen containing a center work island. Bedrooms 2 and 3, a full bath, and a utility room complete this floor. Upstairs, a sumptuous master suite awaits. Double doors extend to a private deck from the master bedroom. His and Hers walk-in closets lead the way to a grand bath featuring an arched whirlpool tub, a double-bowl vanity, and a separate shower.

plan # HPK0400013

Style: Country Cottage
Square Footage: 1,118
Bedrooms: 2
Bathrooms: 2
Width: 44' - 4"
Depth: 47' - 4"
Foundation: Slab

SEARCH ONLINE @ EPLANS.COM

Compact and perfect for starters or empty-nesters, this is a wonderful single-level home. The beautiful facade is supplemented by a stylish and practical covered porch. Just to the left of the entry is a roomy kitchen with bright windows and convenient storage. The octagonal dining room shares a three-sided fireplace with the living room. A covered patio to the rear enhances outdoor living. A fine master suite enjoys a grand bath and is complemented by a secondary bedroom and full bath.

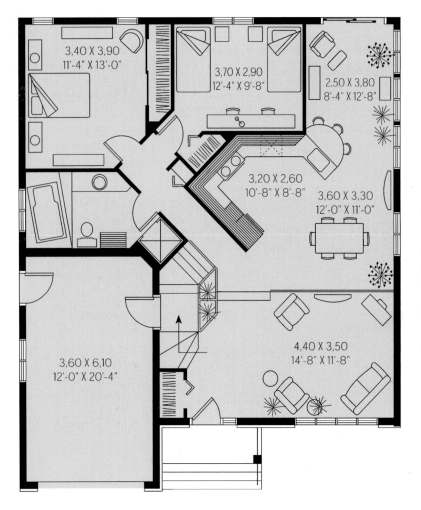

plan # HPK0400014

Style: Contemporary
Square Footage: 1,145
Bedrooms: 2
Bathrooms: 1
Width: 36' - 0"
Depth: 43' - 0"
Foundation: Basement

SEARCH ONLINE @ EPLANS.COM

This brick cottage would fit into any neighborhood and is a darling addition to a narrow space. A coat closet is conveniently located near the front entrance. The living room is creatively set apart from the dining room by a set of short stairs. The open kitchen features a breakfast bar and is within steps of the dining room. A sunroom enjoys the natural light pouring through a wall of windows. Two bedrooms share a full hall bath.

plan # HPK0400015

Style: Traditional
Square Footage: 1,710
Bedrooms: 3
Bathrooms: 2
Width: 53' - 4"
Depth: 54' - 10"

SEARCH ONLINE @ EPLANS.COM

Comfort awaits you in this appealing ranch home. Inside, a formal dining room features elegant ceiling details. The volume great room is designed for daily family gatherings with a raised-hearth fireplace flanked by sparkling windows. Outdoor access and a lazy Susan are thoughtful details designed into the kitchen and bowed dinette. For added flexibility, two secondary bedrooms can be easily converted to a sunroom with French doors, and an optional den. The secluded master suite is enhanced by a boxed ceiling and deluxe skylit dressing room.

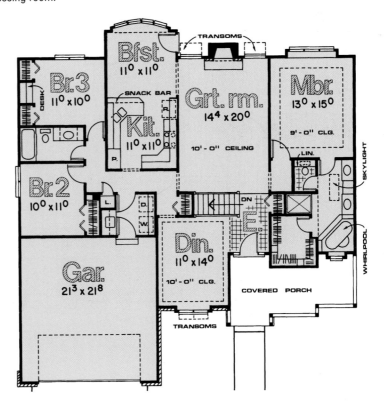

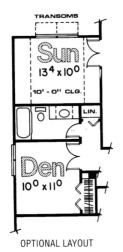

OPTIONAL LAYOUT

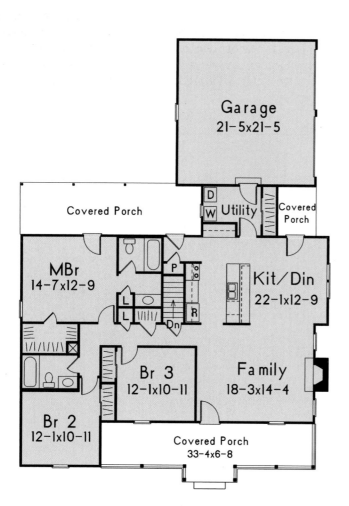

Garage
21-5x21-5

Covered Porch

D
W   Utility   Covered Porch

MBr
14-7x12-9

P

Kit/Din
22-1x12-9

L
L

Dn

R

Br 3
12-1x10-11

Family
18-3x14-4

Br 2
12-1x10-11

Covered Porch
33-4x6-8

plan# HPK0400016

Style: Traditional
Square Footage: 1,501
Bedrooms: 3
Bathrooms: 2
Width: 48' - 0"
Depth: 57' - 4"
Foundation: Crawlspace, Slab, Basement

SEARCH ONLINE @ EPLANS.COM

This ranch-style home provides an inviting front covered porch with rustic accents. Inside, the family room provides a lovely fireplace and is open to a kitchen/dining area that accesses a rear covered porch. Nearby, a utility room leads into the two-car garage. The master bedroom provides spacious views of the rear property and privately accesses the rear covered porch. This bedroom also features a walk-in closet and a full bath with linen storage. Bedrooms 2 and 3 share a full hall bath.

plan # HPK0400017

Style: Farmhouse
Square Footage: 1,787
Bonus Space: 326 sq. ft.
Bedrooms: 3
Bathrooms: 2
Width: 66' - 2"
Depth: 66' - 8"

SEARCH ONLINE @ EPLANS.COM

Cathedral ceilings bring a feeling of spaciousness to this home. The great room features a fireplace, cathedral ceilings, and built-in bookshelves. The kitchen is designed for efficient use with its food preparation island and pantry. The master suite provides a welcome retreat with a cathedral ceiling, a walk-in closet, and a luxurious bath. Two additional bedrooms, one with a walk-in closet, share a skylit bath. A second-floor bonus room is perfect for a study or a play area.

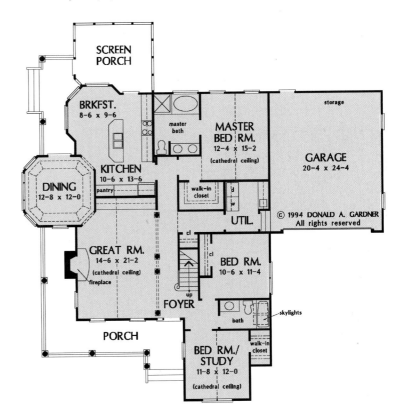

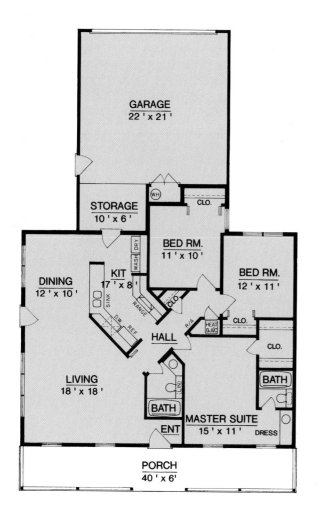

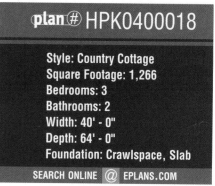

plan # HPK0400018

Style: Country Cottage
Square Footage: 1,266
Bedrooms: 3
Bathrooms: 2
Width: 40' - 0"
Depth: 64' - 0"
Foundation: Crawlspace, Slab

SEARCH ONLINE @ EPLANS.COM

Elegant columns adorn the front porch
of this plan and give it character. Though small in square footage, this home is designed for gracious living. The living and dining rooms are open and surround a galley-style kitchen with access to the two-car garage and its storage space. Bedrooms are on the right side of the plan and include a master suite and two family bedrooms. The master suite has a private bath with a compartmented tub and toilet. It also features a walk-in closet. Family bedrooms share a full hall bath.

plan # HPK0400019

Style: Country Cottage
First Floor: 1,704 sq. ft.
Second Floor: 734 sq. ft.
Total: 2,438 sq. ft.
Bonus Space: 479 sq. ft.
Bedrooms: 3
Bathrooms: 3½
Width: 50' - 0"
Depth: 82' - 6"
Foundation: Crawlspace

SEARCH ONLINE @ EPLANS.COM

Elegant country—that's one way to describe this attractive three-bedroom home. Inside, comfort is clearly the theme, with the formal dining room flowing into the U-shaped kitchen and casual dining taking place in the sunny breakfast area. The spacious, vaulted great room offers a fireplace and built-ins. The first-floor master suite is complete with a walk-in closet, a whirlpool tub, and a separate shower. Upstairs, the sleeping quarters include two family bedrooms with private baths and walk-in closets.

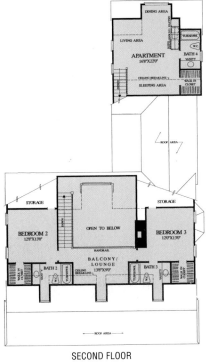

SECOND FLOOR

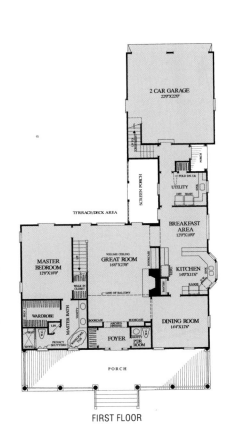

FIRST FLOOR

SECOND FLOOR

plan # HPK0400020

Style: Craftsman
First Floor: 1,896 sq. ft.
Second Floor: 692 sq. ft.
Total: 2,588 sq. ft.
Bedrooms: 3
Bathrooms: 2½
Width: 60' - 0"
Depth: 84' - 10"

SEARCH ONLINE @ EPLANS.COM

This fine three-bedroom home is full of amenities and will surely be a family favorite! A covered porch leads into the great room/dining room. Here, a fireplace reigns at one end, casting its glow throughout the room. A private study is tucked away, perfect for a home office or computer study. The master bedroom suite offers a bayed sitting area, large walk-in closet, and pampering bath. With plenty of counter and cabinet space and an adjacent breakfast area, the kitchen will be a favorite gathering place for casual mealtimes. The family sleeping zone is upstairs and includes two bedrooms, a full bath, a loft/study area, and a huge storage room.

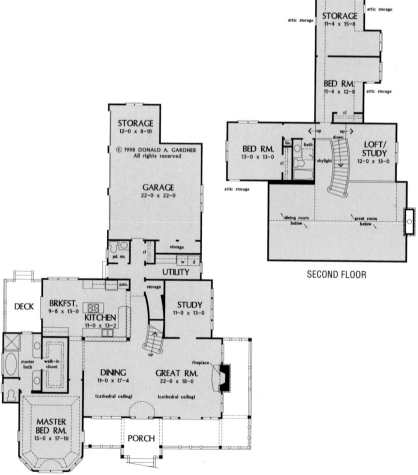

FIRST FLOOR

plan# HPK0400021

Style: Country Cottage
Square Footage: 2,151
Bonus Space: 814 sq. ft.
Bedrooms: 3
Bathrooms: 2
Width: 61' - 0"
Depth: 55' - 8"
Foundation: Crawlspace, Basement

SEARCH ONLINE @ EPLANS.COM

Country flavor is well established on this fine three-bedroom home. The covered front porch welcomes friends and family alike to the foyer, where the formal dining room opens off to the left. The vaulted ceiling in the great room enhances the warmth of the fireplace and wall of windows. An efficient kitchen works well with the bayed breakfast area. The secluded master suite offers a walk-in closet and a lavish bath; on the other side of the home, two family bedrooms share a full bath. Upstairs, an optional fourth bedroom is available for guests or in-laws and provides access to a large recreation room.

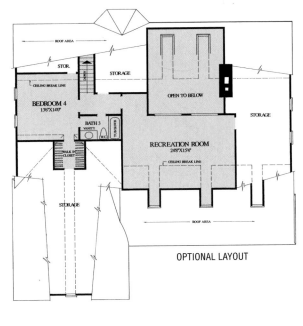

OPTIONAL LAYOUT

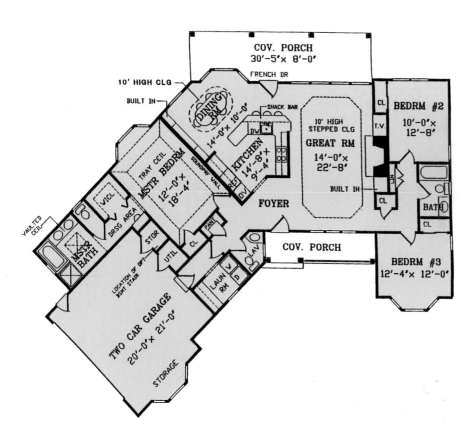

plan # HPK0400022

Style: Country Cottage
Square Footage: 1,709
Bedrooms: 3
Bathrooms: 2½
Width: 70' - 1"
Depth: 60' - 7"
Foundation: Basement, Slab, Crawlspace

SEARCH ONLINE @ EPLANS.COM

This angled, country-style ranch home is designed to fit about any lot. Four bay windows and two dormers distinguish the exterior. A recessed, covered front porch opens to the foyer, which is visually connected to the adjoining great room. The great room features a fireplace and built-ins for media. The great room is a "pavilion-style" area with windows at the front and rear. A dramatic angled kitchen with a snack bar faces the rear porch. A private master suite contains a tray ceiling, a dressing area, two closets, and a compartmented five-fixture bath. Two other bedrooms, one set into an attractive front bay, share a full bath. The unusual-shaped kitchen, which looks out over the covered porch, is easily served by the kitchen. A convenient half-bath is located off the foyer.

plan # HPK0400023

Style: Farmhouse
Square Footage: 1,310
Bedrooms: 3
Bathrooms: 2
Width: 61' - 0"
Depth: 51' - 5"

SEARCH ONLINE @ EPLANS.COM

A multipane bay window, decorative dormers, and a covered porch dress up this one-story cottage. The foyer leads to an impressive great room with a cathedral ceiling and fireplace. The U-shaped kitchen, adjacent to the dining room, provides an ideal layout for food preparation. A large deck offers shelter and admits cheery sunlight through skylights. The luxurious master bedroom, located to the rear of the house, takes advantage of the deck area and is assured privacy from two other bedrooms at the front of the house. These family bedrooms share a full bath.

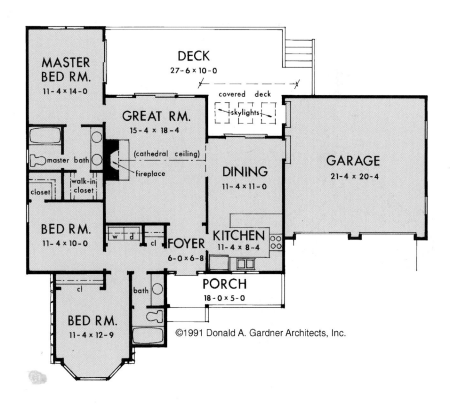

©1991 Donald A. Gardner Architects, Inc.

The large front window highlights the elegance of this home's exterior as well as pours natural light into the cheery and spacious home office, which includes a private entrance, guest bath, two closets, and vaulted ceiling. The delightful great room features a vaulted ceiling, a fireplace, extra storage closets, and patio doors to the sundeck. An extra-large kitchen contains a walk-in pantry, cooktop island, and bay window. The vaulted master suite includes transomed windows, a walk-in closet, and a luxurious bath.

plan# HPK0400025

Style: Traditional
Square Footage: 1,777
Bonus Space: 557 sq. ft.
Bedrooms: 3
Bathrooms: 2
Width: 50' - 0"
Depth: 56' - 0"
Foundation: Basement

A roomy front porch gives this home a country flavor, and the expansive rear view offers plenty of windows. The vaulted great room boasts a fireplace, TV alcove, pass-through snack bar to the kitchen, an atrium with a bay window, and a stairway to the lower-level family room. The kitchen is conveniently located between the formal dining area, which overlooks the rear deck, and the breakfast alcove. It also boasts a walk-in pantry. The oversize master bedroom features a vaulted ceiling, double-entry doors, and a large walk-in closet.

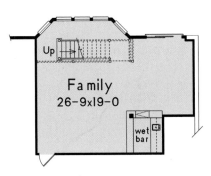

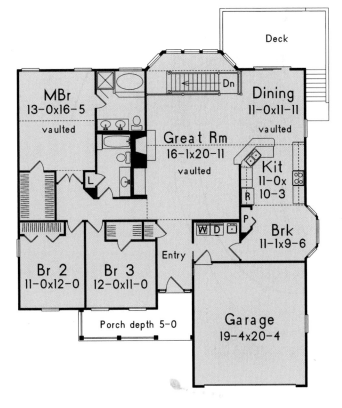

A stylish stucco exterior enhances this home's curb appeal. A sunken great room offers a corner fireplace flanked by wide patio doors. A well-designed kitchen features an ideal view of the great room and fireplace through the breakfast-bar opening. The rear patio offers plenty of outdoor entertaining and relaxing space. The master suite features a private bath and walk-in closet. The master bath contains dual vanities, and the two family bedrooms each access baths. A spacious two-car garage completes this plan.

plan# HPK0400026

Style: SW Contemporary
Square Footage: 1,712
Bedrooms: 3
Bathrooms: 2½
Width: 67' - 0"
Depth: 42' - 4"
Foundation: Crawlspace

SEARCH ONLINE @ EPLANS.COM

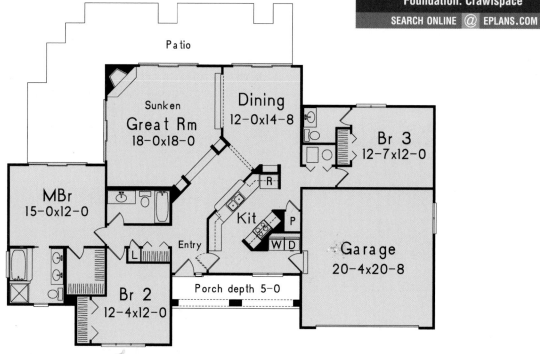

plan# HPK0400027

Style: Seaside
First Floor: 731 sq. ft.
Second Floor: 935 sq. ft.
Total: 1,666 sq. ft.
Lookout: 138 sq. ft.
Bedrooms: 3
Bathrooms: 3
Width: 35' - 0"
Depth: 38' - 0"
Foundation: Pier

SEARCH ONLINE @ EPLANS.COM

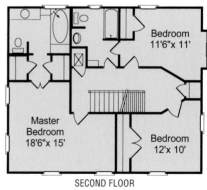

Look Out
9'x 15'

This pier-foundation home has an abundance of amenities to offer, not the least being the loft lookout. Inside, the living room is complete with a corner gas fireplace. The spacious kitchen features a cooktop island, an adjacent breakfast nook, and easy access to the dining room. From this room, a set of French doors leads out to a small deck—perfect for dining alfresco. Upstairs, the sleeping zone consists of two family bedrooms sharing a full hall bath, and a deluxe master suite. Amenities in this suite include two walk-in closets and a private bath.

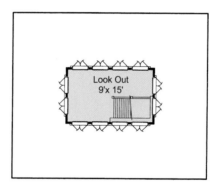

Deck

Dining
9'x 13'8"

Living
14'x 19'

Screen
Porch

FIRST FLOOR

Bedroom
11'6"x 11'

Master
Bedroom
18'6"x 15'

Bedroom
12'x 10'

SECOND FLOOR

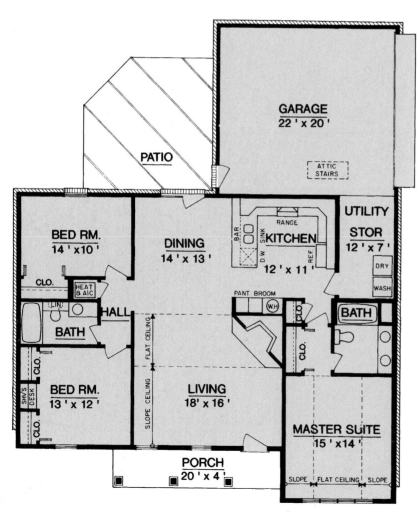

plan# HPK0400028

Style: Traditional
Square Footage: 1,380
Bedrooms: 3
Bathrooms: 2
Width: 46' - 0"
Depth: 56' - 0"
Foundation: Crawlspace, Slab

SEARCH ONLINE @ EPLANS.COM

A Palladian window set in a stucco facade under a hipped roof lends a gracious charm to this three-bedroom home. The welcoming front porch leads to a living room featuring a corner fireplace. The U-shaped kitchen opens directly to the dining room and its patio access. A utility/storage room connects the two-car garage to the kitchen. This plan splits the master suite from the two family bedrooms on the left for added privacy. Note the dual-sink vanity in the master bath.

plan # HPK0400029

Style: European Cottage
Square Footage: 1,475
Bedrooms: 2
Bathrooms: 2½
Width: 38' - 0"
Depth: 79' - 2"
Foundation: Slab

SEARCH ONLINE @ EPLANS.COM

This quaint cottage-style home is enhanced by country European accents and an amenity-filled interior. Double doors open into a petite welcoming foyer. Double doors from the family room and dining room access the back porch. The kitchen features an efficient storage pantry. A powder room and laundry room are placed just outside of the two-car garage. The master bedroom enjoys a private bath and walk-in closet; Bedroom 2 is located near the hall bath.

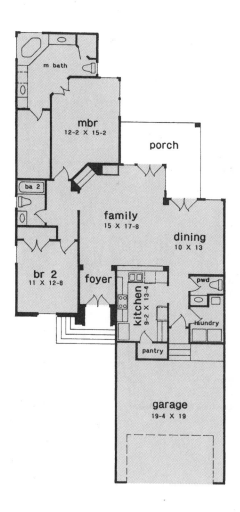

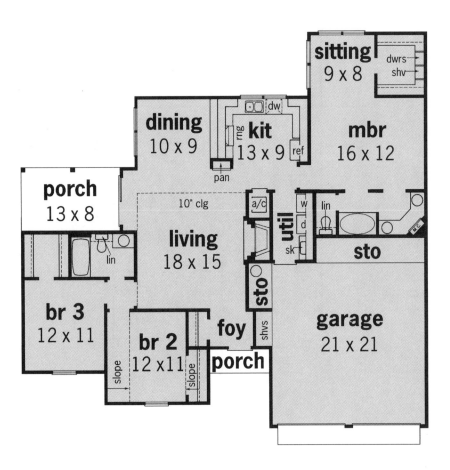

plan# HPK0400030

Style: Traditional
Square Footage: 1,442
Bedrooms: 3
Bathrooms: 2
Width: 54' - 0"
Depth: 50' - 0"
Foundation: Crawlspace, Slab

SEARCH ONLINE @ EPLANS.COM

A French facade accentuates the cozy appeal of this home with corner quoins, shuttered windows, transoms, and a stucco finish. The foyer introduces the spacious and open living room, which flows into the dining room and kitchen. A fireplace warms this area. The U-shaped kitchen features a window sink and a pantry. The kitchen is also within a few steps of the dining area. Two family bedrooms to the left of the plan share a full hall bath. The master bedroom sports a bright sitting bay, a walk-in closet with built-ins, and a roomy bath.

This delightful traditional home offers a pleasant facade with nested gables, shuttered windows, a covered porch, and a fireplace in profile. Enter the vaulted family room and you are immediately greeted by the spaciousness, the enchanting fireplace, and the multitude of windows. To the rear, the U-shaped kitchen adjoins the dining room for efficiency and practicality. The central hallway leads to the two family bedrooms and full bath as well as the master suite with its tray ceiling, two walk-in closets, and vaulted private bath.

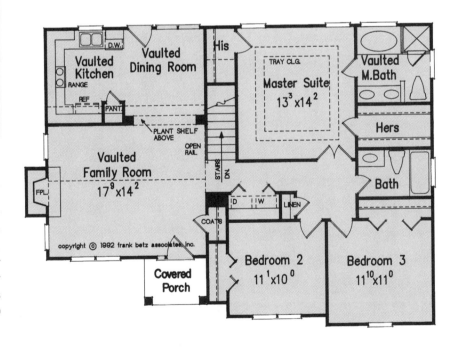

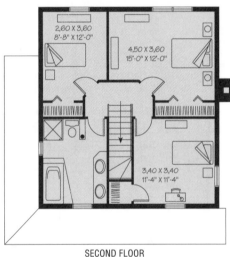

SECOND FLOOR

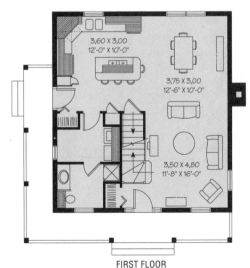

FIRST FLOOR

plan# HPK0400032

Style: Colonial
First Floor: 728 sq. ft.
Second Floor: 728 sq. ft.
Total: 1,456 sq. ft.
Bedrooms: 3
Bathrooms: 2
Width: 26' - 0"
Depth: 28' - 0"
Foundation: Basement

SEARCH ONLINE @ EPLANS.COM

This classic plan offers exceptional curb appeal with a wraparound porch, set off with decorative columns and a glass-paneled entry. Inside, the foyer provides a convenient coat closet and leads to an open living area. A double window allows sunlight to brighten the formal dining space. The well-equipped kitchen includes a food-preparation island with a snack counter. A service area offers access to the wraparound porch and to a laundry and powder room. Upstairs, sleeping quarters include three spacious bedrooms and a full bath with a dual vanity.

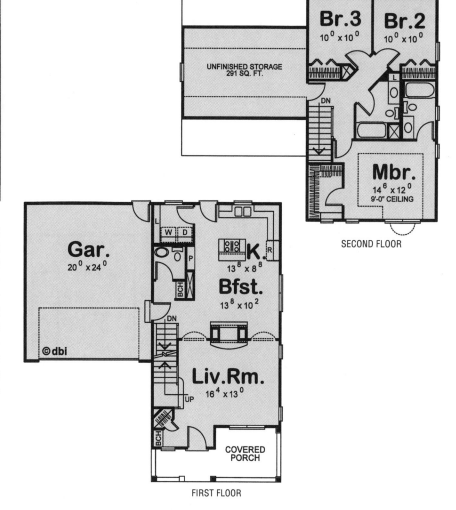

plan# HPK0400033

Style: Farmhouse
First Floor: 762 sq. ft.
Second Floor: 691 sq. ft.
Total: 1,453 sq. ft.
Bedrooms: 3
Bathrooms: 2½
Width: 41' - 4"
Depth: 43' - 0"

SEARCH ONLINE @ EPLANS.COM

This charming country home has an alluring street presence, with a wide covered porch and a lovely second-story Palladian window. Enter to find a foyer with a coat closet and a bench; the living room opens from here with a two-sided fireplace and archways to the rear. The fireplace can be viewed from the open cooktop-island kitchen and warms the breakfast nook. Upstairs, the master suite enjoys a private bath, as two secondary bedrooms share a full bath. Storage space abounds with plenty of room for seasonal equipment and childhood memorabilia.

SECOND FLOOR

FIRST FLOOR

This plan starts with a two-story foyer that opens to a family room with a fireplace and windows overlooking the rear yard. Just off the foyer, a vestibule provides a coat closet and a convenient powder room. The dining room leads to the gourmet kitchen, which includes a pantry and a serving bar. Upstairs, sleeping quarters include two family bedrooms sharing a full bath, and a master suite with a tray ceiling, a vaulted bath, and a walk-in closet.

plan# HPK0400034

Style: Traditional
First Floor: 637 sq. ft.
Second Floor: 730 sq. ft.
Total: 1,367 sq. ft.
Bedrooms: 3
Bathrooms: 2½
Width: 37' - 6"
Depth: 34' - 0"
Foundation: Crawlspace, Basement

SEARCH ONLINE @ EPLANS.COM

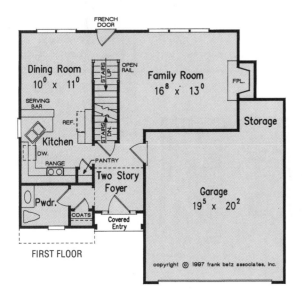

FIRST FLOOR

copyright © 1997 frank betz associates, inc.

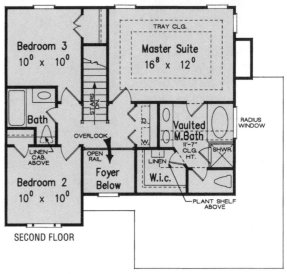

SECOND FLOOR

plan# HPK0400035

Style: Chateau Style
First Floor: 704 sq. ft.
Second Floor: 704 sq. ft.
Total: 1,408 sq. ft.
Bedrooms: 3
Bathrooms: 1½
Width: 38' - 0"
Depth: 32' - 0"
Foundation: Basement

SEARCH ONLINE @ EPLANS.COM

This sharp-looking European design features a charming air reminiscent of Old World cottages. Many Chateau-style features, such as stonework and hipped rooflines, enhance the exterior. An enclosed entryway keeps the home warm. Double doors open into a bay-windowed family room—great for receiving visitors. The snack-bar kitchen is open to the dining area, and a laundry/powder room is just steps away. The large garage completes the first floor. Upstairs, the master bedroom enjoys bayed front-yard views and shares a hall bath with two additional bedrooms.

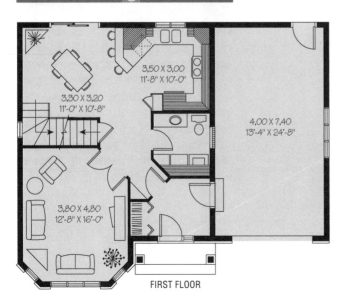

FIRST FLOOR

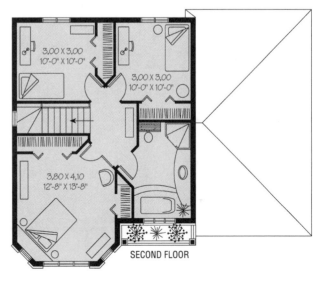

SECOND FLOOR

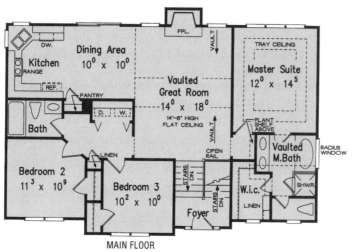

MAIN FLOOR

Dining Area 10⁰ x 10⁰
Kitchen
RANGE
REF.
DW.
PANTRY
Bath
D. W.
FPL.
VAULT
Vaulted Great Room 14⁰ x 18⁰
14'-6" HIGH FLAT CEILING
VAULT
OPEN RAIL
LINEN
Bedroom 2 11³ x 10⁹
STAIRS DN
Bedroom 3 10² x 10⁰
Foyer
STAIRS DN
TRAY CEILING
Master Suite 12⁰ x 14⁵
PLANT SHELF ABOVE
VAULT
Vaulted M.Bath
RADIUS WINDOW
W.i.c.
LINEN
SHWR

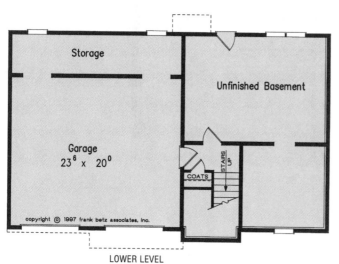

LOWER LEVEL

Storage
Unfinished Basement
Garage 23⁶ x 20⁰
STAIRS UP
COATS
copyright © 1997 frank betz associates, inc.

plan # **HPK0400036**

Style: Country Cottage
Main Level: 1,249 sq. ft.
Lower-level Entry: 46 sq. ft.
Total: 1,295 sq. ft.
Bedrooms: 3
Bathrooms: 2
Width: 45' - 0"
Depth: 31' - 4"
Foundation: Basement

SEARCH ONLINE @ EPLANS.COM

With a double garage and unfinished basement space on the lower level, this design lives like a one-story home, but has the space of two levels. A vaulted great room features a fireplace flanked by windows. The U-shaped kitchen features a large dining area and a corner window sink. Bedrooms are split for privacy, with the master suite to the right of the great room and family bedrooms to the left. Note the many pampering amenities in the master suite.

plan# HPK0400037

Style: Traditional
First Floor: 756 sq. ft.
Second Floor: 676 sq. ft.
Total: 1,432 sq. ft.
Bedrooms: 3
Bathrooms: 2
Width: 38' - 8"
Depth: 32' - 0"
Foundation: Basement

SEARCH ONLINE @ EPLANS.COM

Traditional style doesn't have to mean ordinary, as this country home beautifully proves. Enter through French doors to the elegant foyer, spacious enough for a small chair and entry table. This area also serves as a functional mudroom as you continue to the bright, airy family room. Ample space in the kitchen accommodates multiple cooks, and formal or casual dining options suit any occasion. Bedrooms are located upstairs, along with a majestic spa bath.

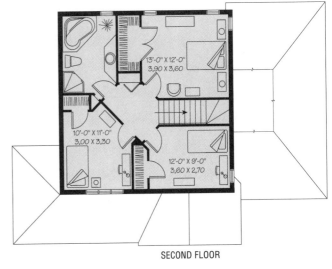

SECOND FLOOR

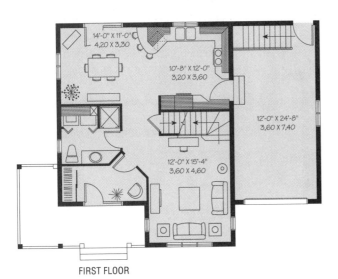

FIRST FLOOR

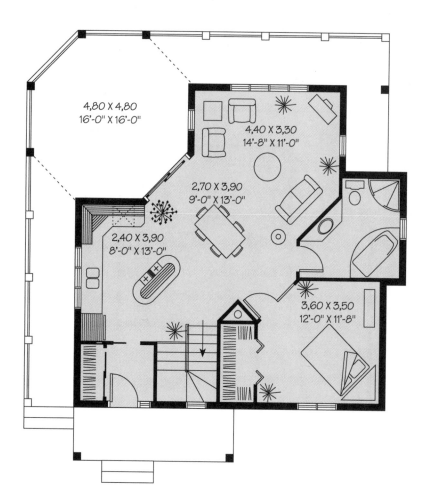

plan # HPK0400038

Style: Victorian
Square Footage: 840
Bedrooms: 1
Bathrooms: 1
Width: 33' - 0"
Depth: 31' - 0"
Foundation: Basement

SEARCH ONLINE @ EPLANS.COM

This charming home is ideal for waterfront property with a generous wraparound porch. The porch features a corner gazebo that's perfect for outdoor living. The vestibule offers an energy- and space-efficient pocket door that opens to the island kitchen and dining room where sliding glass doors open to the gazebo. The living room views in three directions, bringing the outside in. A bedroom and lavish bath complete the floor plan.

plan# HPK0400039

Style: Resort Lifestyles
First Floor: 895 sq. ft.
Second Floor: 576 sq. ft.
Total: 1,471 sq. ft.
Bedrooms: 3
Bathrooms: 2
Width: 26' - 0"
Depth: 36' - 0"
Foundation: Basement

SEARCH ONLINE @ EPLANS.COM

This vacation home enjoys a screened porch and sits on stilts to avoid any water damage. Truly a free-flowing plan, the dining room, living room, and kitchen share a common space, with no walls separating them. An island snack counter in the kitchen provides plenty of space for food preparation. A family bedroom and full bath complete the first level. Upstairs, two additional bedrooms—with ample closet space—share a lavish bath, which includes a whirlpool tub and separate shower.

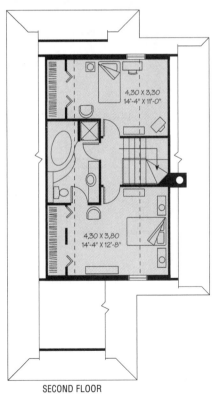

SECOND FLOOR

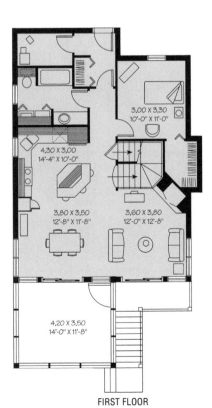

FIRST FLOOR

SECOND FLOOR

FIRST FLOOR

plan# HPK0400040

Style: Cottage
First Floor: 918 sq. ft.
Second Floor: 532 sq. ft.
Total: 1,450 sq. ft.
Bedrooms: 3
Bathrooms: 2
Width: 26' - 4"
Depth: 37' - 0"
Foundation: Basement

SEARCH ONLINE @ EPLANS.COM

Nature enthusiasts are right at home in this engaging two-story home with expansive views and a delightful sunroom. The enclosed vestibule opens to the spacious living/dining room where sunlight abounds. The adjoining, U-shaped island kitchen has access to the angular sunroom for casual yet visually stimulating dining. The utility room is tucked away behind the stairs with the full bath. One bedroom is found on the first floor, and two additional bedrooms share a full bath on the second floor.

plan# HPK0400041

Style: Traditional
Square Footage: 1,185
Bedrooms: 3
Bathrooms: 2
Width: 50' - 0"
Depth: 47' - 4"
Foundation: Basement

SEARCH ONLINE @ EPLANS.COM

Stone accents, gables, and shutters make this traditional/country classic home very charming. The elaborate kitchen features a serving bar, pantry, eating area and access to the washer and dryer. The great room boasts a vaulted ceiling, warming fireplace, built-in plant shelves, and access to the covered side porch. Two family bedrooms and a master suite occupy the right side of the home. The master suite enjoys a tray ceiling, a walk-in closet, and a complete master bath with a vaulted ceiling and an oval garden tub. The two-car garage offers storage space.

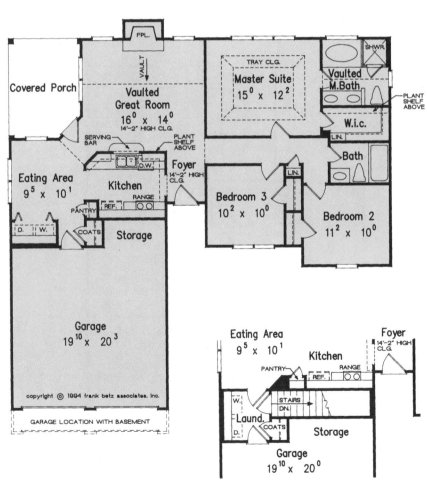

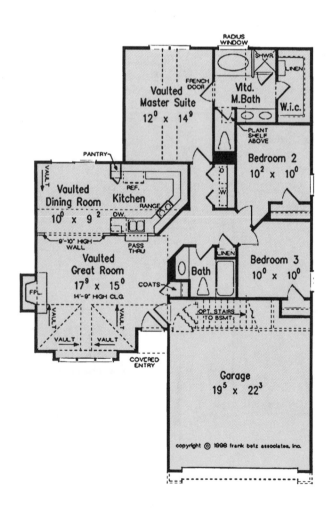

plan# HPK0400042

Style: Country Cottage
Square Footage: 1,209
Bedrooms: 3
Bathrooms: 2
Width: 40' - 0"
Depth: 55' - 6"
Foundation: Crawlspace, Basement

SEARCH ONLINE @ EPLANS.COM

With a box-bay window and stylish siding, this narrow-lot plan is a great choice for a first home or retirement cottage. Enter into the vaulted family room for an impressive presentation. With a pass-through to the kitchen and an extended-hearth fireplace, this room is sure to be a favorite. Follow a short hallway to two family bedrooms— or make one an office—and a vaulted master suite with a pampering bath.

plan # HPK0400043

Style: Ranch
Square Footage: 1,218
Bedrooms: 3
Bathrooms: 2
Width: 54' - 0"
Depth: 36' - 4"
Foundation: Basement

SEARCH ONLINE @ EPLANS.COM

The timeless appeal of western ranch style is scaled down for an affordable home that is sure to please. A covered entry leads to the vaulted great room; rear windows bring in natural light to enhance the feeling of spaciousness. To the left, the dining area, with sliding glass doors to the rear property, flows effortlessly into the kitchen. The sleeping quarters are arranged thoughtfully: the master suite (with a private bath) is to the rear to shelter it from street noise, and two family bedrooms are situated to share a full bath.

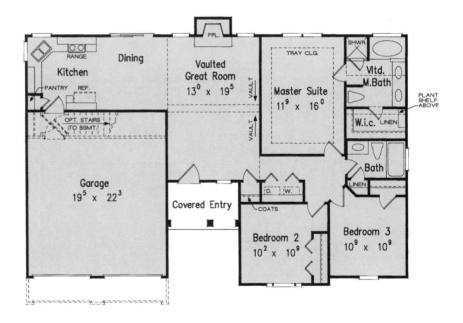

This striking brick home will immediately impress you with its ceilings. A 14-foot-high vaulted ceiling rises above the great room, which, with its warming fireplace, will be the center of all entertaining; the master suite enjoys a majestic tray ceiling. A handy serving bar separates the kitchen from the formal dining area, which opens to the great room. In addition to the lavish master suite, two other bedrooms share a bath. Additional space is available above the garage to build a fourth bedroom.

plan# HPK0400044

Style: Traditional
Square Footage: 1,342
Bonus Space: 350 sq. ft.
Bedrooms: 3
Bathrooms: 2
Width: 52' - 6"
Depth: 39' - 10"
Foundation: Crawlspace, Slab, Basement

SEARCH ONLINE @ EPLANS.COM

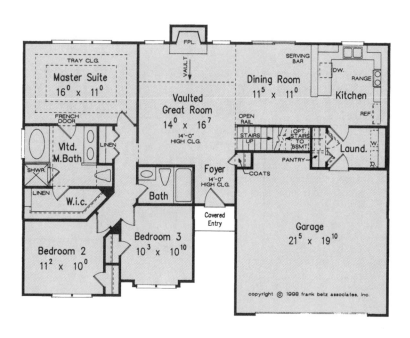

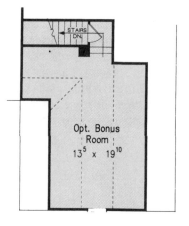

plan# HPK0400045

Style: Traditional
Square Footage: 1,215
Bedrooms: 3
Bathrooms: 2
Width: 40' - 0"
Depth: 49' - 0"
Foundation: Crawlspace, Slab, Basement

SEARCH ONLINE @ EPLANS.COM

This cozy one-story plan offers much more living space than it might appear from the outside. On the right, three bedrooms, including a deluxe master suite, provide ample sleeping room. The left side of the home is organized flexibly, with free-flowing space between the kitchen, dining area, and vault-ceiling family room. The plan comes with a two-car garage and plenty of storage space.

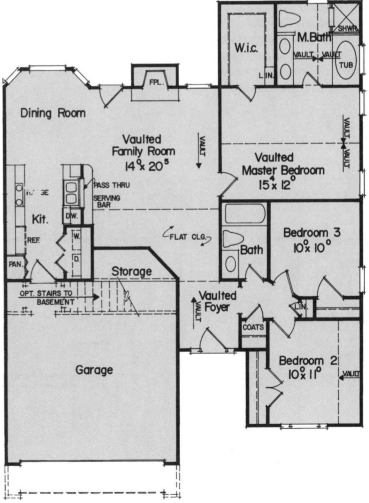

© 1997   Donald A Gardner Architects, Inc.

There's not a bit of wasted space in this cozy, well-designed home. Sunburst windows decorate the exterior and fill the interior with light. Double columns lend elegance to the foyer, which opens to a spacious great room with a cathedral ceiling, a fireplace, and access to the rear porch. The formal dining room features a bay window that offers wide views of the property. Split sleeping quarters include a master suite with a walk-in closet, oversized shower, and garden tub, as well as two secondary bedrooms that share a full bath.

plan# HPK0400046

Style: Traditional
Square Footage: 1,488
Bonus Space: 338 sq. ft.
Bedrooms: 3
Bathrooms: 2
Width: 69' - 7"
Depth: 42' - 0"

SEARCH ONLINE @ EPLANS.COM

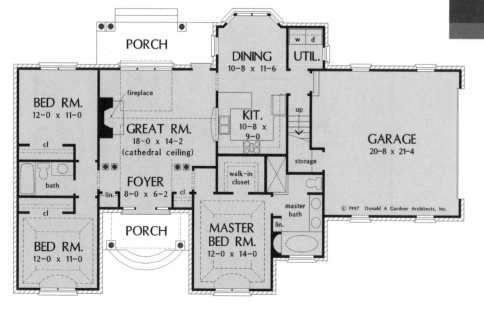

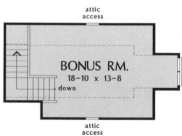

ORDER BLUEPRINTS 24 HOURS, 7 DAYS A WEEK, AT 1-800-521-6797

©2000 Donald A. Gardner, Inc.

plan# HPK0400047

Style: Country
Square Footage: 1,399
Bonus Space: 296 sq. ft.
Bedrooms: 3
Bathrooms: 2
Width: 58' - 0"
Depth: 44' - 4"

SEARCH ONLINE @ EPLANS.COM

Open gables, a covered porch, and shuttered windows bring out the country flavor of this three-bedroom home. Inside, the great room enjoys a cathedral ceiling and a fireplace. Decorative columns set off the formal dining room, which is only steps away from the well-outfitted kitchen. Here, a window sink, a pantry, and a cooktop island overlooking the great room make an ideal food-preparation environment. Two family bedrooms located to the right of the plan share a full bath. The secluded master suite is highlighted by dual vanities, a compartmented shower and toilet, separate tub, walk-in closet, and cathedral ceiling.

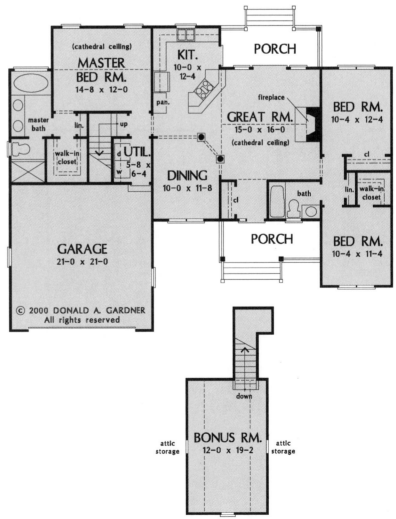

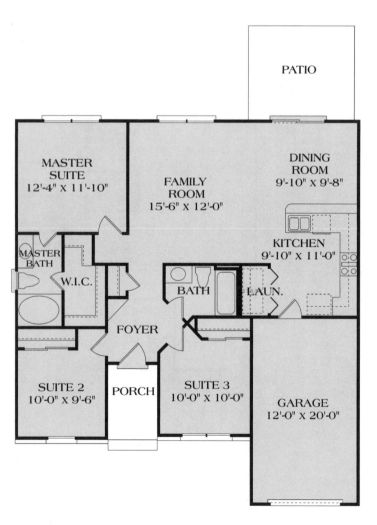

PATIO

MASTER SUITE
12'-4" x 11'-10"

FAMILY ROOM
15'-6" x 12'-0"

DINING ROOM
9'-10" x 9'-8"

MASTER BATH

W.I.C.

KITCHEN
9'-10" x 11'-0"

BATH

LAUN.

FOYER

SUITE 2
10'-0" x 9'-6"

PORCH

SUITE 3
10'-0" x 10'-0"

GARAGE
12'-0" x 20'-0"

plan # HPK0400048

Style: Transitional
Square Footage: 1,151
Bedrooms: 3
Bathrooms: 2
Width: 39' - 3"
Depth: 42' - 1"
Foundation: Slab

SEARCH ONLINE @ EPLANS.COM

With brick, wood, and siding, this home will captivate interest right away. An efficient layout reveals two family bedrooms—or use one as a study—at the front of the home; the master suite is tucked at the rear for privacy. The master bath will soothe and revitalize, and the large walk-in closet is sure to please. The family room opens to the dining room, with easy access to the open kitchen. The convenient laundry room is hidden in one wall of the kitchen.

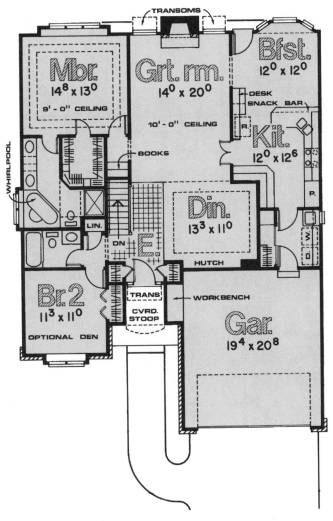

plan # HPK0400049

Style: Traditional
Square Footage: 1,499
Bedrooms: 2
Bathrooms: 2
Width: 42' - 0"
Depth: 54' - 0"

SEARCH ONLINE @ EPLANS.COM

A pleasant mix of materials, shapes, and textures creates an eye-catching facade. A practical use of space is demonstrated by two closets flanking the entry. An optional den/bedroom provides design flexibility. In the lofty great room, windows surround a fireplace. Double doors separate the kitchen from the great room. The master suite features a deluxe bath with a sloped ceiling and plant shelves above an open shower.

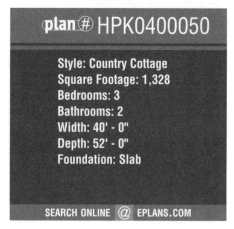

plan# HPK0400050

Style: Country Cottage
Square Footage: 1,328
Bedrooms: 3
Bathrooms: 2
Width: 40' - 0"
Depth: 52' - 0"
Foundation: Slab

SEARCH ONLINE @ EPLANS.COM

This compact home has a lot more packed inside its walls than it might appear from the outside. It enjoys three bedrooms, one of them an amenity-filled master suite; two baths; a well-equipped laundry; and a two-car garage. The grand room, with a warming fireplace, soars two stories high to a vaulted ceiling. It easily opens to the kitchen and a breakfast nook, which opens to a rear deck or patio.

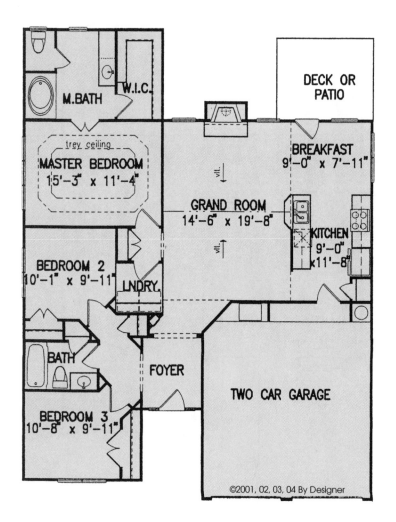

©2001, 02, 03, 04 By Designer

plan # HPK0400051

Style: Country Cottage
Square Footage: 1,477
Bonus Space: 283 sq. ft.
Bedrooms: 3
Bathrooms: 2
Width: 51' - 0"
Depth: 51' - 4"
Foundation: Crawlspace, Basement

SEARCH ONLINE @ EPLANS.COM

This adorable three-bedroom home will provide a pleasant atmosphere for your family. The communal living areas reside on the left side of the plan. The L-shaped kitchen includes a serving bar, which opens to the dining area. The vaulted family room features a fireplace and leads to the sleeping quarters. A master suite and vaulted master bath will pamper homeowners. Two family bedrooms reside across the hall and share a full hall bath. Upstairs, an optional fourth bedroom and full bath are perfect for guests.

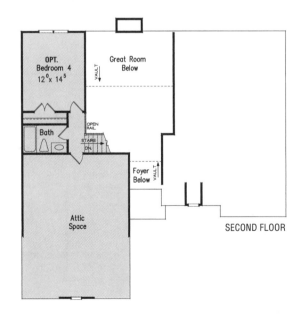

SECOND FLOOR

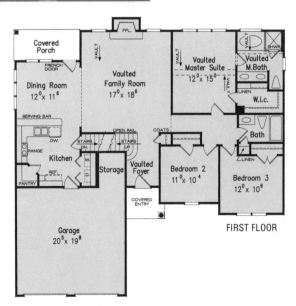

FIRST FLOOR

A comfortable front porch welcomes all to this darling country home. Inside, open spaces and minimal hallways create an illusion of a much larger home. The entry has a convenient coat closet and opens to the gracious living room. Continue through an arch to the dining area and social kitchen, designed to keep conversation flowing. The master suite is a private haven with its own bath and walk-in closet; two bedrooms share a full bath nearby—perfect for young children. Extra storage in the two-car garage is a thoughtful touch.

plan # HPK0400052

Style: Traditional
Square Footage: 1,342
Bedrooms: 3
Bathrooms: 2
Width: 57' - 0"
Depth: 45' - 0"
Foundation: Basement

SEARCH ONLINE @ EPLANS.COM

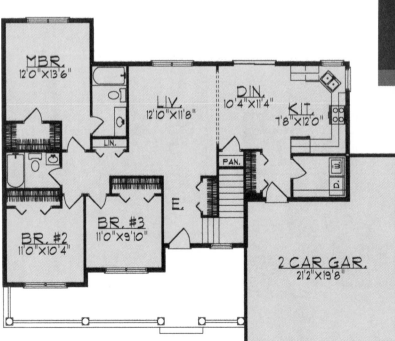

plan # HPK0400053

Style: Contemporary
Square Footage: 1,321
Bedrooms: 3
Bathrooms: 1
Width: 36' - 0"
Depth: 40' - 0"
Foundation: Basement

SEARCH ONLINE @ EPLANS.COM

This stylish contemporary design will work well for an active family. Three bedrooms—two with walk-in closets—share a bath with a shower and tub. The living room and dining area flow together, allowing great versatility in organizing the space. The kitchen is set up so that the cook can reach most everything without difficulty; an ample pantry is conveniently nearby. Off the foyer, which is entered from a small covered porch, is a handy coat closet.

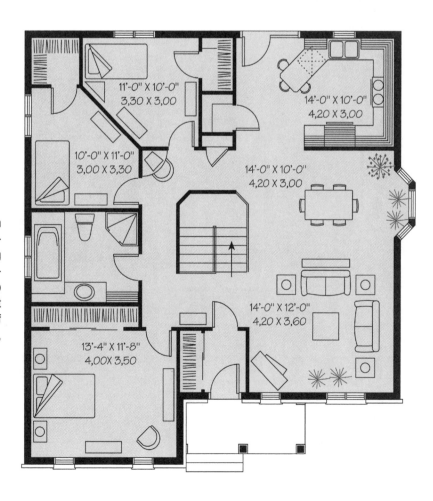

11'-0" X 10'-0"
3,30 X 3,00

14'-0" X 10'-0"
4,20 X 3,00

10'-0" X 11'-0"
3,00 X 3,30

14'-0" X 10'-0"
4,20 X 3,00

14'-0" X 12'-0"
4,20 X 3,60

13'-4" X 11'-8"
4,00 X 3,50

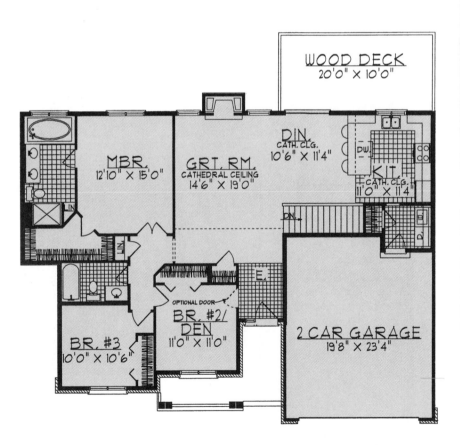

plan # HPK0400054

Style: Traditional
Square Footage: 1,461
Bedrooms: 3
Bathrooms: 2
Width: 56' - 0"
Depth: 42' - 0"
Foundation: Basement

SEARCH ONLINE @ EPLANS.COM

The combination of brick and siding creates a very pleasing exterior. The great room, which includes a fireplace, is the heart of the home. The U-shaped kitchen features a snack bar, and a nearby dining room accesses the wood deck in the backyard. Two family rooms share a full hall bath and a hall linen closet. The master bedroom boasts a large walk-in closet and a private bath with a tub and separate shower.

plan ⊕ HPK0400055

Style: Transitional
Square Footage: 1,151
Bedrooms: 3
Bathrooms: 2
Width: 39' - 2"
Depth: 42' - 5"
Foundation: Slab

SEARCH ONLINE @ EPLANS.COM

This petite home, with a country-style siding exterior, packs a lot of living space into its efficient floor plan. Two family bedrooms, both with easy access to a full bath, flank the foyer; the master suite to the rear of the home features a private bath and large walk-in closet. Family living areas consist of a family room, a kitchen with an adjacent laundry area, and a dining room that opens to the patio.

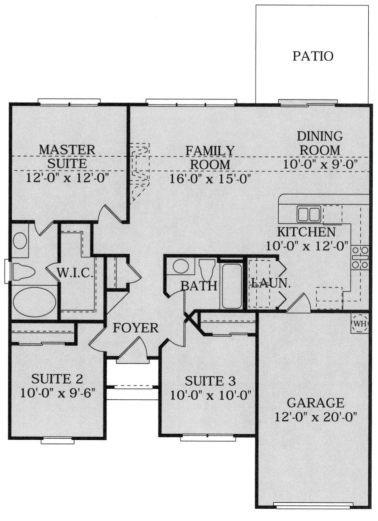

ALTERNATE EXTERIORS

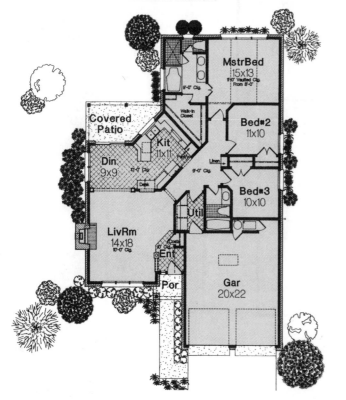

plan # HPK0400056

Style: Traditional
Square Footage: 1,405
Bedrooms: 3
Bathrooms: 2
Width: 40' - 0"
Depth: 60' - 8"
Foundation: Slab

SEARCH ONLINE @ EPLANS.COM

This traditional brick home flaunts a touch of European flavor with its corner quoins. It also presents great curb appeal from the wide muntin window to the sidelight and transom in the entry. The spacious living room includes a warming fireplace. The dining room and U-shaped kitchen are connected by the snack bar and easily access a covered patio. Two family bedrooms reside along the extended hallway. At the end of the hall is the master bedroom, which presents a deluxe private bath and a walk-in closet. The utility room acts as a passage to the two-car garage.

plan # HPK0400057

Style: Bungalow
Square Footage: 1,319
Bedrooms: 3
Bathrooms: 2
Width: 44' - 0"
Depth: 54' - 8"
Foundation: Crawlspace, Basement

SEARCH ONLINE @ EPLANS.COM

Charming and economical to build, this brick ranch design is ideal for first-time homeowners or retirement couples. A tiled foyer leads past the open-rail basement stairs to a vaulted great room. Here a gas fireplace warms the living and entertaining area. The dining room has buffet space and sliding glass doors to the rear deck. A nearby L-shaped island kitchen overlooks the rear deck. Sleeping quarters include two family bedrooms that share a full bath. A two-car garage sits in front of the bedrooms to shelter them from street noise.

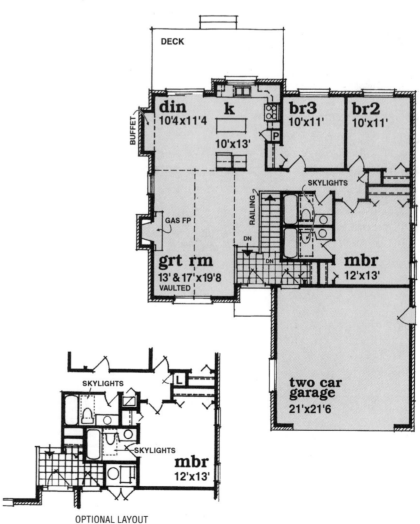

OPTIONAL LAYOUT

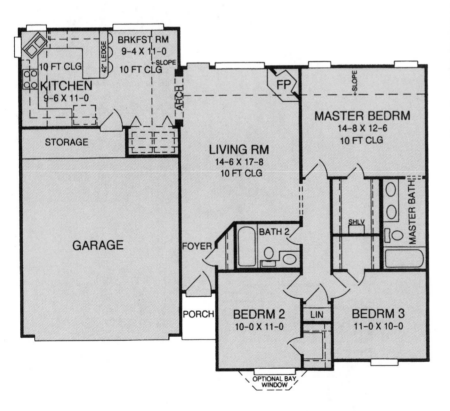

plan⊕ HPK0400058

Style: Traditional
Square Footage: 1,310
Bedrooms: 3
Bathrooms: 2
Width: 49' - 10"
Depth: 40' - 6"
Foundation: Slab, Crawlspace

SEARCH ONLINE @ EPLANS.COM

This charming plan is perfect for families just starting out or for the empty-nester looking to pare down. Every room is designed for maximum livability, from the living room with a corner fireplace to the efficient kitchen with a snack bar and hidden washer and dryer. The master bedroom is fashioned with a dual-vanity bath and a walk-in closet equipped with shelves. Two additional bedrooms each have a walk-in closet and share a hall bath.

plan # HPK0400059

Style: Traditional
Square Footage: 1,282
Bedrooms: 3
Bathrooms: 2
Width: 48' - 10"
Depth: 52' - 6"
Foundation: Crawlspace, Slab

SEARCH ONLINE @ EPLANS.COM

Brick detailing and corner quoins lend charm to this traditional exterior. Inside, a graceful arch announces the living room, complete with a fireplace and a French door to the back property. The angled kitchen is conveniently positioned to offer service to the dining room, and provides a snack counter for easy meals. Split sleeping quarters offer a private wing to the sumptuous master suite, which has a bath with twin-sink vanity.

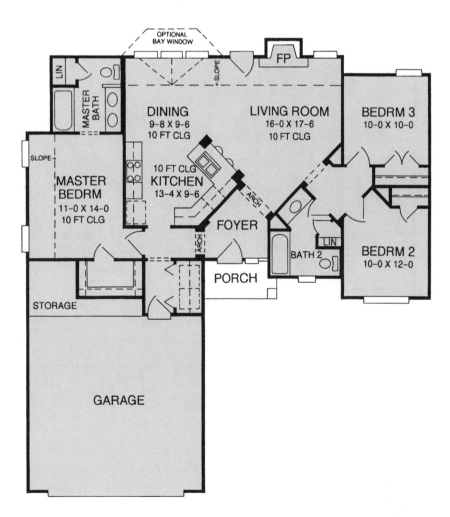

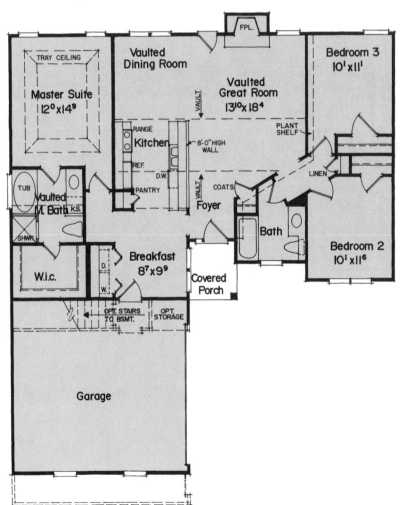

plan# HPK0400060

Style: Traditional
Square Footage: 1,289
Bedrooms: 3
Bathrooms: 2
Width: 46' - 0"
Depth: 52' - 4"
Foundation: Basement, Crawlspace, Slab

SEARCH ONLINE @ EPLANS.COM

The multiple gables, arched picture window, and shutters give this charming home great curb appeal. The foyer leads directly into the vaulted great room, which contains a warming fireplace framed by a window and a door to the backyard. Air flow is at a maximum in the main living area, with a low kitchen wall and open ceiling between the dining room, great room, kitchen, and breakfast area. The galley kitchen has plenty of counter space. A private master suite with tray ceiling has a luxurious bath—complete with a garden tub, shower, and large walk-in closet. On the opposite side of the house are Bedrooms 2 and 3, which share a full bath.

plan# HPK0400061

Style: Country Cottage
Square Footage: 1,432
Bedrooms: 3
Bathrooms: 2
Width: 49' - 0"
Depth: 52' - 4"
Foundation: Crawlspace, Basement, Slab

SEARCH ONLINE @ EPLANS.COM

The beauty of this home lies in its simple yet efficient design and all its extras. Decorative touches include plant shelves, arched openings, and vaulted ceilings. The well-equipped kitchen enjoys a pass-through to the great room, very handy for social get-togethers. It also boasts a walk-in pantry. A tray ceiling, walk-in closet, resplendent bath with a separate glass shower and oval tub add splendor to the master suite. The two secondary bedrooms are secluded on the other side of the plan.

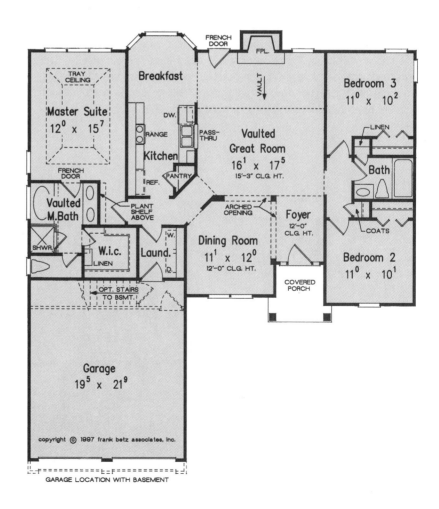

Build on a narrow lot with this plan—it's only 37 feet wide. But that doesn't affect the classic floor plan at all. The recessed entry opens to a tiled hall with a stairway to the basement at one end and kitchen at the other. Straight ahead are the living and dining areas, which combine to form one large, open space. A warm hearth is the focus at one end. Bedrooms are just down a short hallway. Bedroom 3 has a walk-in closet and shares a full bath with Bedroom 2. The master bedroom also contains a walk-in closet but has its own private bath. A laundry room with space for a washer and dryer and a utility closet sits close to the bedrooms for convenience. The two-car garage accesses the main house at the entry hall.

plan# HPK0400062

Style: Ranch
Square Footage: 1,342
Bedrooms: 3
Bathrooms: 2
Width: 37' - 0"
Depth: 59' - 4"
Foundation: Basement

SEARCH ONLINE @ EPLANS.COM

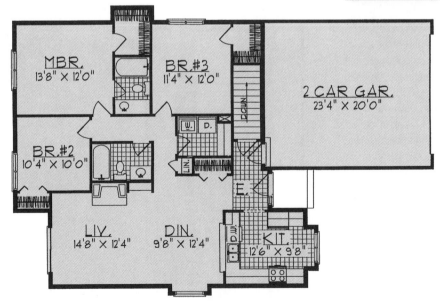

MBR.
13'8" X 12'0"

BR.#3
11'4" X 12'0"

2 CAR GAR.
23'4" X 20'0"

BR.#2
10'4" X 10'0"

LIV.
14'8" X 12'4"

DIN.
9'8" X 12'4"

KIT.
12'6" X 9'8"

plan# HPK0400063

Style: Traditional
Square Footage: 993
Bedrooms: 3
Bathrooms: 2
Width: 57' - 0"
Depth: 30' - 0"
Foundation: Crawlspace, Slab, Basement

SEARCH ONLINE @ EPLANS.COM

Cozy and refined, this home boasts a distinguished pediment, window shutters, and lintels. Within, a vaulted family room—fireplace included—greets you and leads further into the kitchen and dining area. The kitchen is graced with a door that leads to storage space directly off the garage. The dining room has a vaulted ceiling and rear-door access. The master suite is unique with its tray ceiling and His and Hers walk-in closets. Bedrooms 2 and 3 share a full bath and sport front-facing windows.

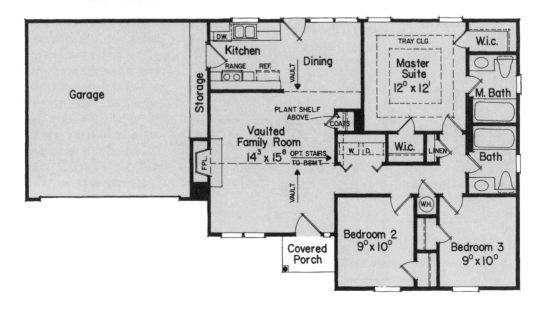

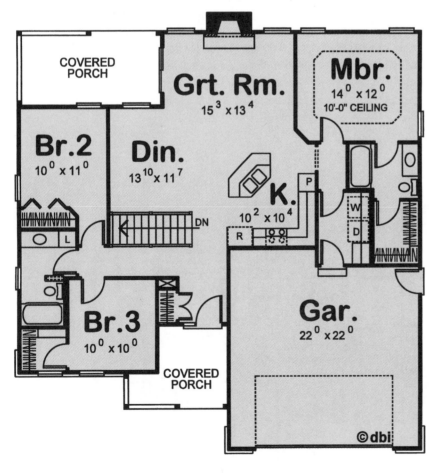

COVERED PORCH

Br.2
10⁰ x 11⁰

Grt. Rm.
15³ x 13⁴

Din.
13¹⁰ x 11⁷

K.
10² x 10⁴

Mbr.
14⁰ x 12⁰
10'-0" CEILING

DN

Br.3
10⁰ x 10⁰

COVERED PORCH

Gar.
22⁰ x 22⁰

©dbi

plan # HPK0400064

Style: Traditional
Square Footage: 1,333
Bedrooms: 3
Bathrooms: 2
Width: 47' - 0"
Depth: 47' - 0"

SEARCH ONLINE @ EPLANS.COM

This home combines an airy floor plan with an uncluttered traditional facade. Space is optimized with the great room, dining room, and kitchen flowing together in one open area, yet each remains distinct. Two family bedrooms—each with its own closet—reside to the left, sharing a full hall bath. The master suite, accented with a tray ceiling, is secluded to the right for privacy. The master bath opens into a walk-in closet. Washer-and-dryer space makes the most of the garage entry, and porches front and back bring the outdoors in.

plan # HPK0400065

Style: Traditional
Square Footage: 1,208
Bedrooms: 3
Bathrooms: 2
Width: 48' - 0"
Depth: 29' - 0"
Foundation: Basement

SEARCH ONLINE @ EPLANS.COM

Here is a rustic cottage that provides plenty of amenities. An open interior takes full advantage of outdoor views and allows flexible space. The family room boasts a fireplace and vistas that extend to the rear property. The dining room features a double window and French-door access to the sundeck. Wrapping counters in the kitchen provide plenty of space for food preparation. The master suite provides a compartmented bath, front-property views, and two wardrobes. The secondary bedrooms share a hall with linen storage.

This stellar single-story symmetrical home offers plenty of living space for any family. The front porch and rear deck make outdoor entertaining delightful. The living and dining rooms are open and spacious for family gatherings. A well-organized kitchen with an abundance of cabinetry and a built-in pantry completes the functional plan. Three bedrooms reside on the left side of the plan.

plan# HPK0400066

Style: Traditional
Square Footage: 1,140
Bedrooms: 3
Bathrooms: 2
Width: 44' - 0"
Depth: 27' - 0"
Foundation: Basement

SEARCH ONLINE @ EPLANS.COM

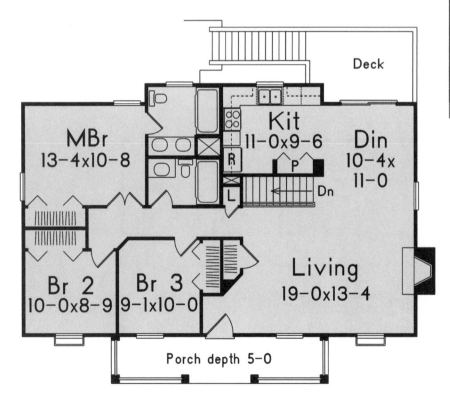

Deck

Kit
11-0x9-6

Din
10-4x
11-0

Dn

MBr
13-4x10-8

R

P

L

Living
19-0x13-4

Br 2
10-0x8-9

Br 3
9-1x10-0

Porch depth 5-0

plan# HPK0400067

Style: Traditional
Square Footage: 1,400
Bedrooms: 3
Bathrooms: 2
Width: 72' - 0"
Depth: 28' - 0"
Foundation: Crawlspace, Basement

SEARCH ONLINE @ EPLANS.COM

Twin bay windows, an elegant Palladian window, and corner quoins help create symmetry to this spectacular Southern home. The formal dining room and living room are filled with natural light from their bay windows. The more casual family room also enjoys wonderful views with its generous window wall. The island kitchen serves both the dining room and the breakfast nook with ease and efficiency. Three bedrooms and a full bath join the lavish master suite on the second floor where the master bedroom delights with a tray ceiling. A second staircase leads from the kitchen to the second-floor utility room. A bonus room over the two-car garage offers an option for future development.

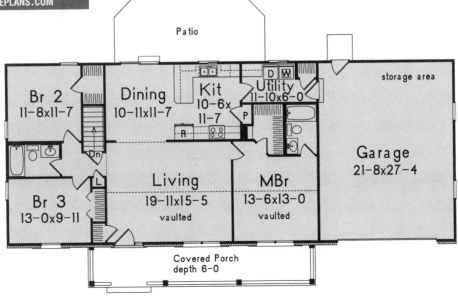

ALTERNATE EXTERIOR

plan# HPK0400068

Style: Transitional
Square Footage: 1,383
Bedrooms: 3
Bathrooms: 2
Width: 50' - 0"
Depth: 39' - 0"
Foundation: Basement, Crawlspace, Slab

SEARCH ONLINE @ EPLANS.COM

Three attractive gables, arch-topped windows, and a covered porch add tons of charm to this fine ranch home. Inside, a vaulted ceiling in the great room and high glass windows on the rear wall combine to create an open, spacious feel. An open dining room sits just off the great room. The ample kitchen layout features a built-in pantry and easy access to the dining room. A generous walk-in closet is found in the master suite, along with a pampering bath. Two secondary suites share a hall bath.

plan# HPK0400069

Style: Traditional
Square Footage: 1,501
Bedrooms: 3
Bathrooms: 2
Width: 48' - 0"
Depth: 66' - 0"
Foundation: Crawlspace,
Basement, Slab

SEARCH ONLINE @ EPLANS.COM

Quaint and pleasing, this ideal design offers versatility. The covered porch provides homeowners with the opportunity to take pleasure in the rising sun or the starry night. Inside, the family room features a fireplace and is open to the kitchen and dining area. The master bedroom includes its own walk-in closet, a private bath, and access to the rear covered porch. Two family bedrooms share a full hall bath and a hall linen closet. The two car-garage entry is located in the utility room.

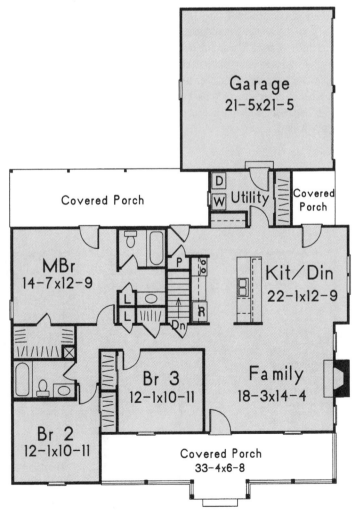

Traditional in every respect, this one-story features shutters, a covered entry, and horizontal siding on the exterior. Its interior is introduced by a tiled entry leading to a formal living room with fireplace on the right and a formal dining room—separated from the entry by a three-foot wall—on the left. Ahead is a convenient coat closet and the large U-shaped kitchen with work island and ample counter space. An attached breakfast nook overlooks the rear yard. The laundry area holds a half bath and access to the two-car garage. The master bedroom is gigantic and has a walk-in closet and bath with soaking tub. Family bedrooms feature wall closets and share the use of a full main bath.

plan # HPK0400070

Style: Bungalow
Square Footage: 1,553
Bedrooms: 3
Bathrooms: 2½
Width: 76' - 0"
Depth: 33' - 0"
Foundation: Basement

SEARCH ONLINE @ EPLANS.COM

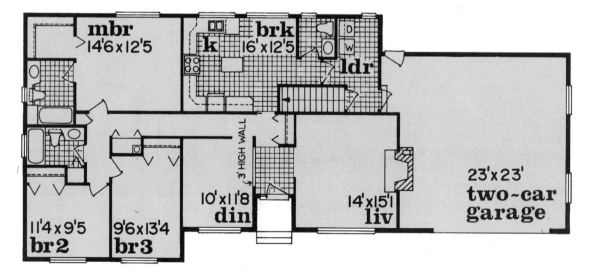

mbr 14'6 x 12'5

k

brk 16' x 12'5

D W

ldr

3' HIGH WALL

11'4 x 9'5 br2

9'6 x 13'4 br3

10' x 11'8 din

14' x 15'1 liv

23' x 23' two~car garage

plan# HPK0400071

Style: Country Cottage
Square Footage: 852 / 852
Bedrooms: 2 / 2
Bathrooms: 1 / 1
Width: 76' - 0"
Depth: 37' - 0"
Foundation: Basement

SEARCH ONLINE @ EPLANS.COM

This country cottage home is a charming and efficient duplex design, economical for any young family. Planter boxes and two covered front porches add a touch of quaint country decor to the exterior. The living room connects to the kitchen, which includes a pantry and a sunny bay window. Access to the single-car garage and the rear patio are conveniently placed nearby. The master bedroom, which features a walk-in closet, and Bedroom 2 share a full hall bath and a hall linen closet.

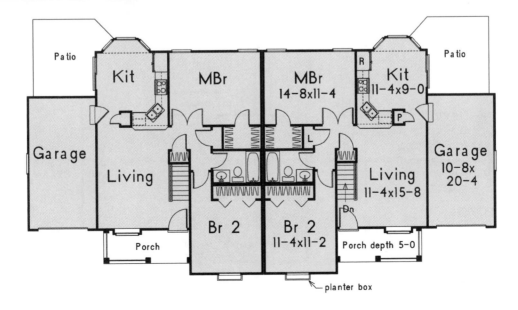

© 1997 Donald A. Gardner Architects, Inc.

A classic country exterior enriches the appearance of this economical home. A grand front porch and two skylit back porches encourage weekend relaxation. The great room features a cathedral ceiling and a fireplace with adjacent built-ins. The master suite enjoys a double-door entry, back-porch access, and a tray ceiling. The master bath has a garden tub set in the corner, a separate shower, twin vanities, and a skylight. Loads of storage, an open floor plan, and walls of windows make this three-bedroom plan very livable.

plan # HPK0400072

Style: Country Cottage
Square Footage: 1,652
Bonus Space: 367 sq. ft.
Bedrooms: 3
Bathrooms: 2
Width: 64' - 4"
Depth: 51' - 0"

SEARCH ONLINE @ EPLANS.COM

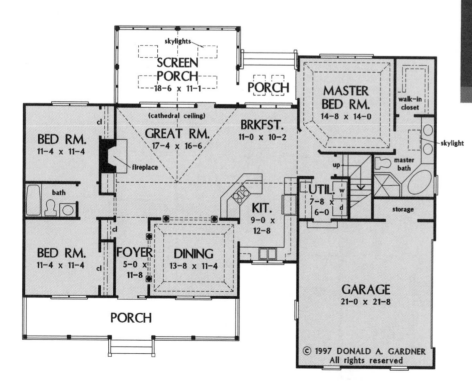

© 1997 DONALD A. GARDNER
All rights reserved

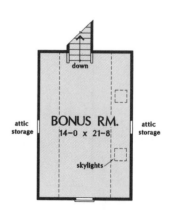

COPYRIGHT LARRY E. BELK

HOLZHAUER INC.

plan # HPK0400073

Style: Traditional
Square Footage: 1,504
Bedrooms: 3
Bathrooms: 2
Width: 55' - 2"
Depth: 46' - 10"
Foundation: Crawlspace, Slab

SEARCH ONLINE @ EPLANS.COM

A sunburst-window motif runs the length of this pretty, contemporary home. Enter to find wonderful ceiling treatments throughout; a coffered ceiling in the great room and vaulted ceilings in the master bedroom and Bedroom 3. Tucked away at the back of the home, the kitchen and dining area allow free movement between rooms for ease of serving. The master suite includes an ample closet and a bath with a tub window. Two additional bedrooms share a hall bath and a convenient hall linen closet. Note the optional covered porch/patio for outdoor fun.

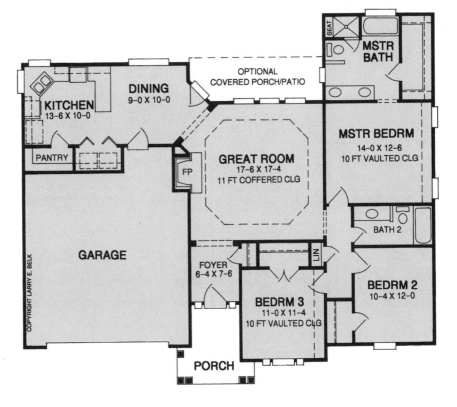

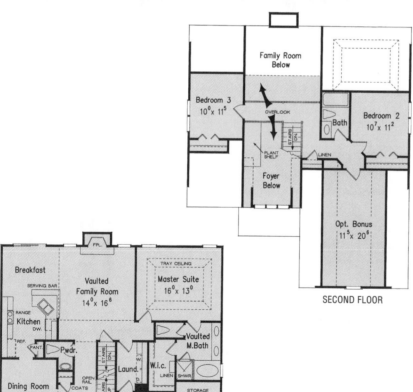

SECOND FLOOR

Family Room Below

Bedroom 3
10^0x 11^5

OVERLOOK

STAIRS DN

PLANT SHELF

Foyer Below

Bath

Bedroom 2
10^7x 11^2

LINEN

Opt. Bonus
11^5x 20^8

Breakfast

FPL.

SERVING BAR

RANGE

Kitchen
DW.

REF.

PANT.

Pwdr.

Vaulted
Family Room
14^0x 16^6

TRAY CEILING

Master Suite
16^0x 13^0

Vaulted
M.Bath

W.i.c.

LINEN SHWR.

STORAGE

Laund.

OPEN RAIL

COATS

STAIRS UP

STAIRS DN

Dining Room
10^0x 11^6

Two Story
Foyer

COVERED
ENTRY

Garage
19^5x 21^9

copyright © 2002 frank betz associates, inc.

FIRST FLOOR

plan# HPK0400074

Style: European Cottage
First Floor: 1,177 sq. ft.
Second Floor: 457 sq. ft.
Total: 1,634 sq. ft.
Bonus Space: 249 sq. ft.
Bedrooms: 3
Bathrooms: 2½
Width: 41' - 0"
Depth: 48' - 4"
Foundation: Crawlspace, Basement

SEARCH ONLINE @ EPLANS.COM

Influenced by Early American architecture, this petite rendition offers all of the amenities you love in a space designed for small lots. A two-story foyer is lit by surrounding sidelights and a multipaned dormer window. The dining room flows conveniently into the efficient kitchen, which opens to the breakfast nook, brightened by sliding glass doors. The vaulted family room is warmed by an extended-hearth fireplace. Past a well-concealed laundry room, the master suite pampers with a vaulted spa bath and immense walk-in closet. Two bedrooms upstairs access future bonus space.

ORDER BLUEPRINTS 24 HOURS, 7 DAYS A WEEK, AT 1-800-521-6797

plan# HPK0400075

Style: Georgian
Square Footage: 1,768
Bonus Space: 347 sq. ft.
Bedrooms: 3
Bathrooms: 2
Width: 54' - 0"
Depth: 59' - 6"
Foundation: Crawlspace, Slab

SEARCH ONLINE @ EPLANS.COM

This attractive Georgian-inspired home incorporates a classic look with modern amenities for a family home that is sure to please. Follow a 14-foot ceiling from the foyer into the great room, where a warming fireplace is framed by radius windows. A creative use of counter space places the kitchen between the dining room, with decorative columns and a box-bay window, and the sunny breakfast nook. Two bedrooms on this side of the home share a full hall bath. On the far left, the master suite reigns. The bedroom is surrounded by luxurious touches, including an octagonal tray ceiling and an arched opening to the sitting room. In the vaulted bath, a garden tub will relax any stress away.

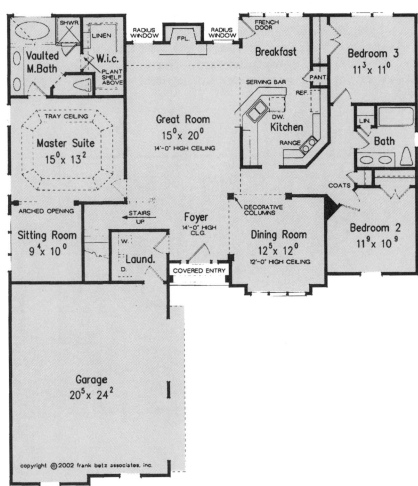

The grand Palladian window lends plenty of curb appeal to this charming home. The wrap-around country porch is perfect for peaceful evenings. The vaulted great room enjoys a large bay window, stone fireplace, pass-through to the kitchen, and awesome rear views through the atrium window wall. The master suite features double entry doors, a walk-in closet, and a fabulous bath. The optional lower level includes a family room.

plan# HPK0400076

Style: Traditional
Square Footage: 1,681
Bonus Space: 415 sq. ft.
Bedrooms: 2
Bathrooms: 2
Width: 55' - 8"
Depth: 46' - 0"
Foundation: Basement

SEARCH ONLINE @ EPLANS.COM

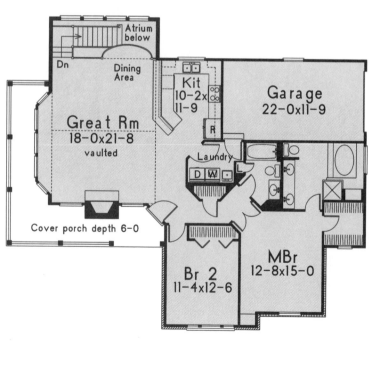

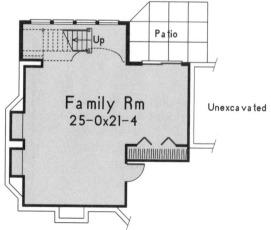

plan# HPK0400077

Style: Traditional
Square Footage: 1,708
Bedrooms: 3
Bathrooms: 2
Width: 80' - 0" '
Depth: 42' - 0"
Foundation: Crawlspace, Basement

SEARCH ONLINE @ EPLANS.COM

The steep side-gabled roof is very distinctive, offering plenty of curb appeal for this one-story home. Outside, the shutters sharply emphasize the windows on all sides of the house. Inside, windows enhance the enormous family room, which enjoys a fireplace and access to the rear porch. The deluxe master bath is accented by the step-up corner tub flanked by double vanities. Spacious closets are found throughout the home.

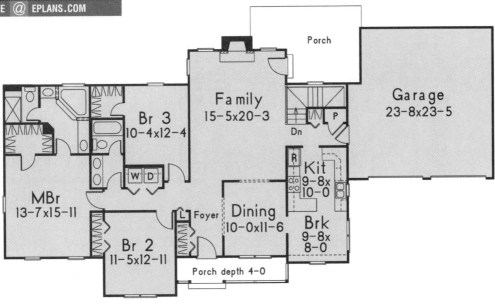

This inviting Colonial-style home will capture your heart with a lovely facade and flowing floor plan. From the foyer and beyond, raised ceilings expand spaces visually. A vaulted great room is warmed by a cozy hearth and opens to the bayed breakfast nook. A serving-bar kitchen helps chefs prepare marvelous meals for any occasion and easily accesses the columned dining room. Tucked to the rear, the vaulted master suite enjoys light from radius windows and the comforts of a pampering spa bath. Two additional bedrooms are located to the far right, near a full bath and laundry room. Bonus space is available for an extra bedroom, study, or play-room—whatever your family desires.

plan# HPK0400078

Style: **Country Cottage**
Square Footage: **1,725**
Bonus Space: **256 sq. ft.**
Bedrooms: **3**
Bathrooms: **2**
Width: **58' - 0"**
Depth: **54' - 6"**
Foundation: **Crawlspace, Basement**

SEARCH ONLINE @ EPLANS.COM

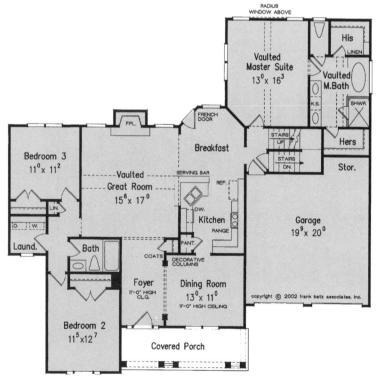

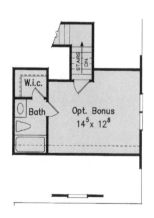

plan # HPK0400079

Style: Traditional
Square Footage: 1,594
Bedrooms: 3
Bathrooms: 2
Width: 52' - 8"
Depth: 55' - 5"
Foundation: Basement

SEARCH ONLINE @ EPLANS.COM

This design is a traditional Western ranch home. A covered porch, split bedrooms, formal and informal dining areas, and sloped ceilings combine to create a delightful home in a moderate square footage. The large island in the kitchen brings definition to the space, and angled windows decorate the eating area. Split bedrooms allow privacy for the master bedroom, which offers a private bath and laundry-room access. Modify one of the family bedrooms into a library to create an exciting option. The open stairway to the full basement allows for easy expansion of the living area.

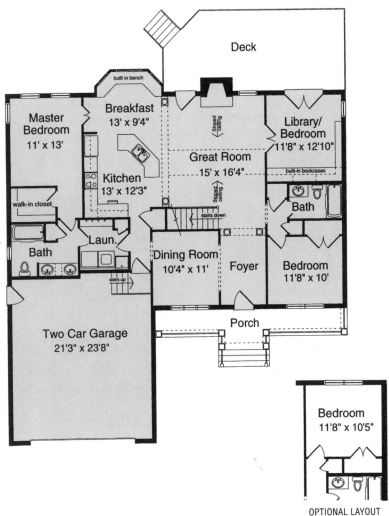

OPTIONAL LAYOUT

© 2002 Donald A. Gardner, Inc.

This smart, traditional plan packs a lot of living space into its modest square footage. A stately columned porch leads to the foyer, which boasts a convenient coat closet to its left. Just ahead, the great room's cathedral ceiling amplifies elegance; its cozy hearth offers the warmth of home. The kitchen features ample counter space and is bookended by a formal dining room and a sunny breakfast nook. The rear deck will provide many seasons of fun and relaxation. Two bedrooms—one that could be converted to a study—share a full bath on the left of the plan. A divine master suite is secluded behind the garage, with a vaulted ceiling, stunning master bath, and walk-in closet. The utility room is convenient to both the kitchen and the garage. Bonus space awaits expansion upstairs.

plan # HPK0400080

Style: Traditional
Square Footage: 1,606
Bonus Space: 338 sq. ft.
Bedrooms: 3
Bathrooms: 2
Width: 50' - 0"
Depth: 54' - 0"

SEARCH ONLINE @ EPLANS.COM

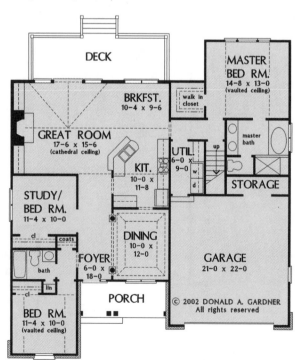

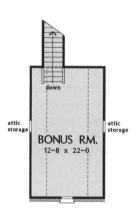

© 2002 Donald A. Gardner, Inc.

plan# HPK0400081

Style: Traditional
Square Footage: 1,711
Bonus Space: 328 sq. ft.
Bedrooms: 3
Bathrooms: 2
Width: 46' - 6"
Depth: 65' - 0"

SEARCH ONLINE @ EPLANS.COM

This striking narrow-lot bungalow features an arched entrance, nostalgic front porch, and hipped roof. A sidelight and fanlight over the front door usher natural light into the home and columns are used to divide space without enclosing it. Featuring a fireplace and built-in cabinetry, the great room accesses both the porch and the dining room. Columns and a tray ceiling define the dining room, which also leads to the side porch through French doors. Above the garage, there is a bonus room for expansion needs. A vaulted ceiling and spacious walk-in closet highlight the master bedroom. The master bath includes a double vanity, garden tub, and separate shower.

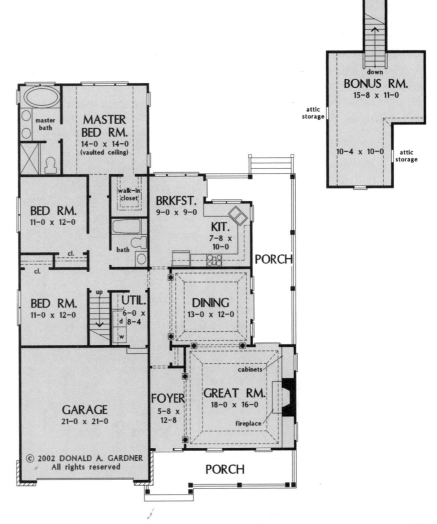

© 2000 Donald A. Gardner, Inc.

Stylish and sensible, this modest-size home makes the most of its square footage and is ready for expansion with a skylit bonus room. Taking the floor plan to new heights is a cathedral ceiling in the great room and tray ceilings in both the dining room and master bedroom. Triplet windows are fashionable additions to the breakfast area and master bedroom, and a box-bay window adds a special touch to the garage. The foyer opens to the great room and dining room for effortless gatherings. A full-size bath is strategically located for easy accessibility from any part of the home. The master suite is a haven, complete with a spacious walk-in closet, His and Her lavatories, a garden tub, and a large shower.

plan # HPK0400082

Style: Traditional
Square Footage: 1,724
Bonus Space: 329 sq. ft.
Bedrooms: 3
Bathrooms: 2
Width: 62' - 4"
Depth: 57' - 10"

SEARCH ONLINE @ EPLANS.COM

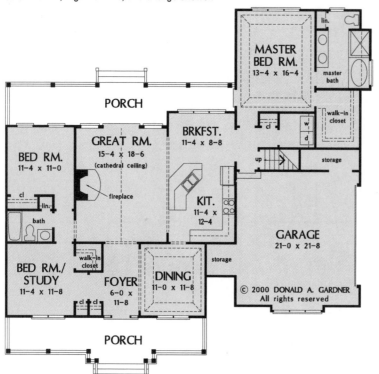

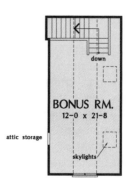

© 2000 Donald A. Gardner, Inc.

B. NATHAN

plan# HPK0400083

Style: Traditional
Square Footage: 1,593
Bonus Space: 332 sq. ft.
Bedrooms: 3
Bathrooms: 2
Width: 50' - 0"
Depth: 54' - 0"

SEARCH ONLINE @ EPLANS.COM

This two- (or three-) bedroom home offers a covered entry and a deck in the rear. The vaulted ceiling in the great room and tray ceiling in the dining room add richness to this charming, indulgent design. The great room, with fireplace and built-ins, features rear-deck access. The arch in the master bedroom's tray ceiling tops a triple window; note the shower seat in the master bath.

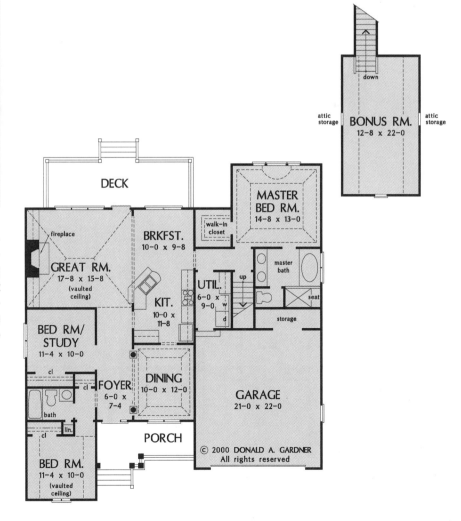

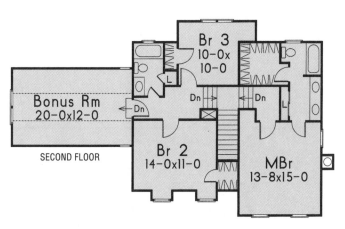

Bonus Rm
20-0x12-0

SECOND FLOOR

Br 3
10-0x
10-0

Dn

Dn

Br 2
14-0x11-0

MBr
13-8x15-0

plan# HPK0400084

Style: Colonial
First Floor: 878 sq. ft.
Second Floor: 822 sq. ft.
Total: 1,700 sq. ft.
Bonus Space: 240 sq. ft.
Bedrooms: 3
Bathrooms: 2½
Width: 53' - 0"
Depth: 31' - 0"
Foundation: Basement,
Crawlspace

SEARCH ONLINE @ EPLANS.COM

Three gable ends add interest to the hipped roof of this Southern-style farmhouse where a front covered porch and a rear deck expand the living spaces to the outdoors. The dining room and family room flank the split staircase that creates privacy for the master suite on the right and the two family bedrooms on the left. Back on the first floor, the kitchen sits behind the staircase with a half-bath and utility room to the left. The sunny breakfast nook, with views in two directions, opens to the rear deck.

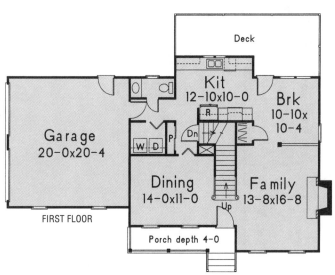

Deck

Kit
12-10x10-0

Brk
10-10x
10-4

Garage
20-0x20-4

W D P

Dn

R

FIRST FLOOR

Dining
14-0x11-0

Family
13-8x16-8

Up

Porch depth 4-0

plan# HPK0400085

Style: Traditional
First Floor: 858 sq. ft.
Second Floor: 741 sq. ft.
Total: 1,599 sq. ft.
Bonus Space: 336 sq. ft.
Bedrooms: 3
Bathrooms: 2½
Width: 50' - 4"
Depth: 36' - 0"
Foundation: Crawlspace,
Basement

SEARCH ONLINE @ EPLANS.COM

The welcoming two-story foyer is flanked by the spacious living room and elegant dining room. A French door in the breakfast area opens to the backyard. Three windows brighten the family room, which has a fireplace. The upper-level master suite, the epitome of luxury, has a tray ceiling and a bath with a vaulted ceiling, a walk-in closet, a separate shower, and a plant shelf. Bonus space over the garage is available for another bedroom or study.

SECOND FLOOR

FIRST FLOOR

OPTIONAL LAYOUT

A striking mix of traditional brick and siding enhances the exterior of this home, enclosing a floor plan of family luxury. A petite porch welcomes you inside to a two-story entry. The U-shaped kitchen with pantry is placed between the breakfast and dining rooms for optimal convenience. The family room with fireplace overlooks the rear patio—a seasonal outdoor necessity. A powder room, laundry, and two-car garage complete the first floor. Upstairs, the master bedroom features a private bath and walk-in closet for the homeowners. Three additional family bedrooms share a full hall bath and a linen storage closet.

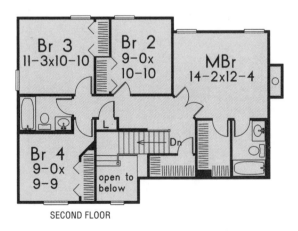

plan # HPK0400086

Style: Traditional
First Floor: 896 sq. ft.
Second Floor: 804 sq. ft.
Total: 1,700 sq. ft.
Bedrooms: 4
Bathrooms: 2½
Width: 39' - 0"
Depth: 42' - 8"
Foundation: Basement

SEARCH ONLINE @ EPLANS.COM

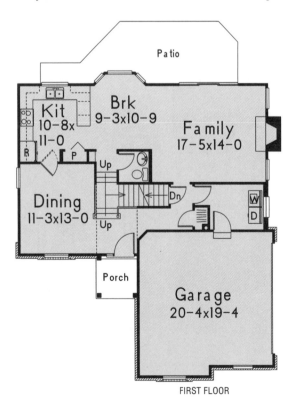

Patio

Kit 10-8x 11-0

Brk 9-3x10-9

Family 17-5x14-0

Dining 11-3x13-0

Up

Dn

Up

Porch

Garage 20-4x19-4

FIRST FLOOR

Br 3 11-3x10-10

Br 2 9-0x 10-10

MBr 14-2x12-4

Br 4 9-0x 9-9

open to below

Dn

SECOND FLOOR

plan # HPK0400087

Style: Traditional
First Floor: 802 sq. ft.
Second Floor: 773 sq. ft.
Total: 1,575 sq. ft.
Bedrooms: 3
Bathrooms: 2½
Width: 36' - 0"
Depth: 46' - 8"
Foundation: Basement

SEARCH ONLINE @ EPLANS.COM

Brick and siding add character to this traditional design. A simple and functional floor plan keeps the casual living space open on the first floor and family quarters private upstairs. An island kitchen offers plenty of counter and storage space, a nearby laundry room, pantry, and adjoining breakfast nook work in unison for a flawless use of space. The master suite enjoys a vaulted ceiling, walk-in closet, and full bath. Two secondary bedrooms share a hall bath.

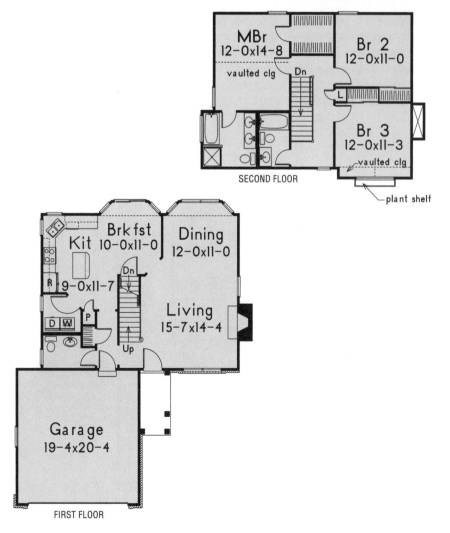

This home's front and rear covered porches allow family and guests maximum enjoyment of the outdoors. Inside, a tiled entry leads to a spacious living room featuring a cozy fireplace; a dining room and a gourmet kitchen are just steps away. The efficient kitchen also comes with a snack bar—great for morning gatherings. The master bedroom, secluded to the rear of the plan, features a walk-in closet, a private bath, and access to the rear porch. The second floor holds two additional bedrooms, a full bath, and a loft area that overlooks the living room.

plan# HPK0400088

Style: Farmhouse
First Floor: 1,029 sq. ft.
Second Floor: 489 sq. ft.
Total: 1,518 sq. ft.
Bonus Space: 339 sq. ft.
Bedrooms: 3
Bathrooms: 2½
Width: 44' - 8"
Depth: 59' - 0"

SEARCH ONLINE @ EPLANS.COM

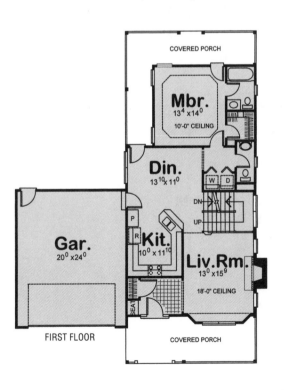

FIRST FLOOR

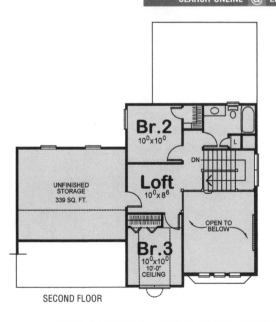

SECOND FLOOR

plan # HPK0400089

Style: Traditional
First Floor: 880 sq. ft.
Second Floor: 755 sq. ft.
Total: 1,635 sq ft.
Bedrooms: 3
Bathrooms: 2½
Width: 36' - 0"
Depth: 54' - 4"
Foundation: Basement, Crawlspace, Slab

SEARCH ONLINE @ EPLANS.COM

With a wrapping front porch that just begs for summer's lazy days, this three-bedroom farmhouse is a step back in time. Arches and columns define the foyer, which opens to the hearth-warmed living room and dining room. At the rear, the family room and island kitchen combine to form a casual space, just right for relaxing. Utility rooms line the back of the two-car garage. Bedrooms are located upstairs, including two secondary bedrooms and a spacious master suite. An additional walk-in closet can be found in the hall and gives access to abundant attic space.

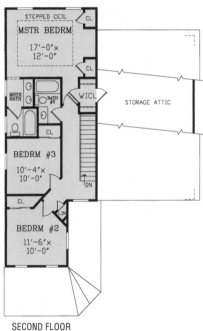

SECOND FLOOR

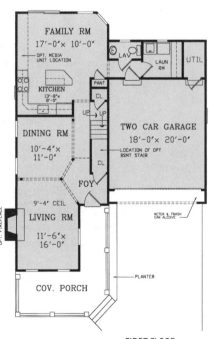

FIRST FLOOR

© 2001 Donald A. Gardner, Inc.

A trio of dormers, a metal porch covering, and a mixture of stone and siding create a modern version of the traditional American home. The front porch is bordered by columns and features a trio of arches. A fireplace and built-ins, along with a cathedral ceiling that flows to the kitchen, highlight the great room. Tray ceilings crown the dining room and master bedroom, visually expanding space. The bonus room makes a perfect playroom for kids, separating the noise from the common living areas and master bedroom. The master bath is complete with a sizable shower, double-sink vanity, and a garden tub.

plan ⊕ HPK0400090

Style: Traditional
Square Footage: 1,674
Bonus Space: 336 sq. ft.
Bedrooms: 3
Bathrooms: 2
Width: 56' - 4"
Depth: 50' - 0"

SEARCH ONLINE @ EPLANS.COM

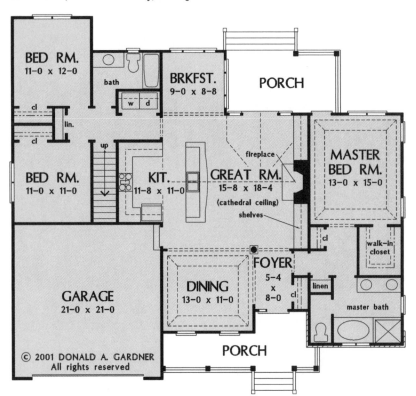

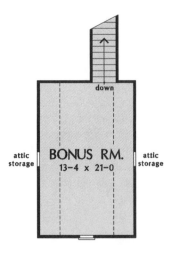

plan # HPK0400091

Style: Country Cottage
Square Footage: 1,692
Bonus Space: 358 sq. ft.
Bedrooms: 3
Bathrooms: 2
Width: 54' - 0"
Depth: 56' - 6"
Foundation: Crawlspace, Basement

SEARCH ONLINE @ EPLANS.COM

This cozy country cottage is enhanced with a front-facing planter box above the garage and a charming covered porch. The foyer leads to a vaulted great room, complete with a fireplace and radius windows. Decorative columns complement the entrance to the dining room, as does a decorative arch. On the left side of the plan resides the master suite, which is resplendent with amenities including a vaulted sitting room with an arched opening, tray ceiling, and French doors to the vaulted full bath. On the right side, two additional bedrooms share a full bath.

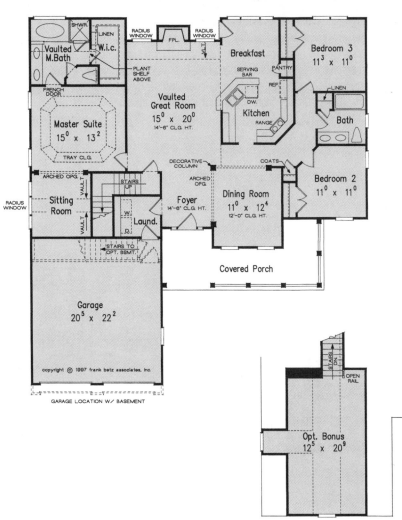

This country ranch duplex takes vacation living to the next level. Each home enjoys two bedrooms, both with spacious closets and lots of privacy, and the living and dining areas are set up for socializing. The compact kitchen is organized for efficient preparation of meals. A spacious front porch brings the outdoors in, and the door to the rear property is ideal for slipping out for impromptu walks. Space for a washer-and-dryer set means you won't be "roughing it" too hard! A full hall bath and linen storage finish off these mirror-image plans.

plan# HPK0400092

Style: Ranch
Square Footage: 768 / 768
Bedrooms: 2 / 2
Bathrooms: 1 / 1
Width: 32' - 0"
Depth: 24' - 0"
Foundation: Crawlspace

SEARCH ONLINE @ EPLANS.COM

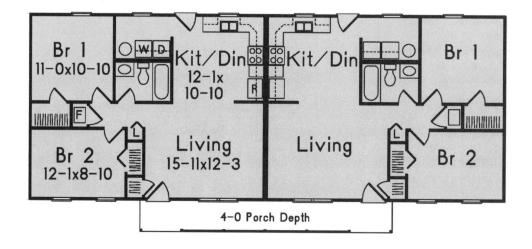

plan # HPK0400093

Style: Country Cottage
First Floor: 1,152 sq. ft.
Second Floor: 567 sq. ft.
Total: 1,719 sq. ft.
Bonus Space: 115 sq. ft.
Bedrooms: 3
Bathrooms: 2½
Width: 36' - 0"
Depth: 64' - 0"
Foundation: Crawlspace, Basement

SEARCH ONLINE @ EPLANS.COM

Simplicity is often the best approach to design. Twin chimneys serve as anchors to the home, and a deep front porch welcomes visitors. Inside, the cathedral ceiling and natural light from the dormers above enliven the great room. The well-appointed master suite also enjoys a private fireplace. Two additional bedrooms are located on the second floor along with the bonus room, which will add 115 square feet if finished.

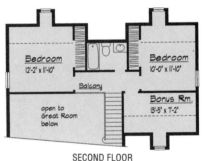

SECOND FLOOR

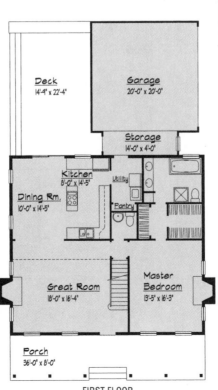

FIRST FLOOR

plan # HPK0400094

Style: Traditional
Square Footage: 1,642
Bedrooms: 3
Bathrooms: 2
Width: 60' - 4"
Depth: 48' - 0"
Foundation: Basement, Slab, Crawlspace

SEARCH ONLINE @ EPLANS.COM

A wonderful covered entry, turned gable, and double dormers create an inviting house with great curb appeal. An open floor plan is sensibly laid out with a centrally located kitchen, open to both the dining room and family room. Vaulted ceilings enlarge the area. The master suite enjoys a private bath, a walk-in closet, and an intriguing sloped ceiling. Two family bedrooms share a full bath. Two closets offer ample space for storing linen. A side patio can be entered from the family room, which boasts a fireplace, or from the two-car garage.

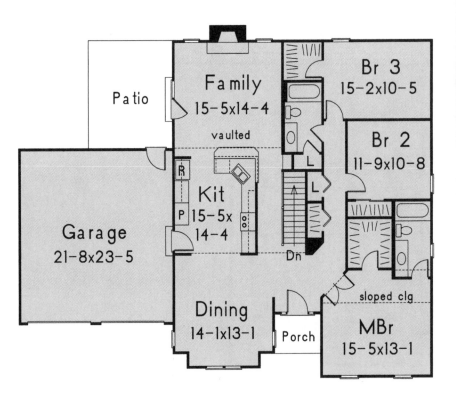

plan # HPK0400095

Style: Traditional
Square Footage: 850 / 850
Bedrooms: 2 / 2
Bathrooms: 1 / 1
Width: 68' - 0"
Depth: 37' - 0"
Foundation: Basement

SEARCH ONLINE @ EPLANS.COM

This attractive duplex home is enhanced by stylish symmetry and mirror-image floor plans. Country dormers and porches welcome you inside to a vaulted living area. The vaulted space continues into the combined kitchen and dining area. The U-shape of the kitchen allows for compact efficiency. Bedroom 1 provides impressive closet space; Bedroom 2 is perfect for a nursery or home office—great for young couples just starting out or empty-nesters. The two bedrooms share a full hall bath. Each unit offers a single-car garage.

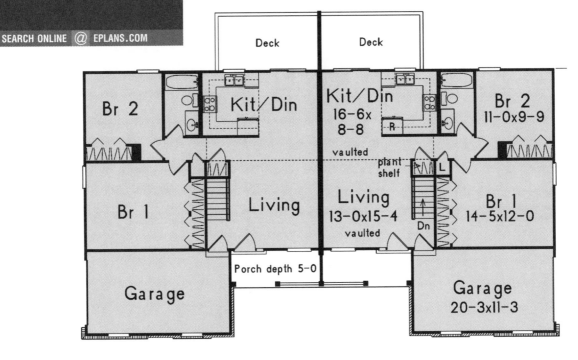

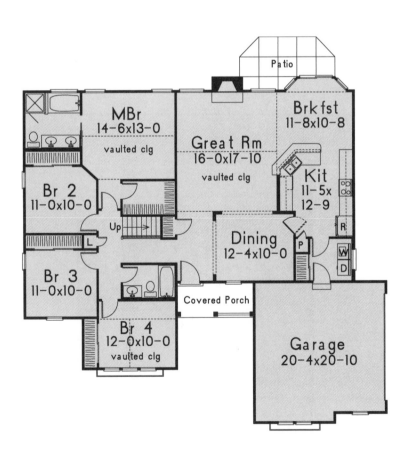

plan # HPK0400096

Style: Traditional
Square Footage: 1,761
Bedrooms: 4
Bathrooms: 2
Width: 57' - 0"
Depth: 52' - 2"
Foundation: Basement

SEARCH ONLINE @ EPLANS.COM

Residing peacefully in a serene mountain setting, this small family home brings quaint style to an efficient floor plan. The covered porch leads inside to formal vistas from the dining and great rooms. Warmed by a cozy fireplace, the vaulted great room connects to the kitchen/breakfast area, opening onto a rear patio. The master bedroom is vaulted and includes a walk-in closet and private bath. Three additional family bedrooms share a full hall bath. A two-car garage completes this charming plan.

plan # HPK0400097

Style: Traditional
Square Footage: 1,791
Bedrooms: 4
Bathrooms: 2
Width: 67' - 4"
Depth: 48' - 0"
Foundation: Basement

SEARCH ONLINE @ EPLANS.COM

The two dormers draw attention to this home as well as flood the kitchen and breakfast nook with plenty of natural light. The steep rooflines lend vaulted ceilings to the interior of this home. The great room and octagonal dining room enjoy views of the covered patio. The amazingly well-lit kitchen features a pass-through to the dining room, a center island, a walk-in pantry and a breakfast room with a large bay window. The bedrooms align along the right side of the plan.

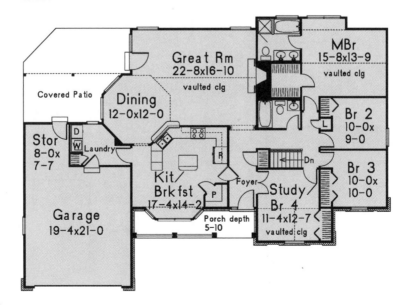

This home offers a beautifully textured facade. Keystones and lintels highlight the beauty of the windows. The vaulted great room and dining room are immersed in light from the atrium window wall. The breakfast bay opens to the covered porch in the backyard. A curved counter connects the kitchen to the great room. Three bedrooms, including a deluxe master suite, share the right side of the plan. All enjoy large windows of their own. The garage is designed for two cars, plus space for a motorcycle or yard tractor.

plan # HPK0400098

Style: Traditional
Square Footage: 1,721
Bedrooms: 3
Bathrooms: 2
Width: 83' - 0"
Depth: 42' - 0"
Foundation: Basement

SEARCH ONLINE @ EPLANS.COM

plan# HPK0400099

Style: Farmhouse
Square Footage: 1,793
Bonus Space: 779 sq. ft.
Bedrooms: 3
Bathrooms: 2
Width: 69' - 10"
Depth: 51' - 8"
Foundation: Basement, Slab, Crawlspace

SEARCH ONLINE @ EPLANS.COM

A wraparound porch and steep roofline, punctuated by small dormers, mark this farmhouse-style ranch home. The inviting foyer leads past a dining room with an enchanting stepped ceiling to the great room, which also enjoys an 11-foot-high ceiling. The delightful master suite includes a tray ceiling, a beautiful bay-window sitting area, two walk-in closets, and a lovely compartmented private bath with a whirlpool tub. Access to the master suite is very private and separated from the two front bedrooms. The high roofline provides for a huge bonus area.

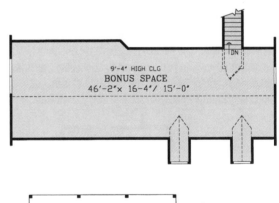

9'-4" HIGH CLG
BONUS SPACE
46'-2" x 16'-4" / 15'-0"
DN

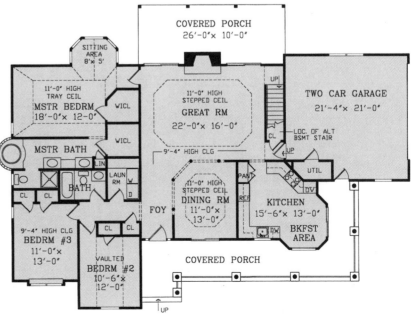

COVERED PORCH
26'-0" x 10'-0"

SITTING AREA
8' x 5'

11'-0" HIGH TRAY CEIL
MSTR BEDRM
18'-0" x 12'-0"

WICL

WICL

MSTR BATH

LIN

LAUN RM

BATH

CL CL

9'-4" HIGH CLG
BEDRM #3
11'-0" x 13'-0"

CL CL

VAULTED
BEDRM #2
10'-6" x 12'-0"

UP

11'-0" HIGH STEPPED CEIL
GREAT RM
22'-0" x 16'-0"

9'-4" HIGH CLG

11'-0" HIGH STEPPED CEIL
DINING RM
11'-0" x 13'-0"

FOY

UP

TWO CAR GARAGE
21'-4" x 21'-0"

LOC. OF ALT BSMT STAIR

UP

PANT

REF

UTIL

DW

KITCHEN
15'-6" x 13'-0"

DW

BKFST AREA

COVERED PORCH

This beautiful home packs tons of amenities in under 2,000 square feet! From the front-porch entrance, the great room, with a fireplace, will greet you. Continue to the bayed breakfast area, bathed in natural light. The kitchen is a chef's delight, with lots of space to whip up magnificent meals and convenient to the carport for unloading groceries. Two bedrooms share a hall bath; the master bedroom enjoys His and Hers closets and a bath with a separate tub and shower. Note the future space, available to suit your needs.

plan # HPK0400100

Style: Traditional
Square Footage: 1,726
Bedrooms: 3
Bathrooms: 2
Width: 51' - 8"
Depth: 70' - 6"
Foundation: Basement, Crawlspace, Slab

SEARCH ONLINE @ EPLANS.COM

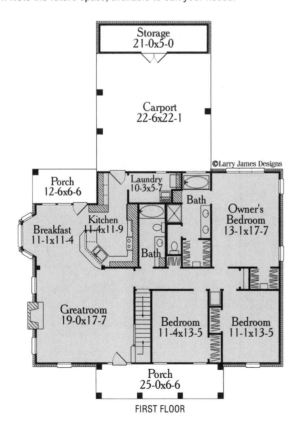

Storage
21-0x5-0

Carport
22-6x22-1

©Larry James Designs

Porch
12-6x6-6

Laundry
10-3x5-7

Bath

Owner's Bedroom
13-1x17-7

Kitchen
11-4x11-9

Breakfast
11-1x11-4

Bath

Greatroom
19-0x17-7

Bedroom
11-4x13-5

Bedroom
11-1x13-5

Porch
25-0x6-6

FIRST FLOOR

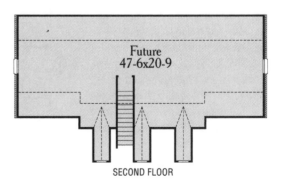

Future
47-6x20-9

SECOND FLOOR

plan # HPK0400101

Style: Ranch
Square Footage: 1,668
Bedrooms: 3
Bathrooms: 2
Width: 54' - 0"
Depth: 30' - 0"
Foundation: Basement

SEARCH ONLINE @ EPLANS.COM

Intriguing bay windows brighten this compact, three-bedroom ranch house, and a covered front porch and rear deck help to spread the living space outward. An impressive tray ceiling in the bedchamber, two huge walk-in closets, and a resplendent bath make the master suite a dream come true. Two other bedrooms share a hall bath. A sloped ceiling and extended-hearth fireplace enhance the coziness of the living room. Food preparation and service will be a cinch in the well-planned kitchen.

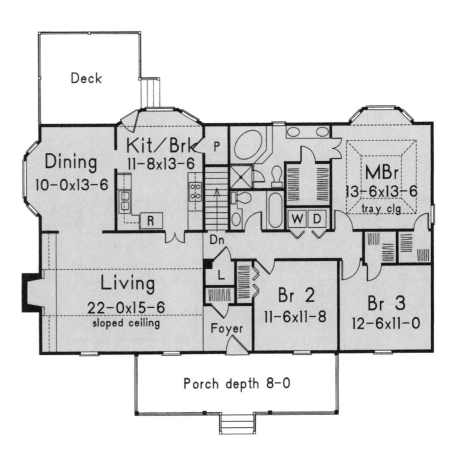

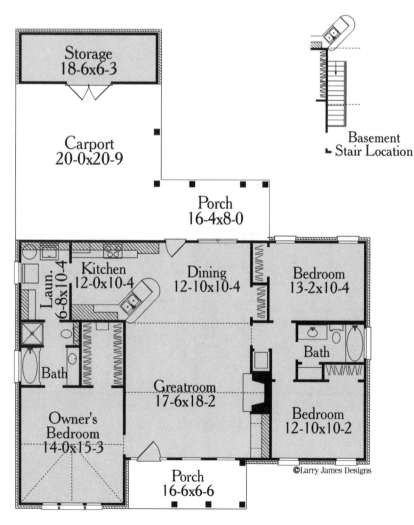

Storage
18-6x6-3

Carport
20-0x20-9

Basement
Stair Location

Porch
16-4x8-0

Laun.
6-8x10-4

Kitchen
12-0x10-4

Dining
12-10x10-4

Bedroom
13-2x10-4

Bath

Bath

Greatroom
17-6x18-2

Bedroom
12-10x10-2

Owner's
Bedroom
14-0x15-3

Porch
16-6x6-6

©Larry James Designs

plan# HPK0400102

Style: Traditional
Square Footage: 1,532
Bedrooms: 3
Bathrooms: 2
Width: 49' - 0"
Depth: 63' - 6"
Foundation: Basement,
Crawlspace, Slab

SEARCH ONLINE @ EPLANS.COM

Take one look at this sweet country home and you'll want to call it your own. A warm brick facade and Palladian-style windows welcome family and friends. A cathedral ceiling in the great room adds grandeur and a centered fireplace adds a cozy element. Continue to the dining area, where a snack bar from the kitchen's workspace peninsula makes serving simple. In the master suite, a cathedral ceiling makes an elegant statement and a private bath pampers. On the far right, two bedrooms share a full bath.

plan # HPK0400103

Style: **Traditional**
Square Footage: **1,604**
Bedrooms: **3**
Bathrooms: **2**
Width: **48' - 8"**
Depth: **48' - 0"**

SEARCH ONLINE @ EPLANS.COM

ALTERNATE EXTERIOR

Cost to build? See page 333
to order complete cost estimate
to build this house in your area!

A thoughtful arrangement makes this uncomplicated three-bedroom plan comfortable. The living and working areas are grouped together for convenience—a great room with cathedral ceiling, dining room with a wet bar pass-through, and kitchen with a breakfast room. The sleeping area features a spacious master suite with a skylit bath, a whirlpool tub, and a large walk-in closet. Two smaller bedrooms accommodate the rest of the family. An alternate exterior is available at no extra cost.

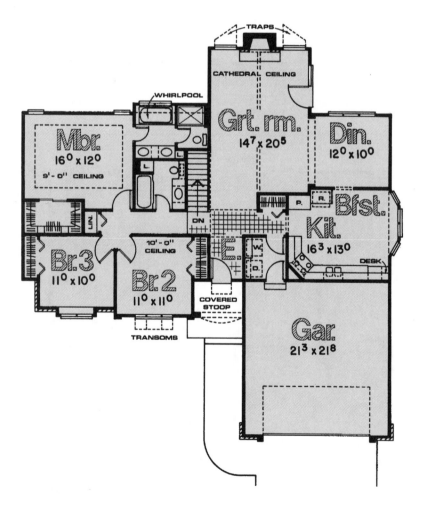

plan # HPK0400104

Style: **Traditional**
Square Footage: **1,583**
Bedrooms: **3**
Bathrooms: **2**
Width: **56' - 0"**
Depth: **55' - 4"**

SEARCH ONLINE @ EPLANS.COM

Crisp rooflines and bright window and column details accentuate the exterior of this elegant three-bedroom ranch home. Once inside, family and friends alike will appreciate the striking 10-foot-high entry with a decorator plant shelf. The great room has a cathedral ceiling and a fireplace flanked by sunny, trapezoid windows. Serving the formal dining room is a generous kitchen with bayed breakfast area. Both secondary bedrooms have spacious closets. A built-in linen closet is an added bonus in the shared hall bath. The luxurious master suite includes special ceiling detail, a spacious walk-in closet with mirrored doors, dual sinks, whirlpool, and a vanity/make-up area with natural light.

plan # HPK0400105

Style: Traditional
Square Footage: 1,790
Bedrooms: 3
Bathrooms: 2
Width: 55' - 0"
Depth: 57' - 0"

SEARCH ONLINE @ EPLANS.COM

Hipped rooflines and an arched front entry dynamically combine to give this one-story home an impressive presence. Further enhancements include the sidelights, curved transom, and tall window that illuminate the front porch. The entry has a convenient bench to sit and remove shoes and coats. The gorgeous master suite boasts a private covered porch and a whirlpool tub. Living areas soar upward with 11-foot ceilings. A curved snack bar ties the kitchen, breakfast alcove, and great room together. The two-car garage comes with lots of storage space.

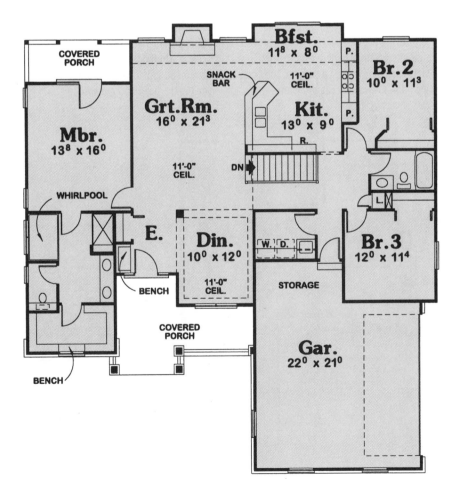

A covered-porch entry to this delightful two-story home gives way to an intriguing foyer with an angled stairway. The formal living and dining rooms are to the left and provide a massive open space for relaxing and entertaining. The island kitchen is open to a breakfast bay and connects to the garage via a laundry and half-bath. Upstairs, an indulgent master suite reigns. It pampers with a huge walk-in closet and a bath with a whirlpool tub, shower, double-sink vanity, separate make-up counter, and compartmented toilet. Two other bedrooms are also on this floor. A window seat and plant shelves are located at the head of the stairs.

plan # HPK0400106

Style: Traditional
First Floor: 884 sq. ft.
Second Floor: 848 sq. ft.
Total: 1,732 sq. ft.
Bedrooms: 3
Bathrooms: 2½
Width: 38' - 8"
Depth: 46' - 8"

SEARCH ONLINE @ EPLANS.COM

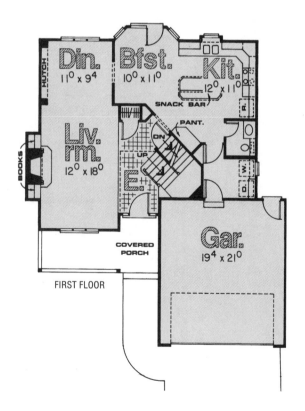

FIRST FLOOR

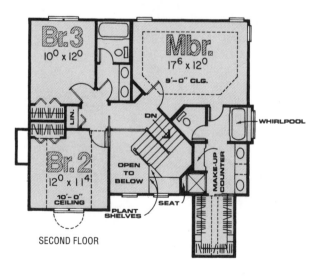

SECOND FLOOR

ORDER BLUEPRINTS 24 HOURS, 7 DAYS A WEEK, AT 1-800-521-6797

plan # HPK0400107

Style: Traditional
First Floor: 964 sq. ft.
Second Floor: 735 sq. ft.
Total: 1,699 sq. ft.
Bedrooms: 3
Bathrooms: 2½
Width: 40' - 0"
Depth: 46' - 0"

SEARCH ONLINE @ EPLANS.COM

A covered front porch offers a warm, friendly welcome into this lovely home. The large living room has a 10-foot ceiling and connects to the formal dining room for exciting entertainment options. Wood floors tie the family room, breakfast nook, and kitchen into one casual living space. The master suite on the second floor begins with double doors and is distinguished by dual closets and a relaxing bath with a whirlpool tub. Two family bedrooms each have boxed windows.

The brick trim and multiple gables combine to offer a creative facade on this spectacular home. A high ceiling through the foyer and great room complements the warmth of the fireplace. Designed for convenience, the modern kitchen serves the formal dining room and breakfast area with equal efficiency. The spacious master bedroom suite features a whirlpool tub, separate shower, double vanities, and a spacious walk-in closet. A den and a family bedroom— or transform the den into a second family bedroom—share a full hall bath.

plan# HPK0400108

Style: Traditional
Square Footage: 1,651
Bedrooms: 2
Bathrooms: 2
Width: 62' - 0"
Depth: 56' - 0"

SEARCH ONLINE @ EPLANS.COM

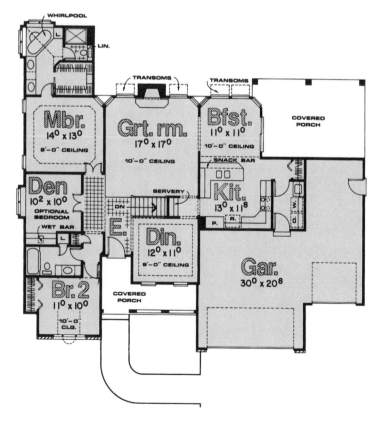

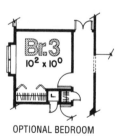

OPTIONAL BEDROOM

plan# HPK0400109

Style: Traditional
Square Footage: 1,595
Bedrooms: 3
Bathrooms: 2
Width: 70' - 0"
Depth: 37' - 4"
Foundation: Basement, Crawlspace, Slab

SEARCH ONLINE @ EPLANS.COM

Wood shutters, glamorous half-round windows, and durable brick give this home its good looks. Entry drama is created with the use of high ceilings in the foyer, dining room, and great room. The dining room is set off by elegant columned openings; formal meals can be kept warm and out of sight in the handy serving station around the corner. The TV center and fireplace in the great room create an attractive wall that complements the sliding French door tandem to the rear. Half-round windows accentuate the radiant bays protruding from the breakfast room and master suite, which boasts a vaulted ceiling and a whirlpool bath. Wider doorways and an alternate garage plan with a ramp instead of a storage area make this home adaptable to wheelchair use.

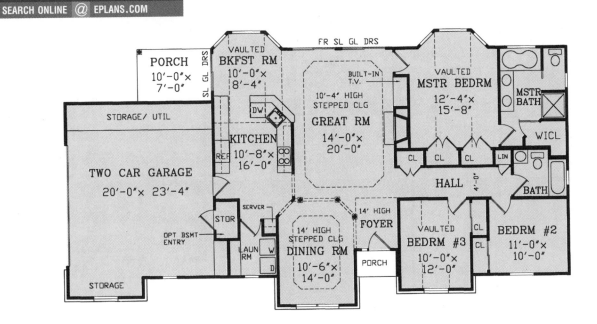

G. MacDonald

Clever zoning and attention to detail allow for great livability in this efficient family plan. From the entry, the great room opens just beyond the staircase and is accented with a fireplace framed by two transom windows. The formal dining room is set at the front of the plan and may be converted to a front parlor. French doors partitioning the kitchen from the great room add quaint, country charm while keeping cooking activities out of sight. The kitchen is equipped with an abundance of counter and cabinet space, a snack bar, and a lovely breakfast room highlighted with corner windows and patio door. The master bedroom offers secluded retreat on the first floor and has a large, compartmented bath and walk-in closet. Upstairs, three family bedrooms share a hall bath.

plan # HPK0400110

Style: Traditional
First Floor: 1,265 sq. ft.
Second Floor: 518 sq. ft.
Total: 1,783 sq. ft.
Bedrooms: 4
Bathrooms: 2½
Width: 48' - 0"
Depth: 48' - 0"

SEARCH ONLINE @ EPLANS.COM

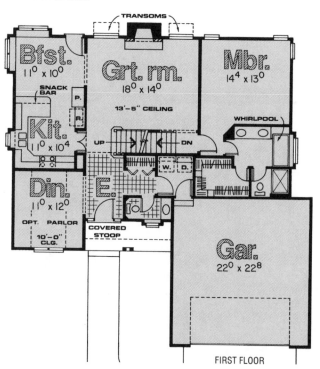

FIRST FLOOR

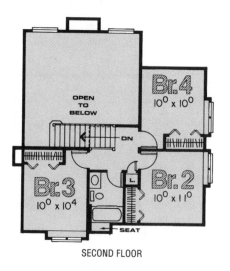

SECOND FLOOR

plan # HPK0400111

Style: Traditional
First Floor: 1,297 sq. ft.
Second Floor: 388 sq. ft.
Total: 1,685 sq. ft.
Bedrooms: 3
Bathrooms: 2½
Width: 52' - 0"
Depth: 45' - 4"

SEARCH ONLINE @ EPLANS.COM

QUOTE ONE®
Cost to build? See page 333
to order complete cost estimate
to build this house in your area!

A lovely covered porch welcomes family and guests to this delightful 1½-story home. The formal dining room with boxed windows and the great room with fireplace are visible from the entry. A powder room for guests is located just beyond the dining room. An open kitchen/dinette features a pantry, planning desk, and snack-bar counter. The elegant master suite is appointed with a formal ceiling and a window seat. A skylight above the whirlpool tub, a decorator plant shelf, and double sinks dress up the master bath. Two family bedrooms on the second floor share a centrally located bath.

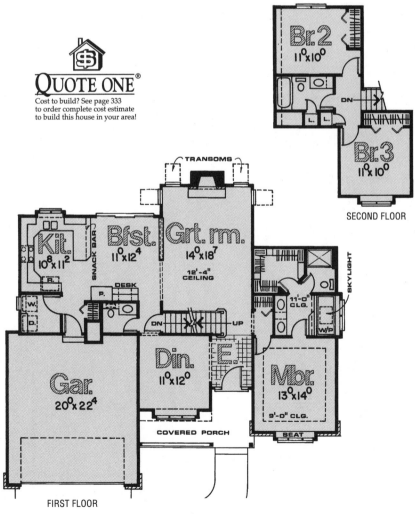

DECK

BREAKFAST
11'-4" X 8'-6"

BEDROOM NO. 3
11'-6" X 11'-0"

GREAT ROOM
14'-0" X 17'-6"

KITCHEN
11'-4" X 10'-0"

MASTER
BEDROOM
12'-4" X 15'-6"

BATH

FOYER
6'-6" X 5'-0"

DN.

HIS

BEDROOM NO. 2
11'-0" X 12'-2"

DINING ROOM
11'-4" X 10'-6"

PWDR.

MASTER
BATH

STOOP

LAUNDRY

HERS

TWO-CAR GARAGE
20'-4" X 19'-4"

QUOTE ONE ®
Cost to build? See page 333
to order complete cost estimate
to build this house in your area!

plan# HPK0400112

Style: French
Square Footage: 1,684
Bedrooms: 3
Bathrooms: 2½
Width: 55' - 6"
Depth: 57' - 6"
Foundation: Walkout Basement

SEARCH ONLINE @ EPLANS.COM

Charming and compact, this home is as beautiful as it is practical. The impressive arch over the double front door is repeated with an arched window in the formal dining room. This room opens to a spacious great room with a fireplace and is near the kitchen and bayed breakfast area. Split sleeping arrangements put the master suite at the right of the plan and two family bedrooms at the left.

plan # HPK0400113

Style: SW Contemporary
Square Footage: 1,624
Bedrooms: 3
Bathrooms: 2
Width: 38' - 0"
Depth: 74' - 4"
Foundation: Slab, Crawlspace, Basement

SEARCH ONLINE @ EPLANS.COM

This stunning stucco design features a three-bedroom layout with plenty of living space for a comfortable family lifestyle. Enter inside—a breakfast room is located to the immediate right. The compact kitchen is conveniently set between the breakfast room and the formal dining area. The dining room accesses a petite rear porch that's perfect for outdoor grilling. A fireplace warms the family room, which combines with the open dining area. The master bedroom is located at the rear of the plan and offers a walk-in closet and private bath. Two additional family bedrooms share a hall bath. A laundry room connecting to the garage completes the floor plan.

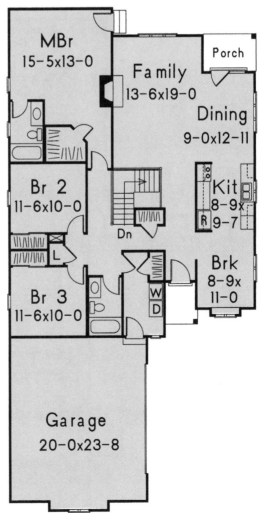

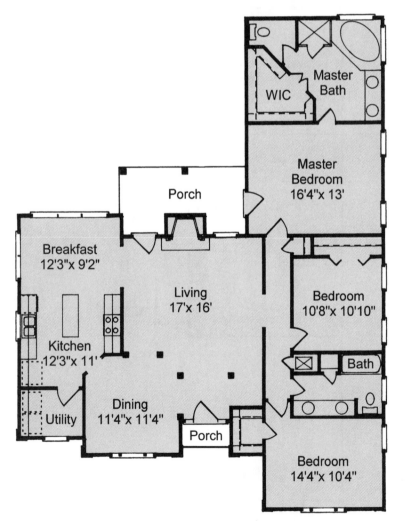

Master Bath

WIC

Master Bedroom
16'4"x 13'

Porch

Breakfast
12'3"x 9'2"

Living
17'x 16'

Bedroom
10'8"x 10'10"

Kitchen
12'3"x 11'

Bath

Dining
11'4"x 11'4"

Utility

Porch

Bedroom
14'4"x 10'4"

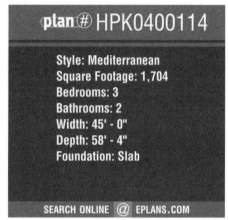

plan# HPK0400114

Style: Mediterranean
Square Footage: 1,704
Bedrooms: 3
Bathrooms: 2
Width: 45' - 0"
Depth: 58' - 4"
Foundation: Slab

SEARCH ONLINE @ EPLANS.COM

A variety of angles and abundant windows make this home interesting and stylish. A spacious living room is the focal point, separated from the dining room by columns and featuring a massive fireplace. The dining room is easily served by the island kitchen, which opens to the sunny breakfast nook. The elegant master bedroom in back includes a private entrance to the porch, a walk-in closet and a sumptuous bath. Two secondary bedrooms share a full bath.

plan# HPK0400115

Style: Floridian
Square Footage: 1,550
Bedrooms: 3
Bathrooms: 2
Width: 43' - 0"
Depth: 59' - 0"
Foundation: Slab

SEARCH ONLINE @ EPLANS.COM

Enjoy resort-style living in this striking Sun Country home. Guests will always feel welcome when entertained in the formal living and dining areas, but the eat-in country kitchen overlooking the family room will be the center of attention. Enjoy casual living in the large family room and out on the patio with the help of an optional summer kitchen and a view of the fairway. Built-in shelves and an optional media center provide decorating options. The master suite features a volume ceiling and a spacious master bath.

ALTERNATE EXTERIOR

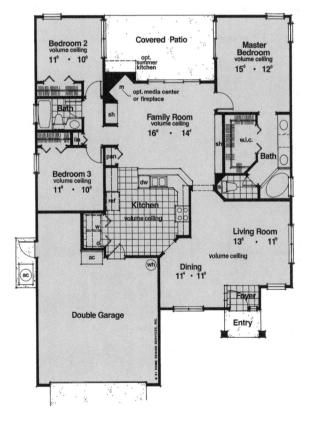

Though small in square footage, this home feels large because of volume ceilings. The expanded ceilings begin in the formal living and dining areas just off the entry. Centered between the formal areas and the casual family room, the L-shaped kitchen features a pantry and eat-in breakfast area. Split-bedroom planning puts the master suite on one side of the home, separate from two family bedrooms. The master suite sports a large bath area with double vanity, separate tub and shower, and huge walk-in closet. The blueprint package includes both exteriors.

plan # HPK0400116

Style: Floridian
Square Footage: 1,750
Bedrooms: 3
Bathrooms: 2
Width: 42' - 6"
Depth: 55' - 8"
Foundation: Slab

SEARCH ONLINE @ EPLANS.COM

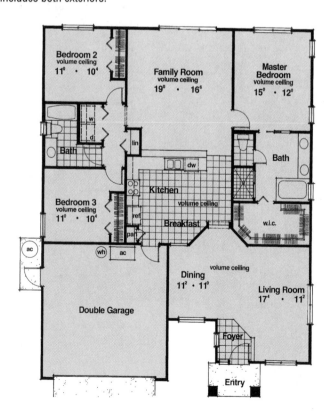

ALTERNATE EXTERIOR

plan # HPK0400117

Style: Traditional
Square Footage: 1,817
Bedrooms: 3
Bathrooms: 2
Width: 50' - 0"
Depth: 63' - 0"
Foundation: Slab

SEARCH ONLINE @ EPLANS.COM

First impressions make a grand statement in this volume-look home. A traditional split entry finds the living room on the left and the dining room on the right. The latter shares a large, open space with the family room, made more impressive with its volume ceiling. The tiled kitchen and breakfast room are the height of charm and efficiency. On one side of the plan, the master bedroom boasts a private sitting space and lavish bath with shutter doors at the soaking tub and a room-sized walk-in closet. At the other side of the house, two family bedrooms each afford ample closet space and room to grow. A "kid's" door leads to the covered patio at the rear of the plan. Note the handy laundry room leading to the two-car garage.

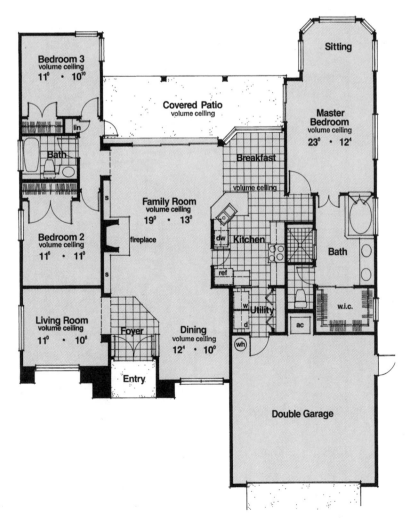

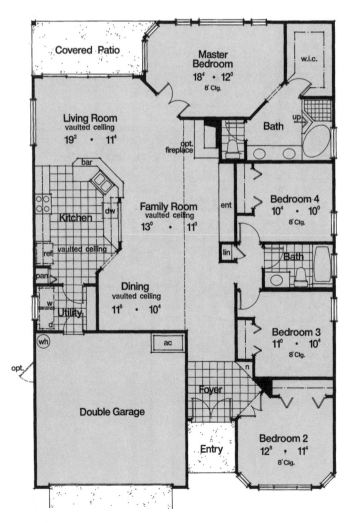

plan# HPK0400118

Style: Contemporary
Square Footage: 1,834
Bedrooms: 4
Bathrooms: 2
Width: 40' - 0"
Depth: 60' - 0"
Foundation: Slab

SEARCH ONLINE @ EPLANS.COM

Loaded with four bedrooms and expansive views from every room of the house, this creative design is perfect for the growing family. Inside the foyer, double doors open to a bedroom or den. Two other bedrooms are off a hall to the right; to the left, the plan hosts the open living area that includes the dining room, family room, living room, and kitchen. Sliding glass doors open from the living room to the rear covered patio. The master bedroom boasts a curved window, a walk-in closet, and a bath with double-bowl vanity.

ORDER BLUEPRINTS 24 HOURS, 7 DAYS A WEEK, AT 1-800-521-6797

Checkout Receipt/Reçu

Louis Riel Library

04 Jan 2021 01:20

****

_ Build it smart : 300 easy-to-build hom
_ CALL #: 728.370222 BUI 2004
 33097057346428
Due Date/Date de retour 25 Jan 2021

__ TOTAL: 1

****

J.N. HANSEN P.T.L.

plan # HPK0400119

Style: Contemporary
First Floor: 1,230 sq. ft.
Second Floor: 649 sq. ft.
Total: 1,879 sq. ft.
Bedrooms: 3
Bathrooms: 2½
Width: 38' - 0"
Depth: 53' - 6"
Foundation: Slab

SEARCH ONLINE @ EPLANS.COM

The tiled foyer of this two-story home opens to a living/dining space with a soaring ceiling, a fireplace in the living room, and access to a covered patio that invites outdoor livability. The kitchen has an oversized, sunny breakfast area with a volume ceiling. The master bedroom offers privacy with its sumptuous bath; a corner soaking tub, dual lavatories, and a compartmented toilet lend character to the room. Upstairs, one of the family bedrooms features a walk-in closet. A loft overlooking the living spaces could become a third family bedroom. Both bedrooms share a generous hall bath.

SECOND FLOOR

FIRST FLOOR

Amenities abound in this delightful two-story home. The foyer opens directly into the fantastic grand room, which offers a warming fireplace and two sets of double doors to the rear deck. The dining room also accesses this deck and a second deck shared with Bedroom 2. A convenient kitchen and another bedroom also reside on this level. Upstairs, the master bedroom reigns supreme. Entered through double doors, it pampers with a luxurious bath, walk-in closet, morning kitchen, and private observation deck.

plan # HPK0400120

Style: Floridian
First Floor: 1,342 sq. ft.
Second Floor: 511 sq. ft.
Total: 1,853 sq. ft.
Bedrooms: 3
Bathrooms: 2
Width: 44' - 0"
Depth: 40' - 0"
Foundation: Pier

SEARCH ONLINE @ EPLANS.COM

SECOND FLOOR

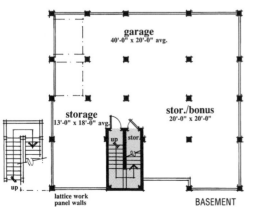

BASEMENT

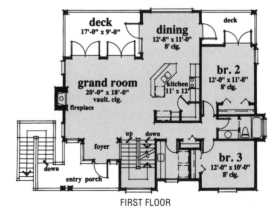

FIRST FLOOR

plan# HPK0400121

Style: Contemporary
Square Footage: 1,868
Bedrooms: 4
Bathrooms: 2
Width: 45' - 0"
Depth: 66' - 0"
Foundation: Slab

ALTERNATE EXTERIOR

This innovative plan features an angled entry into the home, lending visual impact to the facade and giving the interior floor plan space for a fourth bedroom. A fabulous central living area with a volume ceiling includes a dining area with kitchen access, a great room with a built-in media center, and access to the rear covered patio. The bayed breakfast area with another volume ceiling shares natural light with the tiled kitchen. The kitchen and breakfast nook overlook the outdoor living space, which even offers an optional summer kitchen—great for entertaining. A plush master suite opens from the great room through a privacy door and offers vistas to the rear and side grounds.

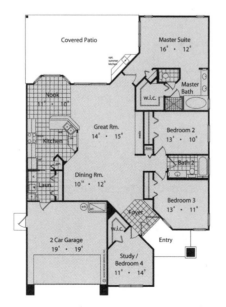

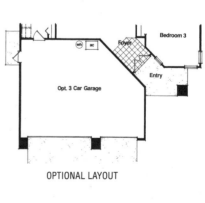

OPTIONAL LAYOUT

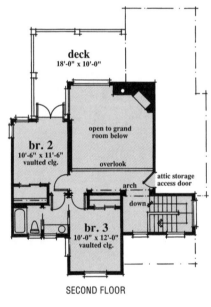

deck
18'-0" x 10'-0"

br. 2
10'-6" x 11'-6"
vaulted clg.

open to grand
room below

overlook

attic storage
access door

arch

down

br. 3
10'-0" x 12'-0"
vaulted clg.

SECOND FLOOR

down

covered porch
18'-0" x 10'-0"

master
13'-0" x 15'-0"
vaulted clg.

corner
fireplace

entertainment
center

w.i.c.

dining
11'-0" x 13'-0"
8'-0" clg.

great room
16'-0" x 18'-0"
2 story clg.

arch

arch

eating
bar

arch

arch

butlers
pantry

w/d

kitchen

foyer

storage

up

10' x 16'

covered entry porch

FIRST FLOOR

plan # HPK0400122

Style: Floridian
First Floor: 1,290 sq. ft.
Second Floor: 548 sq. ft.
Total: 1,838 sq. ft.
Bedrooms: 3
Bathrooms: 2½
Width: 38' - 0"
Depth: 51' - 0"
Foundation: Crawlspace

SEARCH ONLINE @ EPLANS.COM

A romantic air flirts with the clean, simple lines of this seaside getaway, set off by stunning shingle accents and sunburst transom. Horizontal siding complements an insulated metal roof to create a charming look that calls up a sense of 19th-Century style. Inside, an unrestrained floor plan harbors cozy interior spaces and offers great outdoor views through wide windows and French doors. At the heart of the home, the two-story great rooms features a corner fireplace, an angled entertainment center, and an eating bar shared with the gourmet kitchen. Columns and sweeping archways define the formal dining room, and French doors open to the veranda, inviting dreamy ocean breezes inside.

plan# HPK0400123

Style: Cottage
First Floor: 871 sq. ft.
Second Floor: 1,047 sq. ft.
Total: 1,918 sq. ft.
Bedrooms: 3
Bathrooms: 2½
Width: 32' - 0"
Depth: 47' - 0"
Foundation: Crawlspace

SEARCH ONLINE @ EPLANS.COM

With its shingle-and-siding exterior, this home has an air of oceanfront living. A large covered porch accesses a spacious gathering room, complete with a fireplace and optional shelving units. An archway leads from the gathering room to the dining room, which is highlighted with a wall of windows and boasts a doorway to the kitchen. The breakfast area overlooks a screened porch and flows smoothly into a U-shaped kitchen. The sleeping quarters reside upstairs and include two family suites, two full baths, a master suite with a tray ceiling, and a convenient laundry room.

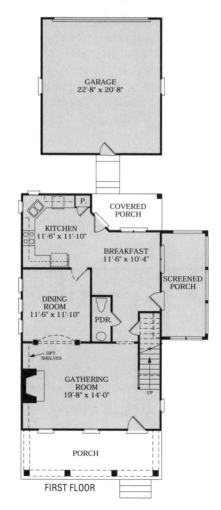

FIRST FLOOR

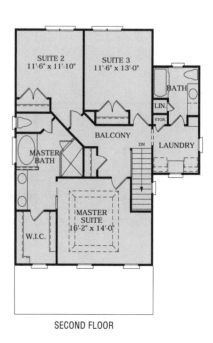

SECOND FLOOR

This home is quite a "looker" with its steeply sloping rooflines and large sunburst and multi-pane windows. This plan not only accommodates a narrow lot, but it also fits a sloping site. The angled corner entry gives way to a two-story living room with a tiled hearth. The dining room shares an interesting angled space with this area and enjoys easy service from the efficient kitchen. The family room offers double doors to a refreshing balcony. A powder room and laundry room complete the main level. Upstairs, a vaulted master bedroom enjoys a private bath; two other bedrooms share a bath.

plan# HPK0400124

Style: NW Contemporary
First Floor: 1,022 sq. ft.
Second Floor: 813 sq. ft.
Total: 1,835 sq. ft.
Bedrooms: 3
Bathrooms: 2½
Width: 36' - 0"
Depth: 33' - 0"
Foundation: Slab

SEARCH ONLINE @ EPLANS.COM

DINING
11/0 X 11/0 +/-

REF.
DN. UP
D. W

PANTRY

FAMILY
13/6 X 17/6

DN.

TWO STORY
LIVING
13/0 X 14/4

DECK

FIRST FLOOR

BR. 2
10/2 X 13/0

DN.

SHLVS.

BR. 3
10/8 X 11/8

LIN.

VAULTED
MASTER
13/6 X 12/6

LIVING RM.
BELOW

SECOND FLOOR

plan# HPK0400125

Style: Traditional
First Floor: 972 sq. ft.
Second Floor: 843 sq. ft.
Total: 1,815 sq. ft.
Bonus Space: 180 sq. ft.
Bedrooms: 3
Bathrooms: 2½
Width: 45' - 0"
Depth: 37' - 0"
Foundation: Crawlspace

SEARCH ONLINE @ EPLANS.COM

A brick arch and a two-story bay window adorn the facade of this comfortable family home. Inside, the formal bayed living room and dining room combine to make entertaining a breeze. At the rear of the home, family life is easy with the open floor plan of the family room, breakfast nook, and efficient kitchen. A fireplace graces the family room, and sliding glass doors access the outdoors from the nook. A powder room is conveniently located in the entry hall. Upstairs, three bedrooms include the master suite with a pampering bath. A full hall bath with twin vanities is shared by the family bedrooms. A bonus room is available for future development as a study, library, or fourth bedroom.

FIRST FLOOR

SECOND FLOOR

BR. 3
11/0 X 10/8

BR. 2
11/0 X 10/0

LOFT

DN

FOYER
BELOW

LIVING
BELOW

LIN

VAULTED
MASTER
15/2 X 12/0

SECOND FLOOR

plan# HPK0400126

Style: Craftsman
Main Level: 1,106 sq. ft.
Upper Level: 872 sq. ft.
Total: 1,978 sq. ft.
Bedrooms: 3
Bathrooms: 2½
Width: 38' - 0"
Depth: 35' - 0"
Foundation: Slab, Basement

SEARCH ONLINE @ EPLANS.COM

Though this home gives the impression of the Northwest, it will be the winner in any neighborhood. From the foyer, the two-story living room is just a couple of steps up and features a through-fireplace. The U-shaped kitchen has a cooktop work island, an adjacent nook, and easy access to the formal dining room. A spacious family room shares the fireplace with the living room, is enhanced by built-ins and also offers a quiet deck for stargazing. The upstairs consists of two family bedrooms sharing a full bath and a vaulted master suite complete with a walk-in closet and sumptuous bath. A two-car, drive-under garage has plenty of room for storage.

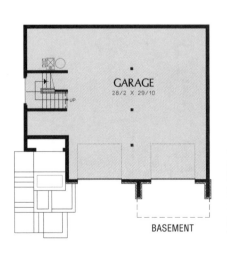

GARAGE
28/2 X 29/10

UP

BASEMENT

OPT FR
DRS.

DINING
10/6 X 12/0+

15/0 X 9/0

DW

PAN REF

DN

UP

DN

NOOK
13/10 X 8/4

2 STORY
LIVING
13/0 X 14/0

FAMILY
13/10 X 20/8

DECK

FIRST FLOOR

plan # HPK0400127

Style: Traditional
First Floor: 968 sq. ft.
Second Floor: 977 sq. ft.
Total: 1,945 sq. ft.
Bedrooms: 4
Bathrooms: 2½
Width: 40' - 0"
Depth: 46' - 0"
Foundation: Crawlspace

SEARCH ONLINE @ EPLANS.COM

This traditional home offers lovely formal rooms for entertaining. The living room has a centered fireplace and access to the front covered porch. A gourmet kitchen with a cooktop island serves the dining room. French doors open the morning nook to the outdoors; a second fireplace warms the family room. Upstairs, the master suite has a corner walk-in closet and an oversized shower. Three secondary bedrooms are connected by a stair hall.

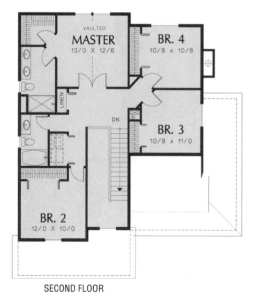

SECOND FLOOR

FIRST FLOOR

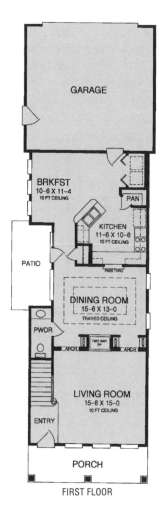

GARAGE

BRKFST
10-6 X 11-4
10 FT CEILING

PAN

KITCHEN
11-6 X 10-6
10 FT CEILING

PATIO

PASS THRU

DINING ROOM
15-6 X 13-0
TRAYED CEILING

PWDR

TWO WAY FP

ARCH   ARCH

LIVING ROOM
15-6 X 15-0
10 FT CEILING

ENTRY

PORCH

FIRST FLOOR

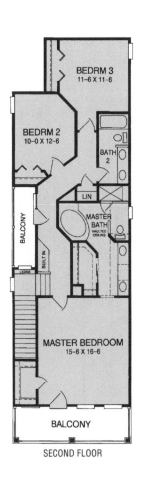

BEDRM 3
11-6 X 11-6

BEDRM 2
10-0 X 12-6

BATH 2

BALCONY

LIN

MASTER BATH
VAULTED CEILING

BUILT IN

LEDGE

MASTER BEDROOM
15-6 X 16-6

BALCONY

SECOND FLOOR

plan# HPK0400128

Style: Traditional
First Floor: 904 sq. ft.
Second Floor: 1,058 sq. ft.
Total: 1,962 sq. ft.
Bedrooms: 3
Bathrooms: 2½
Width: 22' - 0"
Depth: 74' - 0"
Foundation: Slab, Crawlspace

SEARCH ONLINE @ EPLANS.COM

Reminiscent of the popular town houses of the past, this fine clapboard home is perfect for urban or riverfront living. Two balconies grace the second floor—one at the front and one on the side. A two-way fireplace between the formal living and dining rooms provides visual impact. Built-in bookcases flank an arched opening between these rooms. A pass-through from the kitchen to the dining room simplifies serving, and a walk-in pantry provides storage. On the second floor, the master bedroom opens to a large balcony, and the relaxing master bath is designed with a separate shower and an angled whirlpool tub. Two secondary bedrooms and a full bath are located at the rear of the plan.

plan # HPK0400129

Style: Traditional
Square Footage: 1,879
Bonus Space: 965 sq. ft.
Bedrooms: 3
Bathrooms: 2
Width: 45' - 0"
Depth: 62' - 0"
Foundation: Crawlspace, Slab, Basement

SEARCH ONLINE @ EPLANS.COM

A sunburst over the entry door, columns supporting the covered porch, three dormers, and shutters give this home a comforting air. Inside, the living room contains a warming fireplace framed by windows. Sunshine or moonlight fills the formal dining room through bay windows—making any meal a glowing experience. The kitchen adjoins the dining room with a snack bar and shares the natural lighting of both the sunroom and the dining area. Nearby, the master suite has a private bath with a walk-in closet, separate shower, large oval tub, and two-sink vanity. Two bedrooms share a full bath accessed via the living room.

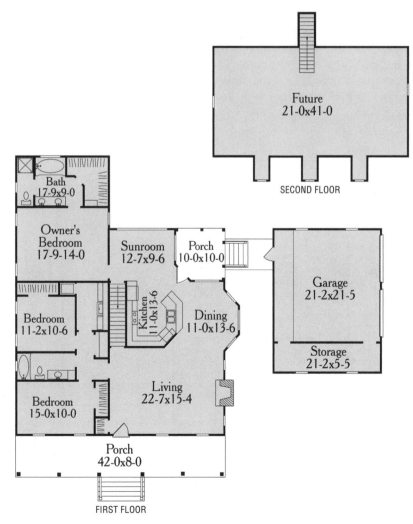

© 1998   Donald A Gardner, Inc.

Gable treatments along with stone and horizontal siding give a definite country flavor to this two-story home. Inside, the foyer opens to a great room, which boasts a fireplace, built-ins, and a magnificent view of the backyard beyond an inviting rear porch. The kitchen is designed for high style with a column-defined cooktop island and serving-bar access to the dining area. The master suite finishes this level and includes two walk-in closets and a private bath. Two bedrooms share a full bath and bonus space on the second floor.

plan# HPK0400130

Style: Country Cottage
First Floor: 1,336 sq. ft.
Second Floor: 523 sq. ft.
Total: 1,859 sq. ft.
Bonus Space: 225 sq. ft.
Bedrooms: 3
Bathrooms: 2½
Width: 45' - 0"
Depth: 53' - 0"

SEARCH ONLINE @ EPLANS.COM

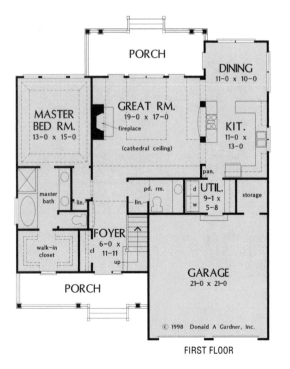

FIRST FLOOR

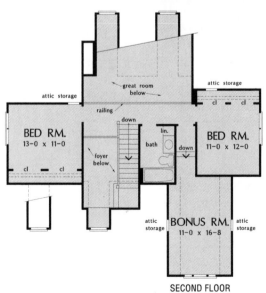

SECOND FLOOR

ORDER BLUEPRINTS 24 HOURS, 7 DAYS A WEEK, AT 1-800-521-6797

©1999 Donald A. Gardner, Inc.

plan # HPK0400131

Style: Traditional
First Floor: 1,454 sq. ft.
Second Floor: 533 sq. ft.
Total: 1,987 sq. ft.
Bonus Space: 428 sq. ft.
Bedrooms: 3
Bathrooms: 2½
Width: 57' - 0"
Depth: 50' - 4"

SEARCH ONLINE @ EPLANS.COM

Arched windows, gables, and dormers combine for maximum curb appeal. Inside, an innovative floor plan makes this home remarkably family-friendly. Elegant columns divide the home's foyer from its formal dining room, which is separated from the kitchen by a sizable pantry. The great room features a cathedral ceiling, a fireplace with flanking built-ins, and a wall of windows that overlooks the back porch. The master suite enjoys privacy on the first floor as well as a cathedral ceiling, private bath, and walk-in closet. Two more bedrooms upstairs share a hall bath, large linen closet, and access to the bonus room.

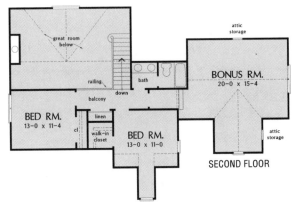

SECOND FLOOR

FIRST FLOOR

©1999 Donald A. Gardner, Inc.

© 1994 Donald A. Gardner Architects, Inc.

Interesting room arrangements make this home unique and inviting. From the wide front porch, enter the foyer to find the family bedrooms and a shared full bath on the left and a small hallway on the right that leads to the sunny kitchen. Ahead of the foyer and the kitchen is a combination great room and dining area that features a fireplace, access to the large back porch, and plenty of windows and skylights. A large utility area with access to the garage and an abundance of storage space completes the first floor. The second floor is reserved for a grand master suite that features plenty of closet space, a separate loft or study area, and a wonderful master bath with a bumped-out whirlpool tub.

plan # HPK0400132

Style: Traditional
First Floor: 1,234 sq. ft.
Second Floor: 609 sq. ft.
Total: 1,843 sq. ft.
Bedrooms: 3
Bathrooms: 2½
Width: 58' - 0"
Depth: 44' - 0"

SEARCH ONLINE @ EPLANS.COM

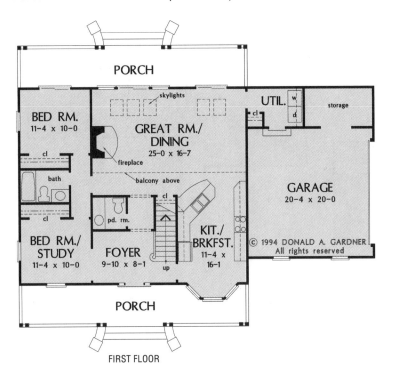

FIRST FLOOR

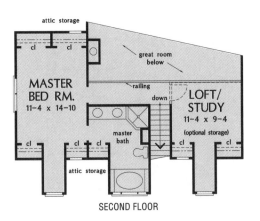

SECOND FLOOR

plan # HPK0400133

Style: Farmhouse
First Floor: 1,356 sq. ft.
Second Floor: 542 sq. ft.
Total: 1,898 sq. ft.
Bonus Space: 393 sq. ft.
Bedrooms: 3
Bathrooms: 2½
Width: 59' - 0"
Depth: 64' - 0"

SEARCH ONLINE @ EPLANS.COM

The welcoming charm of this country farmhouse is expressed by its many windows and its covered wraparound porch. A two-story foyer is enhanced by a Palladian window in a clerestory dormer above to let in natural lighting. The first-floor master suite allows privacy and accessibility. The master bath includes a whirlpool tub, separate shower, double-bowl vanity, and walk-in closet. The first floor features nine-foot ceilings throughout with the exception of the kitchen area, which sports an eight-foot ceiling. The second floor contains two additional bedrooms, a full bath, and plenty of storage space. The bonus room provides room to grow.

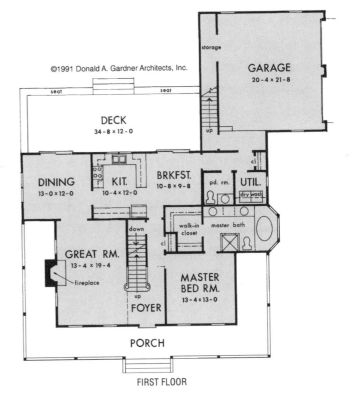

©1991 Donald A. Gardner Architects, Inc.

FIRST FLOOR

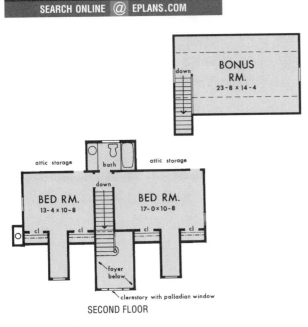

SECOND FLOOR

© 1992 Donald A. Gardner Architects, Inc.

B. NATHAN

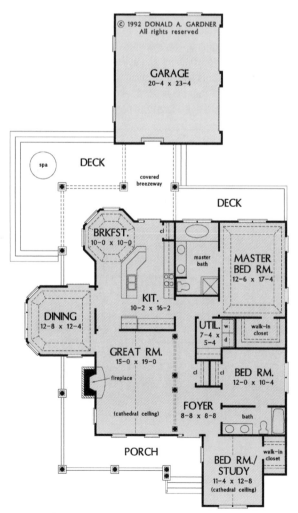

GARAGE
20-4 x 23-4

DECK

spa

covered breezeway

DECK

BRKFST.
10-0 x 10-0

cl

master bath

MASTER BED RM.
12-6 x 17-4

KIT.
10-2 x 16-2

DINING
12-8 x 12-4

UTIL.
7-4 x 5-4

w
d

walk-in closet

GREAT RM.
15-0 x 19-0

fireplace

cl

BED RM.
12-0 x 10-4

(cathedral ceiling)

FOYER
8-8 x 8-8

bath

PORCH

BED RM./ STUDY
11-4 x 12-8
(cathedral ceiling)

walk-in closet

plan# HPK0400134

Style: Traditional
Square Footage: 1,858
Bedrooms: 3
Bathrooms: 2
Width: 50' - 0"
Depth: 59' - 8"

SEARCH ONLINE @ EPLANS.COM

The wraparound covered porch adds charm as it provides a generous amount of outdoor living space. Inside, the foyer opens to the great room with its cathedral ceiling and cozy fireplace. To the rear, the formal dining room and breakfast nook are situated near the island kitchen for efficiency and convenience. The sleeping quarters are on the right where the master suite enjoys a luxurious private bath with a double-sink vanity.

plan# HPK0400135

Style: Farmhouse
Square Footage: 1,864
Bonus Space: 420 sq. ft.
Bedrooms: 3
Bathrooms: 2½
Width: 71' - 0"
Depth: 56' - 4"

SEARCH ONLINE @ EPLANS.COM

Quaint and cozy on the outside with porches front and back, this three-bedroom country home surprises with an open floor plan featuring a large great room with a cathedral ceiling. A central kitchen with an angled counter opens to the breakfast and great rooms for easy entertaining. The privately located master bedroom enjoys a cathedral ceiling and access to the deck. Two secondary bedrooms share a full hall bath. A bonus room makes expanding easy.

BONUS RM.
14-4 x 23-8

SECOND FLOOR

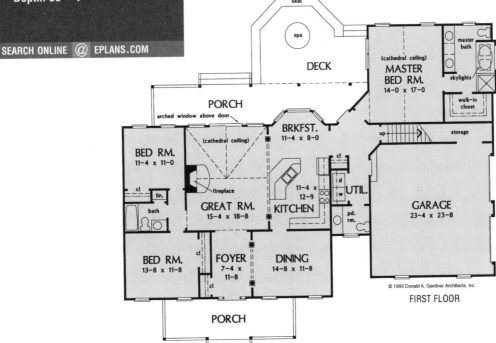

FIRST FLOOR

© 1993 Donald A. Gardner Architects, Inc.

This romantic cottage design is ideal for any countryside setting. Lively Victorian details enhance the exterior. A wrapping porch with a gazebo-style sitting area encourages refreshing outdoor relaxation; interior spaces are open to each other. The kitchen with a snack bar is open to both the dining area and the living room. A powder bath with laundry facilities completes the first floor. The second floor offers space for three family bedrooms with walk-in closets and a pampering whirlpool bath.

plan# HPK0400136

Style: Victorian
First Floor: 960 sq. ft.
Second Floor: 841 sq. ft.
Total: 1,801 sq. ft.
Bedrooms: 3
Bathrooms: 1½
Width: 36' - 0"
Depth: 30' - 0"
Foundation: Basement

SEARCH ONLINE @ EPLANS.COM

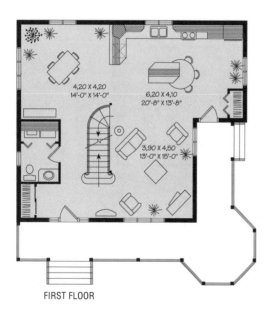

FIRST FLOOR

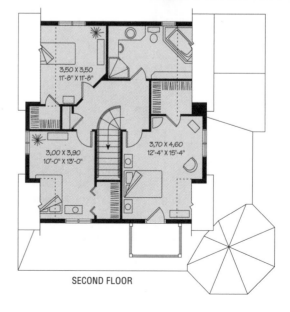

SECOND FLOOR

plan # HPK0400137

Style: Lakefront
First Floor: 1,212 sq. ft.
Second Floor: 620 sq. ft.
Total: 1,832 sq. ft.
Bedrooms: 3
Bathrooms: 2
Width: 38' - 0"
Depth: 40' - 0"
Foundation: Basement

SEARCH ONLINE @ EPLANS.COM

This comfortable vacation design provides two levels of relaxing family space. The main level offers a spacious wrapping front porch and an abundance of windows, filling interior spaces with the summer sunshine. A two-sided fireplace warms the living room/dining room combination and a master bedroom that features a roomy walk-in closet. Nearby, the hall bath offers a relaxing whirlpool tub. The kitchen is open and features an island snack bar and pantry storage. A cozy sunroom accesses the wrapping deck. Upstairs, two additional bedrooms feature ample closet space and share a second-floor bath.

FIRST FLOOR

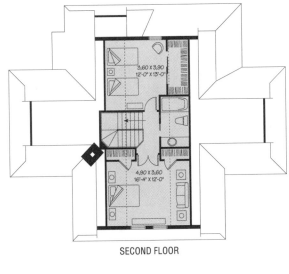

SECOND FLOOR

3,50 X 2,90
11'-8" X 9'-8"

3,60 X 3,00
12'-0" X 10'-0"

3,60 X 4,50
12'-0" X 15'-0"

2,40 X 3,00
8'-0" X 10'-0"

SECOND FLOOR

3,90 x 6,80
13'-0" x 22'-8"

5,30 X 3,60
17'-8" X 12'-0"

3,20 X 3,60
10'-8" X 12'-0"

3,60 X 5,00
12'-0" X 16'-8"

2,40 X 3,10
8'-0" X 10'-4"

FIRST FLOOR

plan # HPK0400138

Style: Farmhouse
First Floor: 974 sq. ft.
Second Floor: 929 sq. ft.
Total: 1,903 sq. ft.
Bedrooms: 3
Bathrooms: 2½
Width: 48' - 0"
Depth: 41' - 2"
Foundation: Basement

SEARCH ONLINE @ EPLANS.COM

A wraparound porch and a wide variety of windows ornament the facade of this country home. Special amenities on the first floor include a fireplace—focused on the living room, but still visible from the cozy dining area—a bay-windowed sitting area to the front of the plan, and a large walk-in closet near the breakfast nook. Upstairs, three bedrooms—one a master suite with a private bath—all access a petite sitting area.

plan# HPK0400139

Style: Victorian
First Floor: 1,044 sq. ft.
Second Floor: 894 sq. ft.
Total: 1,938 sq. ft.
Bonus Space: 228 sq. ft.
Bedrooms: 3
Bathrooms: 2½
Width: 58' - 0"
Depth: 43' - 6"
Foundation: Basement

SEARCH ONLINE @ EPLANS.COM

This charming country traditional home provides a well-lit home office, harbored in a beautiful bay with three windows. The second-floor bay brightens the master bath, which has a double-bowl vanity, a step-up tub, and a dressing area. The living and dining rooms share a two-sided fireplace. The gourmet kitchen has a cooktop island counter and enjoys outdoor views through sliding glass doors in the breakfast area. A sizable bonus room above the two-car garage can be developed into hobby space or a recreation room.

SECOND FLOOR

FIRST FLOOR

This wonderful design begins with the wraparound porch. Explore further and find a two-story entry with a coat closet and plant shelf above and a strategically placed staircase alongside. The island kitchen with a boxed window over the sink is adjacent to a large bay-windowed dinette. The great room includes many windows and a fireplace. A powder room and laundry room are both conveniently placed on the first floor. Upstairs, the large master suite contains His and Hers walk-in closets, corner windows, and a bath area featuring a double vanity and whirlpool tub. Two pleasant secondary bedrooms have interesting angles, and a third bedroom in the front features a volume ceiling and an arched window.

QUOTE ONE®

Cost to build? See page 333
to order complete cost estimate
to build this house in your area!

plan # HPK0400140

Style: Traditional
First Floor: 919 sq. ft.
Second Floor: 927 sq. ft.
Total: 1,846 sq. ft.
Bedrooms: 4
Bathrooms: 2½
Width: 44' - 0"
Depth: 40' - 0"

SEARCH ONLINE @ EPLANS.COM

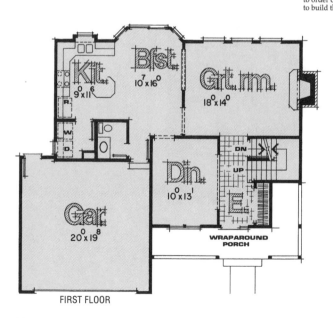

FIRST FLOOR

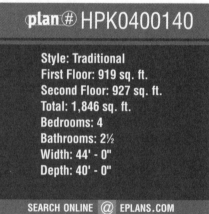

SECOND FLOOR

plan# HPK0400141

Style: Traditional
First Floor: 1,421 sq. ft.
Second Floor: 578 sq. ft.
Total: 1,999 sq. ft.
Bedrooms: 4
Bathrooms: 2½
Width: 52' - 0"
Depth: 47' - 4"

SEARCH ONLINE @ EPLANS.COM

QUOTE ONE®
Cost to build? See page 333
to order complete cost estimate
to build this house in your area!

Growing families will love this unique plan. Start with the living areas—a spacious great room with high ceilings, windows overlooking the backyard, a see-through fireplace to the kitchen area, and access to the rear deck. The dining room with hutch space accommodates formal occasions. The hearth kitchen features a well-planned work space and a bayed breakfast area. The master suite with a whirlpool tub and walk-in closet is found downstairs; three family bedrooms are upstairs. A two-car garage and handy laundry room complete the plan.

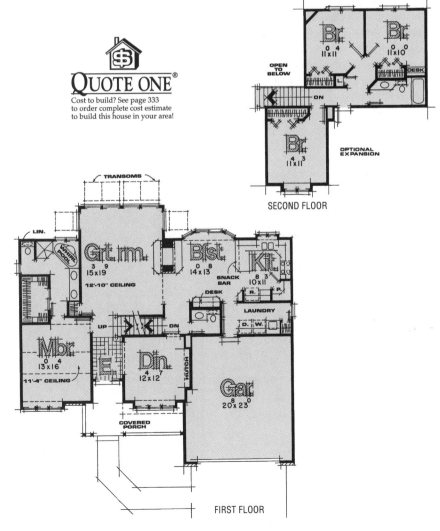

SECOND FLOOR

FIRST FLOOR

This plan's facade offers traditional, homespun appeal, yet its interior boasts elegance and convenience. Graceful ceiling detail brings the great room, dining room, and master bedroom to new heights of style. The kitchen, just a few steps away from the dining room, flows into a windowed breakfast room that accesses the rear porch—as does the great room. Two bedrooms share a bath to the left of the plan. The spacious master suite, tucked behind the garage on the right, offers ample closet space and a deluxe bath with twin vanities and a compartmented bath and shower. Bonus space awaits expansion above the two-car garage.

plan# HPK0400142

Style: Traditional
Square Footage: 1,955
Bonus Space: 329 sq. ft.
Bedrooms: 3
Bathrooms: 2
Width: 56' - 0"
Depth: 58' - 4"

SEARCH ONLINE @ EPLANS.COM

plan # HPK0400143

Style: Traditional
Square Footage: 1,926
Bedrooms: 3
Bathrooms: 2
Width: 57' - 0"
Depth: 62' - 6"

SEARCH ONLINE @ EPLANS.COM

Here's a comfortable family home with an inviting country style that makes it a winner in any neighborhood. Created for today's busy lifestyles, the center of this design is the large island kitchen. A serving bar faces the breakfast area, and the dining room is conveniently around the corner (so dirty dishes are out of sight). An octagonal family room ushers in natural light and warms with a corner fireplace. On the right, two bedrooms share a full bath that hosts private vanities. The master suite is secluded on the left, with a sloped ceiling and a relaxing spa bath.

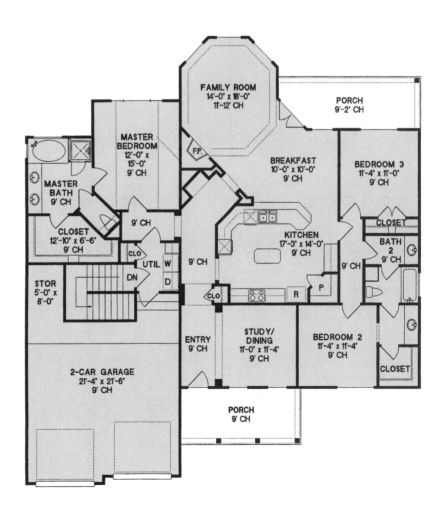

GARAGE
20'-0" x 22'-0"

plan# HPK0400144

Style: Craftsman
First Floor: 1,060 sq. ft.
Second Floor: 914 sq. ft.
Total: 1,974 sq. ft.
Bedrooms: 3
Bathrooms: 3
Width: 32' - 0"
Depth: 35' - 0"
Foundation: Crawlspace

SEARCH ONLINE @ EPLANS.COM

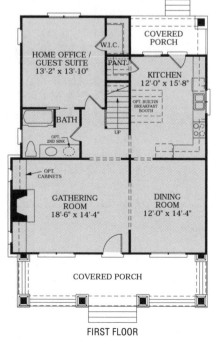

HOME OFFICE /
GUEST SUITE
13'-2" x 13'-10"

W.I.C.

COVERED
PORCH

PANT.

KITCHEN
12'-0" x 15'-8"

BATH

OPT. BUILT-IN
BREAKFAST
BOOTH

OPT.
2ND SINK

UP

OPT.
CABINETS

GATHERING
ROOM
18'-6" x 14'-4"

DINING
ROOM
12'-0" x 14'-4"

COVERED PORCH

FIRST FLOOR

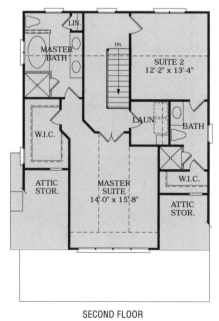

LIN.

MASTER
BATH

DN

SUITE 2
12'-2" x 13'-4"

W.I.C.

LAUN.

BATH

W.I.C.

ATTIC
STOR.

MASTER
SUITE
14'-0" x 15'-8"

ATTIC
STOR.

SECOND FLOOR

This charming Craftsman design offers a second-story master bedroom with four windows under the gabled dormer. The covered front porch displays column and pier supports. The hearth-warmed gathering room opens to the dining room on the right, where the adjoining kitchen offers enough space for an optional breakfast booth. A home office/guest suite is found in the rear. The second floor holds the lavish master suite and a second bedroom suite with its own private bath.

plan⊕# HPK0400145

Style: Craftsman
Square Footage: 1,997
Bedrooms: 4
Bathrooms: 2½
Width: 60' - 0"
Depth: 51' - 0"
Foundation: Crawlspace

SEARCH ONLINE @ EPLANS.COM

Elements of the shingle style reside in this lovely traditional home, which captures a sense of casual dignity. The foyer opens to the formal rooms and to a secluded den or guest room. A vaulted family room adjoins a galley-style kitchen and a morning nook that accesses the outdoors. Sleeping quarters are connected by a hall leading back to the foyer. The master bedroom enjoys a private bath—with garden tub, separate shower, dual basins, and compartmented toilet—and a walk-in closet. The laundry room provides convenient access to the three-car garage.

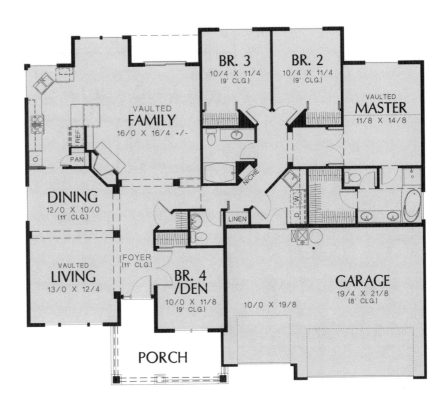

FIRST FLOOR

Second Floor plan:

GREAT RM.
BELOW

DN.

LIN.

BR. 2
10/8 X 13/0

BR. 3
11/0 X 13/0

FOYER
BELOW

PLANT SHELF

SECOND FLOOR

plan# HPK0400146

Style: **Bungalow**
First Floor: **1,396 sq. ft.**
Second Floor: **523 sq. ft.**
Total: **1,919 sq. ft.**
Bedrooms: **4**
Bathrooms: **2½**
Width: **44' - 0"**
Depth: **51' - 0"**
Foundation: **Crawlspace**

SEARCH ONLINE @ EPLANS.COM

Double pillars herald the entry to this charming design. They are offset from the front door and introduce a porch that leads to the den (or make it a fourth bedroom). Living areas center on the casual life and include a great room, with a fireplace, that opens directly to the dining room. The kitchen is L-shaped for convenience and features an island cooktop. The master suite on the first floor sports a vaulted ceiling and bath with spa tub and separate shower. The upper floor holds two secondary bedrooms and a full bath. The open staircase is decorated with a plant shelf that receives light from double windows over the foyer.

plan # HPK0400147

Style: Farmhouse
Square Footage: 1,822
Bedrooms: 3
Bathrooms: 2
Width: 58' - 0"
Depth: 66' - 8"
Foundation: Basement

SEARCH ONLINE @ EPLANS.COM

A quaint mix of materials and an enticing floor plan lend this home modern interest with traditional perks. Inside, the foyer is flanked by a dining room and an optional study/office. The vaulted living room is warmed by a fireplace and connects to the kitchen/nook area. The master suite is secluded and includes a private bath and walk-in closet. Family bedrooms located on the opposite side of the home share a hall bath that accesses the rear porch. Grilling and seasonal activities will be enjoyed on the porch.

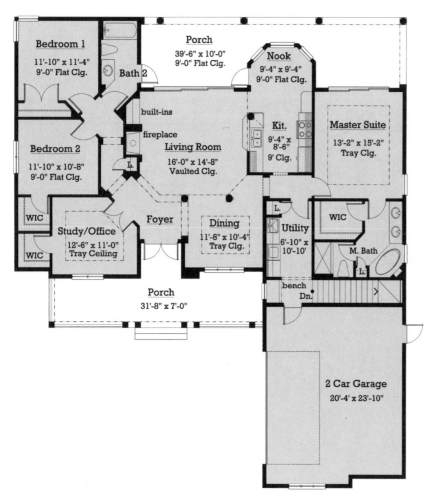

Bedroom 1
11'-10" x 11'-4"
9'-0" Flat Clg.

Bath 2

Porch
39'-6" x 10'-0"
9'-0" Flat Clg.

Nook
9'-4" x 9'-4"
9'-0" Flat Clg.

built-ins

fireplace

Kit.
9'-4" x
8'-6"
9' Clg.

Master Suite
13'-2" x 15'-2"
Tray Clg.

Living Room
16'-0" x 14'-8"
Vaulted Clg.

Bedroom 2
11'-10" x 10'-8"
9'-0" Flat Clg.

WIC

Foyer

Dining
11'-8" x 10'-4"
Tray Clg.

Utility
6'-10" x
10'-10"

WIC

M. Bath

WIC

Study/Office
12'-6" x 11'-0"
Tray Ceiling

Porch
31'-8" x 7'-0"

bench
Dn.

2 Car Garage
20'-4' x 23'-10"

plan # HPK0400148

Style: Country Cottage
Square Footage: 1,822
Bedrooms: 3
Bathrooms: 2
Width: 58' - 0"
Depth: 66' - 8"
Foundation: Basement

SEARCH ONLINE @ EPLANS.COM

The captivating charm of this popular farmhouse is reminiscent of a gentler time. Its compact size makes use of every inch and provides a spacious feel. The centrally located living room has a fireplace and an entertainment center. Both the formal dining room and the breakfast nook are accented with columns and abundant natural light. The study or office located at the front of the design features a tray ceiling. The comforting master bath features double vanities, a garden tub, and a full-sized shower. Two additional bedrooms—one with a walk-in closet—share a full bath.

plan # HPK0400149

Style: Farmhouse
Square Footage: 1,822
Bedrooms: 3
Bathrooms: 2
Width: 58' - 0"
Depth: 67' - 2"
Foundation: Basement

SEARCH ONLINE @ EPLANS.COM

Stone bays and wood siding make up the exterior facade on this one-story home. The interior revolves around the living room with an attached dining room and the galley kitchen with a breakfast room. The master suite has a fine bath and a walk-in closet. One of three family bedrooms on the left side of the plan could be used as a home office.

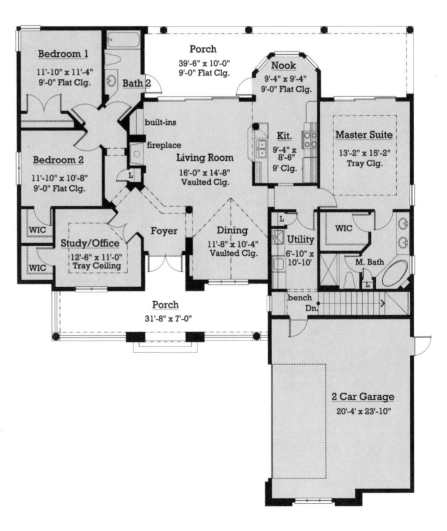

A rustic exterior of shingles, siding, and stone provides a sweet country look. Inside, the foyer is flanked by a dining room and family bedrooms. Bedrooms 2 and 3 share a full hall bath. The master suite, located on the opposite side of the home for privacy, boasts a tray ceiling and a pampering bath with an oversized tub. The kitchen opens to a breakfast room that accesses the rear sundeck. The enormous living room is warmed by a central fireplace. The laundry room and double-car garage complete this plan.

plan# HPK0400150

Style: Traditional
Square Footage: 1,869
Bonus Space: 336 sq. ft.
Bedrooms: 3
Bathrooms: 2
Width: 54' - 0"
Depth: 60' - 6"
Foundation: Basement, Crawlspace, Slab

SEARCH ONLINE @ EPLANS.COM

plan # HPK0400151

Style: Farmhouse
Square Footage: 1,848
Bedrooms: 3
Bathrooms: 2
Width: 58' - 0"
Depth: 60' - 0"
Foundation: Crawlspace

SEARCH ONLINE @ EPLANS.COM

This farmhouse is embellished with European touches. Fieldstone and stucco, arch-top windows, and shutters invite a little bit of everything good into this design. The covered porch is a sweet treat for mild evenings. Inside, the dining room is graced with a stepped ceiling and defining column. The living room captures rear views through multiple windows and rear-porch access. A master suite, to the right, is secluded for privacy. The country kitchen is a delight of casual space featuring interaction between the family room with built-in entertainment center and the breakfast nook—all featuring vaulted ceilings. Two family bedrooms are found to the left and share a full bath.

This simple country design uses both siding and brick for a strong but uncomplicated exterior. The porch leads to an entry chamber with a coat closet and internal door. The living space includes the living room, dining room, and eat-in kitchen with a walk-in pantry. The second floor is home to the sleeping quarters. One option has a master bedroom with a sitting bay and two family bedrooms, all sharing a large bath. Another option includes a private master bath and a separate bath for the family bedrooms.

plan# HPK0400152

Style: Traditional
First Floor: 881 sq. ft.
Second Floor: 926 sq. ft.
Total: 1,807 sq. ft.
Bedrooms: 3
Bathrooms: 1½
Width: 32' - 0"
Depth: 40' - 0"
Foundation: Basement

SEARCH ONLINE @ EPLANS.COM

FIRST FLOOR

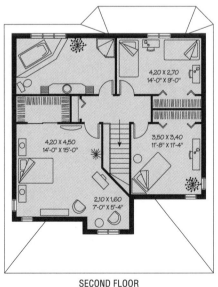

SECOND FLOOR

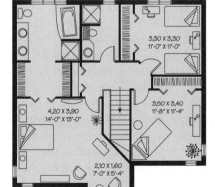

OPTIONAL LAYOUT

plan # HPK0400153

Style: Traditional
First Floor: 1,113 sq. ft.
Second Floor: 835 sq. ft.
Total: 1,948 sq. ft.
Optional Bedroom: 245 sq. ft.
Bedrooms: 3
Bathrooms: 2½
Width: 54' - 0"
Depth: 34' - 8"
Foundation: Basement

SEARCH ONLINE @ EPLANS.COM

The covered porch on this charming two-story home provides a place to relax and enjoy peaceful summer evenings. Warmed by the fireplace and lit by a bay window and glass door, the rear of this home becomes a favorite gathering place for family activities. The island kitchen offers a pantry. The option of a three- or four-bedroom second floor is available with this plan. Choose the plan that best fits your family's needs and you will receive the same master bedroom suite with a luxurious bath and walk-in closet. A balcony overlooks the entry in both options providing added excitement to the family-size home.

SECOND FLOOR

FIRST FLOOR

OPTIONAL LAYOUT

A brick one-story garage with a flowerbox window lends this two-story home a cottage feel. Inside, efficient use of space and flexibility add to the appeal. A formal dining room opens from the two-story foyer, and leads to a cleverly designed kitchen. A serving bar connects the kitchen and breakfast nook. The hearth-warmed family room is just steps away. Four bedrooms—three family bedrooms and a roomy master suite—fill the second level. Note the option of turning Bedroom 4 into a sitting area for the master suite.

plan# HPK0400154

Style: Country Cottage
First Floor: 947 sq. ft.
Second Floor: 981 sq. ft.
Total: 1,928 sq. ft.
Bedrooms: 4
Bathrooms: 2½
Width: 41' - 0"
Depth: 39' - 4"
Foundation: Crawlspace, Basement

SEARCH ONLINE @ EPLANS.COM

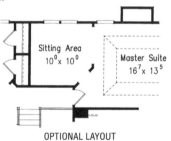

Sitting Area
10^0 x 10^0

Master Suite
16^7 x 13^5

OPTIONAL LAYOUT

FIRST FLOOR

SECOND FLOOR

ORDER BLUEPRINTS 24 HOURS, 7 DAYS A WEEK, AT 1-800-521-6797

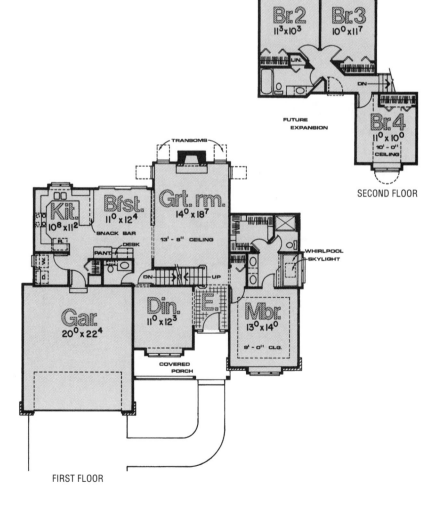

plan # HPK0400155

Style: Traditional
First Floor: 1,297 sq. ft.
Second Floor: 558 sq. ft.
Total: 1,855 sq. ft.
Bedrooms: 4
Bathrooms: 2½
Width: 52' - 0"
Depth: 45' - 4"

SEARCH ONLINE @ EPLANS.COM

The covered front porch of this home opens to a great floor plan. From the entry, go left to reach the formal dining room with its boxed window. Straight back is the great room with a handsome fireplace and tall windows. A snack bar, pantry, and planning desk in the kitchen make it convenient and appealing. The breakfast room has sliding glass doors to the rear yard. The master bedroom is on the first floor and has a luxurious bath with a skylit whirlpool tub. Upstairs are three more bedrooms and a full bath.

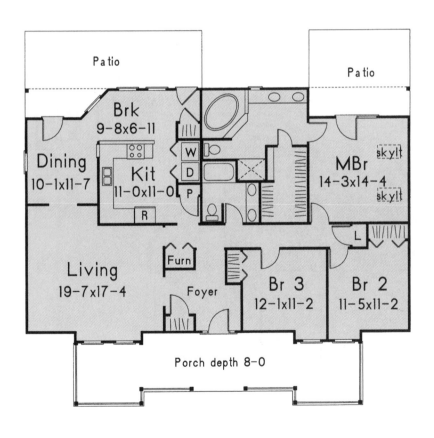

Patio

Patio

Brk
9-8x6-11

Dining
10-1x11-7

Kit
11-0x11-0

W
D
P

skylt

MBr
14-3x14-4

skylt

R

L

Living
19-7x17-4

Furn

Foyer

Br 3
12-1x11-2

Br 2
11-5x11-2

Porch depth 8-0

plan# HPK0400156

Style: Traditional
Square Footage: 1,832
Bedrooms: 3
Bathrooms: 2
Width: 56' - 0"
Depth: 35' - 4"
Foundation: Crawlspace,
Basement, Slab

SEARCH ONLINE @ EPLANS.COM

The expansive front porch and two rear patios extend the living space of this compact, one-story home. The kitchen wonderfully enjoys counters that face the living and dining rooms and the sunny breakfast alcove. Skylights and a private entry to the rear patio are highlights of the lovely master suite. Two other bedrooms share a hall bath. A washer and dryer are conveniently located to the rear of the kitchen.

plan # HPK0400157

Style: Country Cottage
Square Footage: 1,915
Bedrooms: 3
Bathrooms: 2
Width: 46' - 0"
Depth: 60' - 2"
Foundation: Crawlspace

SEARCH ONLINE @ EPLANS.COM

A sunny bay window and a shady recessed entry create an elegant impression in this lovely design. The sleeping quarters are arranged for privacy along the perimeter of the spacious living areas. The kitchen provides a generous work space, and the dining room is open to the gathering room with its fireplace. To the rear, a covered veranda is accessible from the dining room and the master suite. Note the lavish bath and huge walk-in closet in this suite.

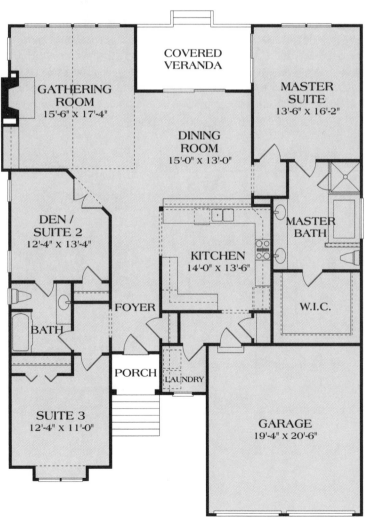

A covered porch with a recessed entry is crowned with the addition of a front gable. A symmetrical plan of living areas places the living and dining rooms to either side of the foyer, with the family room directly ahead. A graceful arched opening and a fireplace flanked by windows are complemented by extra-high ceilings in the foyer and family room. An efficiently designed kitchen features an abundance of counter and cabinet space along with a serving bar to the breakfast nook. The master suite is separated from the two family bedrooms for privacy.

plan# HPK0400158

Style: Country Cottage
Square Footage: 1,856
Bedrooms: 3
Bathrooms: 2
Width: 59' - 0"
Depth: 54' - 6"
Foundation: Slab, Crawlspace, Basement

SEARCH ONLINE @ EPLANS.COM

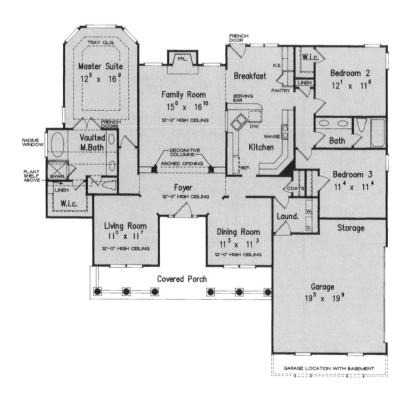

OPTIONAL LAYOUT

plan# HPK0400159

Style: Traditional
Square Footage: 1,833
Bedrooms: 3
Bathrooms: 2
Width: 62' - 0"
Depth: 30' - 0"
Foundation: Basement

SEARCH ONLINE @ EPLANS.COM

This desirable home is modest in size but large on attractive features. A vaulted living room delights with a warming fireplace at one end. Enjoying rear views, the nearby dining room will cater both formal and family occasions. A sunny breakfast bay opens to a rear deck allowing leisurely weekend breakfasts to be enjoyed alfresco. A private master suite boasts a walk-in closet, dual-sink vanity, and corner tub. Two family bedrooms, one with a three-window bay, are located on the other side of the house.

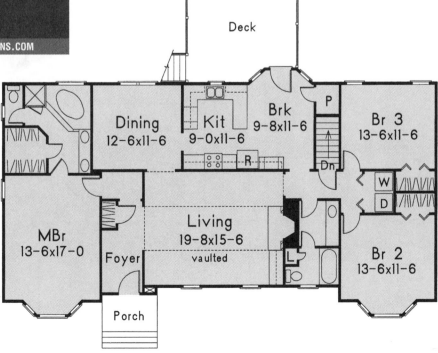

Gables at varying heights, a traditional front porch, and shuttered windows give a small-town look to this family home. The two-story foyer leads to the dining room on the left or to the family room, which is straight ahead past the powder room, coat closet, and entrance to the garage. The family room is open to the kitchen, which boasts a work island, corner window sink, and access to the laundry room. The second floor contains a master suite with two walk-in closets, two family bedrooms that share a bath but have private walk-in closets, an over-look to the foyer below, and an optional bonus room.

plan# HPK0400160

Style: Country Cottage
First Floor: 916 sq. ft.
Second Floor: 895 sq. ft.
Total: 1,811 sq. ft.
Bonus Space: 262 sq. ft.
Bedrooms: 3
Bathrooms: 2½
Width: 44' - 0"
Depth: 38' - 0"
Foundation: Crawlspace, Basement, Slab

SEARCH ONLINE @ EPLANS.COM

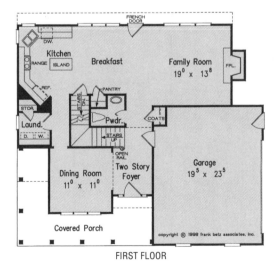

FIRST FLOOR

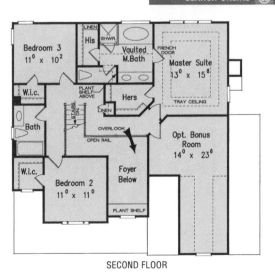

SECOND FLOOR

plan # HPK0400161

Style: Colonial
First Floor: 830 sq. ft.
Second Floor: 1,060 sq. ft.
Total: 1,890 sq. ft.
Bedrooms: 3
Bathrooms: 2½
Width: 41' - 0"
Depth: 40' - 6"
Foundation: Walkout Basement

SEARCH ONLINE @ EPLANS.COM

The pleasing character of this house does not stop behind its facade. The foyer opens to a great room with a fireplace and also to the eat-in kitchen. Stairs lead from the great room to the second floor, where a laundry room is conveniently placed near the bedrooms. The master suite spares none of the amenities: a full bath with a double vanity, shower, tub, and walk-in closet. Bedrooms 2 and 3 share a full bath.

SECOND FLOOR

FIRST FLOOR

FIRST FLOOR

SECOND FLOOR

plan # HPK0400162

Style: Traditional
First Floor: 1,335 sq. ft.
Second Floor: 515 sq. ft.
Total: 1,850 sq. ft.
Bonus Space: 368 sq. ft.
Bedrooms: 3
Bathrooms: 2½
Width: 44' - 0"
Depth: 57' - 4"
Foundation: Crawlspace, Basement

SEARCH ONLINE @ EPLANS.COM

This European design boasts a layout perfect for a narrow lot. A covered front porch welcomes you inside to a two-story foyer that leads to the vaulted great room. The kitchen with a pantry and serving bar easily serves the dining and breakfast rooms. The first-floor master suite is topped by a tray ceiling and includes a private bath with a walk-in closet. A laundry room leading to the two-car garage completes the first floor. Upstairs, two additional bedrooms are separated by a bridge overlook and share a hall bath. The optional bonus room is great for a home office, storage room, or guest suite.

plan# HPK0400163

Style: Traditional
First Floor: 915 sq. ft.
Second Floor: 963 sq. ft.
Total: 1,878 sq. ft.
Bedrooms: 3
Bathrooms: 2½
Width: 52' - 0"
Depth: 37' - 6"
Foundation: Slab, Crawlspace, Basement

SEARCH ONLINE @ EPLANS.COM

A covered front porch and fanciful shutters combine to give this home plenty of curb appeal. The two-story foyer is decorated by a corner niche for collectibles and opens to the formal living and dining rooms. Extras in the kitchen include built-in corner shelves, a pantry, and an angled work space open to the informal area of the house. A sunny breakfast room provides access to the rear property, and the two-story family room features a corner fireplace. Upstairs, two family bedrooms share a full hall bath. A lavish master suite boasts a large walk-in closet and a vaulted bath with a plant shelf, a garden tub, and twin vanities. The laundry room is nearby.

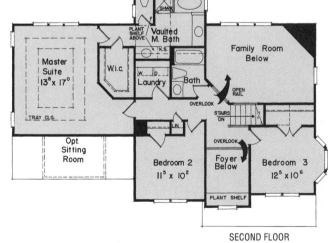

SECOND FLOOR

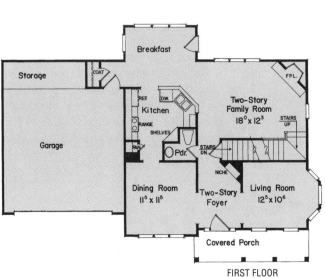

FIRST FLOOR

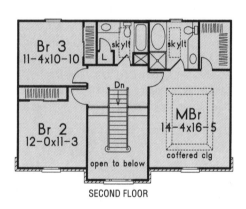

SECOND FLOOR

plan# HPK0400164

Style: Traditional
First Floor: 1,137 sq. ft.
Second Floor: 859 sq. ft.
Total: 1,996 sq. ft.
Bedrooms: 3
Bathrooms: 2½
Width: 68' - 4"
Depth: 27' - 4"
Foundation: Slab, Crawlspace, Basement

SEARCH ONLINE @ EPLANS.COM

A distinctive facade balances traditional angles with European details. The living room and ornate dining room create formal spaces for entertaining. A spacious gourmet kitchen provides a desirable work island, pantry, and breakfast space. The central fireplace draws in warmth from the casual family room. The master suite is outfitted with a private bath and walk-in closet. Two secondary bedrooms share a skylit bath.

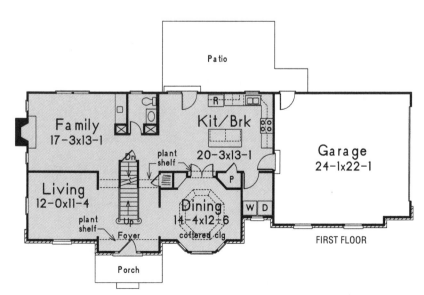

FIRST FLOOR

plan # HPK0400165

Style: Transitional
First Floor: 1,036 sq. ft.
Second Floor: 861 sq. ft.
Total: 1,897 sq. ft.
Bedrooms: 3
Bathrooms: 2½
Width: 48' - 0"
Depth: 38' - 0"
Foundation: Basement

SEARCH ONLINE @ EPLANS.COM

The refined exterior of this distinctive plan introduces a charming and livable home. Highlights of the floor plan include a furniture alcove in the formal dining room, a high ceiling, and French doors topped with arched windows in the great room, a wood rail at the split stairs, a walk-in pantry in the kitchen, and a laundry room that's roomy enough to do a family-size laundry with helpers. The view from the foyer through the great room to the rear yard enhances indoor-outdoor entertaining. The spacious kitchen and breakfast area encourage relaxed gatherings. The second floor features a window seat at the top of the stairs and a computer desk in the extra-large hallway. The deluxe master suite offers a whirlpool tub, separate vanities, a shower stall, and a spacious walk-in closet.

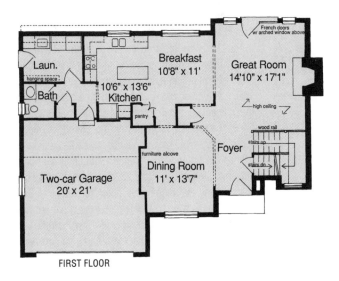

FIRST FLOOR

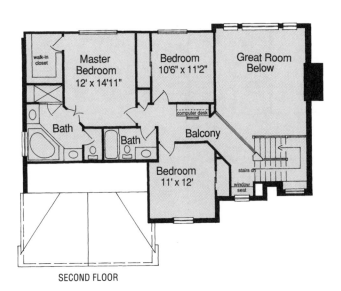

SECOND FLOOR

With zoned living at the core of this floor plan, livability takes a convenient turn. Living areas are to the left of the plan; sleeping areas are to the right. The formal dining room is open to the central hallway and foyer and features graceful columned archways to define its space. The great room contains angled corners and a magnificent central fireplace and offers ample views to the rear grounds. Steps away is a well-lit breakfast room with private rear-porch access and an adjoining C-shaped kitchen with a unique angled counter space and sink. Sleeping quarters are clustered around a private hallway, which offers a guest bath. The master suite includes a resplendent bath with a garden tub, dual lavatories, and a walk-in closet. Two family bedrooms share a full bath that features a compartmented toilet and tub.

plan # HPK0400167

Style: Traditional
First Floor: 918 sq. ft.
Second Floor: 908 sq. ft.
Total: 1,826 sq. ft.
Bedrooms: 3
Bathrooms: 2
Width: 48' - 0"
Depth: 35' - 4"
Foundation: Basement

SEARCH ONLINE @ EPLANS.COM

Rich with a brick facade, floods of natural light, and a comfortable, warm interior, this home may just be perfect. Enter to a foyer with a separate interior door, creating a mudroom-style entry. The family room is on the right, warmed by a cozy hearth and lit by a tall Palladian window. In the kitchen, an island snack bar is great for casual meals, or dine in luxury in the bright, bayed dining room. Three generous bedrooms are located upstairs, the master boasting dual walk-in closets. A shared bath will pamper and soothe with a corner whirlpool tub and twin sinks.

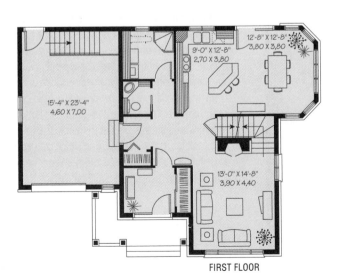

FIRST FLOOR

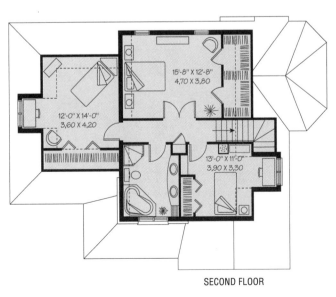

SECOND FLOOR

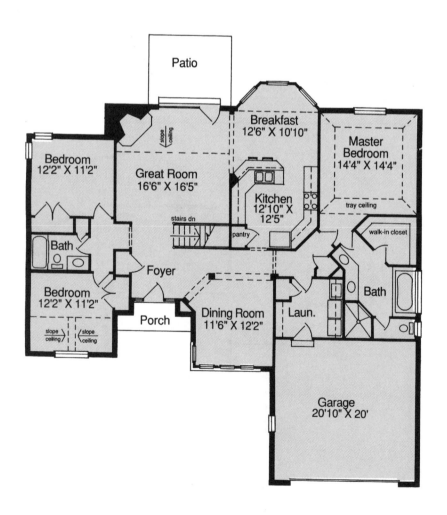

plan # HPK0400168

Style: Transitional
Square Footage: 1,955
Bedrooms: 3
Bathrooms: 2
Width: 59' - 0"
Depth: 58' - 0"
Foundation: Basement

SEARCH ONLINE @ EPLANS.COM

This dynamite brick one-story home holds a floor plan with plenty of space for the family. The great room is the hub of the home and features patio access and a corner fireplace for warmth. A formal dining room, defined by columns, sits at the front of the plan, and a more casual breakfast room connects directly to the gourmet kitchen. The master suite sits behind the two-car garage and contains a walk-in closet and a bath with separate tub and shower. Family bedrooms on the far left side of the plan share a full hall bath.

plan# HPK0400169

Style: Traditional
First Floor: 1,368 sq. ft.
Second Floor: 492 sq. ft.
Total: 1,860 sq. ft.
Bedrooms: 3
Bathrooms: 2½
Width: 50' - 0"
Depth: 47' - 1"
Foundation: Slab

SEARCH ONLINE @ EPLANS.COM

This narrow-lot, two-story home shows an abundance of exterior charm. Of particular note is the transom above the front door with glass sidelights. The two-story brick gable in front creates a massive appearance. Inside, the foyer opens directly to a formal dining room and a large great room that offers windows to the rear and a fireplace and built-in TV shelf. The family dining area features a cone ceiling and fantastic view of the rear yard. The first-floor master suite has a cathedral ceiling and two walk-in closets in the bath area. There is a covered patio off the master suite and also off the casual dining room. Two family bedrooms and a full bath complete the second floor.

SECOND FLOOR

FIRST FLOOR

European and contemporary accents dazzle the exterior of this charming design. An arched entry welcomes you inside, and the two-story turret adds an Old World touch. A two-story living room is located to the left and features a warming fireplace. The island snack-bar kitchen is open to the dining area. A laundry/powder room is placed just outside of the garage. Upstairs, the master bedroom provides a bayed sitting area and a huge walk-in closet. Two additional bedrooms share a full hall bath with the master suite.

plan# HPK0400170

Style: European Cottage
First Floor: 1,050 sq. ft.
Second Floor: 917 sq. ft.
Total: 1,967 sq. ft.
Bedrooms: 3
Bathrooms: 2
Width: 44' - 0"
Depth: 42' - 0"
Foundation: Basement

SEARCH ONLINE @ EPLANS.COM

FIRST FLOOR

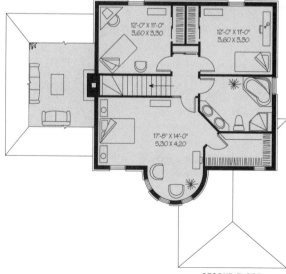

SECOND FLOOR

plan# HPK0400171

Style: Traditional
Square Footage: 1,834
Bedrooms: 3
Bathrooms: 2
Width: 55' - 0"
Depth: 60' - 4"
Foundation: Slab

SEARCH ONLINE @ EPLANS.COM

Corner quoins, French shutters, and rounded windows provide an Old World feel to this modern cottage design. A stunning brick facade hints at the exquisite beauty of the interior spaces. The great room is warmed by a fireplace and accesses the rear porch. The casual kitchen/dinette area provides pantry space. The master suite offers a private bath and enormous walk-in closet. Two family bedrooms on the opposite side of the home share a full hall bath and linen storage. A double garage and laundry room are located nearby.

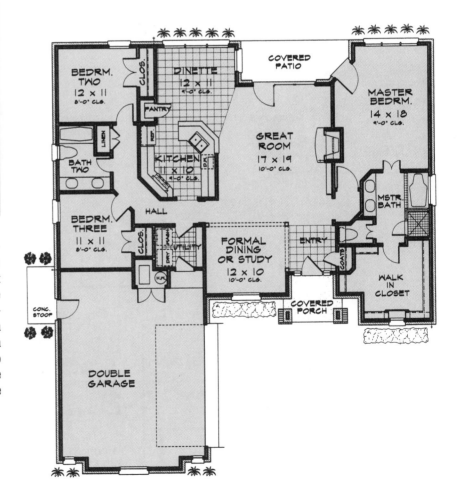

The cozy atmosphere of this delightful bungalow is warm and inviting. The impressive view from the foyer includes the great room with a fireplace and triple windows across the rear. The formal dining room adds dimension to the entry and is conveniently located near the kitchen. French doors and skylights flood the breakfast area with natural light and a recessed alcove provides for efficient furniture placement. Split bedrooms offer privacy to the master bedroom, with a large walk-in closet and a lavish bath. Two secondary bedrooms and a full basement expand this plan to create a home that's perfect for the empty-nester or the growing family.

plan# HPK0400173

Style: Traditional
Square Footage: 1,812
Bedrooms: 4
Bathrooms: 2
Width: 50' - 0"
Depth: 62' - 2"
Foundation: Crawlspace, Slab

SEARCH ONLINE @ EPLANS.COM

Brick adds warmth and character to the exterior of this lovely one-story home. Inside, columns grace the entrance to the formal living room and dining room. Built-in bookcases flank a bright fireplace in the living room. The kitchen easily serves casual and formal dining areas alike. Split-bedroom planning places the private master suite to the right of the plan. A sitting area highlights the master bedroom and the private bath enjoys many amenities. The left side of the home contains three family bedrooms, a full bath, and a utility room.

Classic good looks and a modern floor plan designed for family living are making this traditional home one of our best sellers. A stately brick facade, keystone arches, and a dormer window set this home apart from the crowd, but the spirit of the plan is inside. Raised ceilings throughout the first floor lend a feeling of spaciousness. A sunny living room and vaulted dining room surround the foyer; ahead, the family room enjoys a vaulted ceiling and a cozy corner fireplace. A modified galley kitchen serves the bayed nook with an eating bar and the dining room through a butler's pantry. The opulent master suite is graced with a spa bath with a corner tub, and a vast walk-in closet. Two additional bedrooms share a bath upstairs.

plan # HPK0400174

Style: Traditional
First Floor: 1,448 sq. ft.
Second Floor: 449 sq. ft.
Total: 1,897 sq. ft.
Bedrooms: 3
Bathrooms: 2½
Width: 48' - 0"
Depth: 46' - 0"

SEARCH ONLINE @ EPLANS.COM

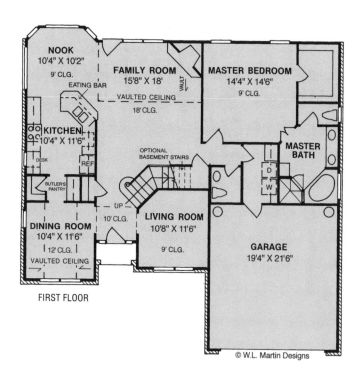

FIRST FLOOR

© W.L. Martin Designs

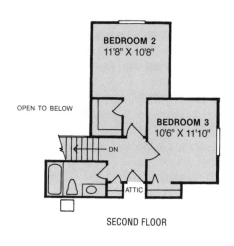

SECOND FLOOR

plan # HPK0400175

Style: Traditional
Square Footage: 1,943
Bedrooms: 2
Bathrooms: 2
Width: 35' - 0"
Depth: 75' - 0"
Foundation: Slab

SEARCH ONLINE @ EPLANS.COM

This traditional-style home begins with a private side entrance and a covered entry porch. A large living room with a corner fireplace opens to the patio area. A laundry area is nestled between the garage, the U-shaped kitchen, and the skylit dinette. Both the study and the master suite feature tray ceilings. The master suite also enjoys a double-sink vanity, a tub and separate shower, and two walk-in closets. A second bedroom features a walk-in closet and accesses a full hall bath.

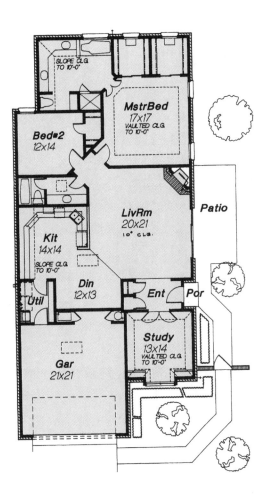

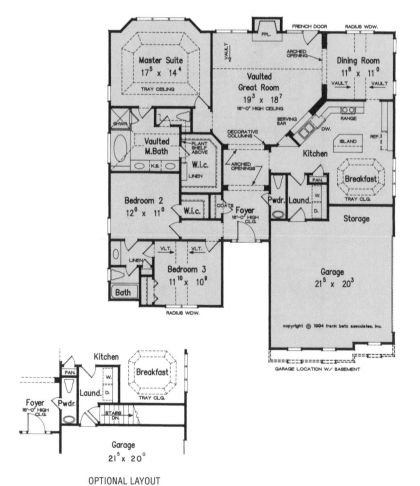

Master Suite
17⁵ x 14⁴
TRAY CEILING

Vaulted
Great Room
19³ x 18⁷
16'-0" HIGH CEILING

Dining Room
11⁸ x 11⁰

Vaulted
M.Bath

W.i.c.

Kitchen

Breakfast
TRAY CLG.

Bedroom 2
12⁰ x 11⁰

Foyer
16'-0" HIGH
CLG.

Pwdr. Laund.

Storage

Bedroom 3
11¹⁰ x 10⁹

Bath

Garage
21⁵ x 20³

copyright © 1994 frank betz associates, inc.

GARAGE LOCATION W/ BASEMENT

Kitchen

Breakfast
TRAY CLG.

Foyer
16'-0" HIGH
CLG.

Pwdr.

Laund.

STAIRS
DN.

Garage
21⁵ x 20⁰

OPTIONAL LAYOUT

plan# HPK0400176

Style: Country Cottage
Square Footage: 1,884
Bedrooms: 3
Bathrooms: 2½
Width: 50' - 0"
Depth: 55' - 4"
Foundation: Slab, Crawlspace, Basement

SEARCH ONLINE @ EPLANS.COM

Arched openings, decorative columns, and elegant ceiling details throughout highlight this livable floor plan. The country kitchen includes a spacious work area, preparation island, serving bar to the great room, and a breakfast nook with a tray ceiling. Set to the rear for gracious entertaining, the dining room opens to the great room. Note the warming fireplace and French-door access to the backyard in the great room. The master suite is beautifully appointed with a tray ceiling, bay window, compartmented bath, and walk-in closet. Two family bedrooms, a laundry room, and a powder room complete this gracious design.

plan ⊕ # HPK0400177

Style: Country Cottage
Square Footage: 1,845
Bonus Space: 409 sq. ft.
Bedrooms: 3
Bathrooms: 2½
Width: 56' - 0"
Depth: 60' - 0"
Foundation: Crawlspace, Basement, Slab

SEARCH ONLINE @ EPLANS.COM

The stucco exterior and combination rooflines give a stately appearance to this traditional home. Inside, the well-lit foyer leads to an elegant living room with a vaulted ceiling, fireplace, radius window, and French door that opens to the rear property. Two family bedrooms share a full bath on the right side of the home; an impressive master suite resides to the left for privacy. A formal dining room and an open kitchen with plenty of counter space complete the plan.

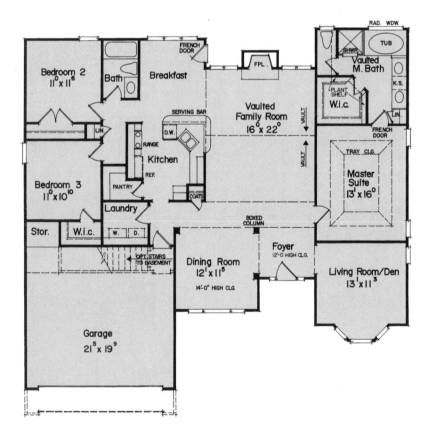

plan # HPK0400178

Style: Traditional
Square Footage: 1,875
Bedrooms: 3
Bathrooms: 2
Width: 56' - 0"
Depth: 50' - 6"
**Foundation: Basement,
Crawlspace, Slab**

SEARCH ONLINE @ EPLANS.COM

An oversized picture window gives a cheerful first impression to this well-appointed family home. Boxed columns frame the formal dining room to one side of the foyer. A living room or den is to the other side. A vaulted ceiling soars over the family room. A lovely fireplace flanked by windows and a wraparound serving bar make this room the heart of family gatherings. The kitchen has all the amenities, including a sunny breakfast nook. The master suite is split from the two family bedrooms and features a lush compartmented bath and walk-in closet. Two family bedrooms, a hall bath, and laundry room complete this favorite plan.

© HOME DESIGN SERVICES, INC.

J.N. HANSEN P.E.

plan# HPK0400179

Style: Mediterranean
Square Footage: 2,253
Bedrooms: 4
Bathrooms: 3
Width: 58' - 0"
Depth: 66' - 8"
Foundation: Slab

SEARCH ONLINE @ EPLANS.COM

Corner quoins combined with arch-top windows and a columned entry lend an exciting facade to this four-bedroom home. The foyer is entered through double doors and introduces the open dining and living-room area. The master suite occupies the right side of the plan and enjoys a sun-strewn sitting room, two walk-in closets, and a luxurious bath complete with a garden tub and separate shower. The kitchen sits conveniently near the dining room and features a pantry, desk, and view through the breakfast nook windows. Two family bedrooms, sharing a full bath, reside near the kitchen. A third bedroom or guest suite is located by the family room and features a private bath. The family room contains a warming fireplace and media wall, which will make it a wonderful gathering place for the family.

plan# HPK0400180

Style: Italianate
Square Footage: 2,089
Bedrooms: 4
Bathrooms: 3
Width: 61' - 8"
Depth: 50' - 4"
Foundation: Slab

SEARCH ONLINE @ EPLANS.COM

This four-bedroom, three-bath home offers the finest in modern amenities. The huge family room, which opens up to the patio with 12-foot pocket sliding doors, provides space for a fireplace and media equipment. Two family bedrooms share a full bath; one bedroom has a private bath with patio access, making it the perfect guest room. The master suite, located just off the kitchen and nook, is private yet easily accessible. The double-door entry, bed wall with glass above, step-down shower, and private toilet room, walk-in linen closet, and lavish vanity make this a very comfortable master suite!

plan # HPK0400181

Style: Floridian
Square Footage: 2,253
Bedrooms: 4
Bathrooms: 3
Width: 58' - 0"
Depth: 66' - 8"
Foundation: Slab

SEARCH ONLINE @ EPLANS.COM

The functional use of angles in this house makes for a plan that is exciting and full of large spaces. A formal living/dining area greets guests as they enter. The mitered glass throughout the rear of the home creates unlimited views to the outdoor living space and pool. Double doors lead to the master suite. A grand bath here boasts His and Hers walk-in closets, a wraparound vanity, a corner tub, and a shower. The best feature of this home is the split-bedroom design, featuring a bedroom with a private bath, perfect for guest or family-member visits. The remaining two bedrooms share their own bath off the hall.

plan # HPK0400182

Style: Contemporary
Square Footage: 2,271
Bedrooms: 4
Bathrooms: 3
Width: 63' - 0"
Depth: 51' - 4"
Foundation: Slab

SEARCH ONLINE @ EPLANS.COM

Transoms and pediments adorn this new contemporary exterior, and a grand entry opens through double doors to a tiled foyer. Formal rooms enjoy tray ceilings, and the family living area offers an extended-hearth fireplace and sliding glass door access to a covered patio. A sunny breakfast nook boasts a bay window and a private door to the patio, and the nearby kitchen employs natural light let in by many rear windows. Split sleeping quarters thoughtfully position the master suite to the rear of the plan for privacy; family bedrooms enjoy their own wing with two full baths.

plan # HPK0400183

Style: Traditional
Square Footage: 2,160
Bedrooms: 3
Bathrooms: 2
Width: 68' - 0"
Depth: 64' - 0"
Foundation: Crawlspace, Slab

SEARCH ONLINE @ EPLANS.COM

Steep rooflines and columns make this home one to remember. Starburst windows align along the exterior and offer a nice touch of sophistication. Extra amenities run rampant through this one-story home. The sunroom can be enjoyed during every season. An eating nook right off the kitchen brightens the rear of the home. Utility and storage areas are also found at the rear of the home. A cozy study privately accesses the side porch. The master bedroom is complete with dual vanities and His and Hers closets. Two family bedrooms reside to the left of the plan.

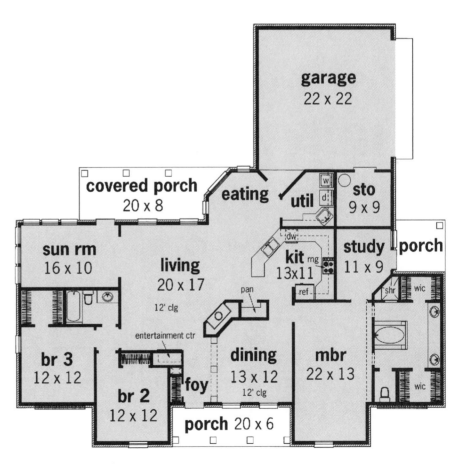

COPYRIGHT LARRY E. BELK

plan# HPK0400184

Style: European Cottage
Square Footage: 2,010
Bedrooms: 3
Bathrooms: 2
Width: 68' - 10"
Depth: 52' - 0"
Foundation: Slab

SEARCH ONLINE @ EPLANS.COM

An arched entrance, a sunburst, and sidelights around the four-panel door provide a touch of class to this European-style home. An angled bar opens the kitchen and breakfast room to the living room with bookcases and a fireplace. The master suite boasts a sloped ceiling and private bath with a five-foot turning radius, dual-sink vanity, and a separate tub and shower. Two family bedrooms provide ample closet space and share a full hall bath and linen closet. Don't miss the two-car garage located to the far right of the plan.

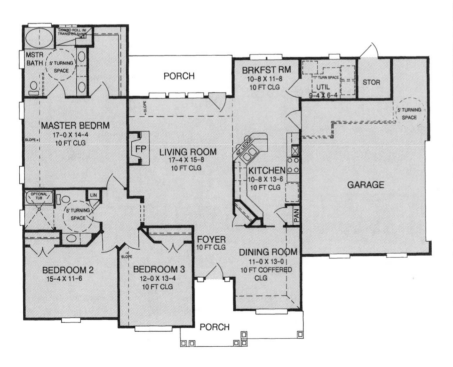

plan # HPK0400185

Style: French
Square Footage: 2,150
Bedrooms: 3
Bathrooms: 2½
Width: 64' - 0"
Depth: 60' - 4"
Foundation: Walkout Basement

SEARCH ONLINE @ EPLANS.COM

This home draws its inspiration from both French and English Country homes. The great room and dining room combine to form an impressive gathering space, with the dining area subtly defined by columns and a large triple window. The kitchen, with its work island, adjoins the breakfast area and keeping room with a fireplace. The home is completed by a master suite with a bay window and a garden tub. Space on the lower level can be developed later.

Quote One®

Cost to build? See page 333
to order complete cost estimate
to build this house in your area!

© The Sater Design Collection, Inc.

plan # HPK0400186

Style: Italianate
Square Footage: 2,191
Bedrooms: 3
Bathrooms: 2½
Width: 62' - 10"
Depth: 73' - 6"
Foundation: Slab

SEARCH ONLINE @ EPLANS.COM

Perfect for a corner lot, this Mediterranean villa is a beautiful addition to any neighborhood. Low and unassuming on the outside, this plan brings modern amenities and classic stylings together for a great family home. The study and two-story dining room border the foyer; an elongated gallery introduces the great room. Here, a rustic beamed ceiling, fireplace, and art niche are thoughtful touches. The step-saving U-shaped kitchen flows into a sunny bayed breakfast nook. To the far right, two bedrooms share a full bath. The master suite is separated for privacy, situated to the far left. French-door access to the veranda and a sumptuous bath make this a pleasurable retreat.

plan⊕ HPK0400187

Style: European Cottage
Square Footage: 2,007
Bedrooms: 3
Bathrooms: 2½
Width: 40' - 0"
Depth: 94' - 10"
Foundation: Slab

SEARCH ONLINE @ EPLANS.COM

An ornate stucco facade with brick highlights refines this charming French cottage. The double-door entrance sits to the side—perfect for a courtyard welcome. A dining and family room utilize an open layout for easy traffic flow. The circular kitchen space features an island and complementary breakfast bay. Bedrooms 2 and 3 share a hall bath. The master suite, apart from the main living areas, enjoys privacy and a full bath with a spacious walk-in closet. The rear porch encourages outdoor relaxation.

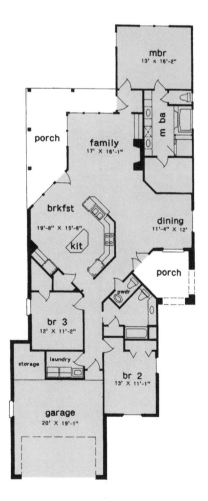

plan# HPK0400188

Style: European Cottage
Square Footage: 2,236
Bedrooms: 3
Bathrooms: 2½
Width: 63' - 0"
Depth: 67' - 0"
Foundation: Crawlspace, Basement

SEARCH ONLINE @ EPLANS.COM

The master suite of this one-story traditional will be a haven for any homeowner. Separate tray ceilings split a generous sitting room from the main bedroom and a fireplace warms both areas. The vaulted master bath includes a three-sided mirror, a corner whirlpool tub, His and Hers sinks, and a walk-in closet with built-in linen storage. The master suite also includes French-door access to the rear yard. The rest of the home is equally impressive. Radius windows highlight the central living room, arches create a dramatic entrance to the dining room, and the open kitchen area includes a cooktop island, a sunny breakfast area, and a serving bar to the vaulted family room with its cozy fireplace. Two bedrooms and a full bath with dual basins complete this amenity-filled design.

plan⊕ HPK0400189

Style: European Cottage
Square Footage: 2,077
Bedrooms: 3
Bathrooms: 2½
Width: 66' - 0"
Depth: 54' - 0"
Foundation: Walkout Basement

SEARCH ONLINE @ EPLANS.COM

This American classic begins with a recessed entry that announces a modern interior designed for entertaining as well as relaxed gatherings. The foyer leads to the living room, which opens through French doors to the back property, and to a banquet-sized dining room, defined by a splendid colonnade. The spacious kitchen has a work island and a sunlit breakfast area that shares the warmth of a hearth in the great room. French doors open to the master suite, which features a lovely bay window and a lavish bath.

ALTERNATE EXTERIOR

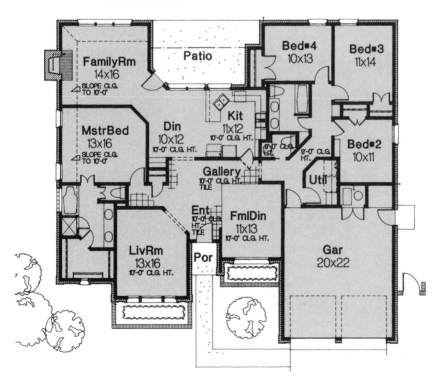

plan# HPK0400190

Style: French
Square Footage: 2,140
Bedrooms: 4
Bathrooms: 2½
Width: 60' - 0"
Depth: 54' - 0"
Foundation: Slab

SEARCH ONLINE @ EPLANS.COM

A copper hood over the living-room windows and graceful round-top windows in the formal dining room lend elegance to this impressive design. The entryway leads to a tiled gallery, which connects the living and dining rooms. The family room at the rear of the house contains a fireplace and a vaulted ceiling and accesses a glass door to a covered patio. The master suite offers complete privacy, and three additional bedrooms provide ample space for a growing family.

plan # HPK0400191

Style: Traditional
Square Footage: 2,065
Bedrooms: 4
Bathrooms: 2½
Width: 60' - 0"
Depth: 65' - 10"
Foundation: Crawlspace, Slab

SEARCH ONLINE @ EPLANS.COM

ALTERNATE EXTERIOR

Two exteriors are available for this delightful one-story home. Brick, shutters, and corner quoins provide European ambiance; gables and horizontal wood siding offer a more traditional facade—the choice is yours. With an 11-foot ceiling, a warming fireplace, and built-in bookcases, the great room will certainly be the family's favorite. The kitchen is bookended by the formal dining room and the sunny breakfast nook with an exit to the patio. Three bedrooms cluster on the left with a full bath, and the master suite, with a pair of walk-in closets and a lavish bath, is secluded on the right for privacy.

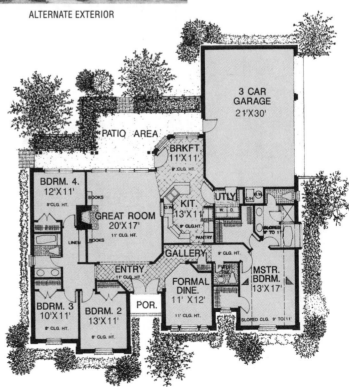

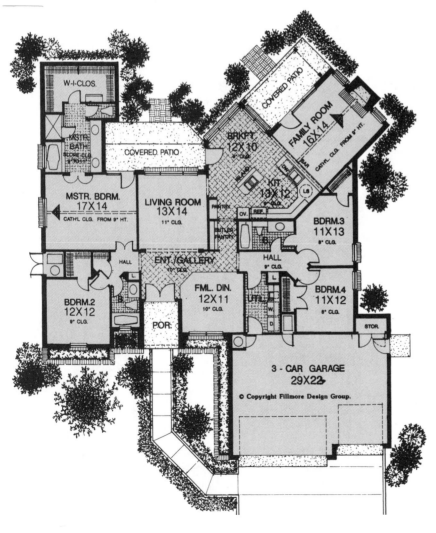

plan# HPK0400192

Style: French
Square Footage: 2,282
Bedrooms: 4
Bathrooms: 3
Width: 63' - 10"
Depth: 71' - 1"
Foundation: Crawlspace, Slab

SEARCH ONLINE @ EPLANS.COM

The stone entryway and steep rooflines accent the rustic nature of this home's facade. French doors lead guests and homeowners into an elegant entry and gallery. This home offers plenty of living space throughout. The large angled kitchen, featuring an island, extends to the open breakfast nook. A fireplace warms the family room in the winter and offers access to the covered rear patio for convenient summer outdoor entertaining. Another covered patio can be privately accessed through the master suite and the breakfast nook. Three family bedrooms and one master bedroom complete this plan.

plan# HPK0400193

Style: Colonial
Square Footage: 2,150
Bedrooms: 3
Bathrooms: 2½
Width: 64' - 0"
Depth: 64' - 3"
Foundation: Walkout Basement

SEARCH ONLINE @ EPLANS.COM

This attractive brick cottage home with an arched covered entry gives family and friends a warm welcome. The jack-arch window detailing adds intrigue to the exterior. The foyer, dining room, and great room are brought together, defined by decorative columns. To the right of the foyer, a bedroom with a complete bath could double as a home office or children's den. The spacious kitchen has a centered work island and an adjacent keeping room with a fireplace—ideal for families that like to congregate at mealtimes. The abundance of windows throughout the back of the home provides a grand view of the back property. The master suite enjoys privacy to the rear of the home. A garden tub, large walk-in closet, and two vanities make a perfect homeowner retreat.

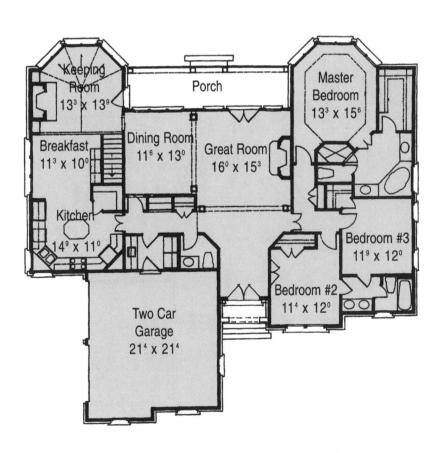

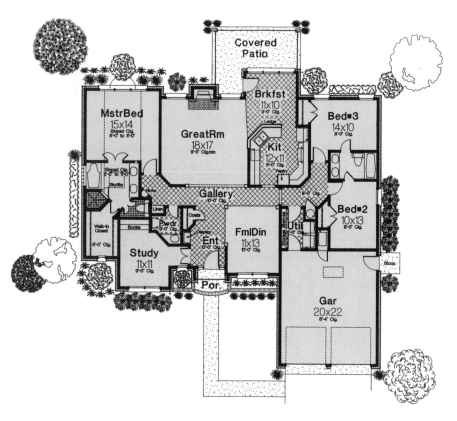

plan# HPK0400194

Style: French
Square Footage: 2,061
Bedrooms: 3
Bathrooms: 2½
Width: 60' - 0"
Depth: 57' - 1"
Foundation: Slab, Crawlspace

SEARCH ONLINE @ EPLANS.COM

This one-living-area plan is perfect for the contemporary family with a taste for classic design. The exterior is traditional with a combination of brick and stone, enhanced by eyebrow windows. The large great room is open to the kitchen and dinette. Full-view doors lead to a large covered patio. Off the entry, a home office/study includes plenty of built-ins. The master bedroom features a sloped ceiling that spans from 8 to 11 feet. The private master bath completes this plan with an 11-foot ceiling and a walk-in closet.

plan# HPK0400195

Style: Transitional
Square Footage: 2,041
Basement: 1,802 sq. ft.
Bedrooms: 3
Bathrooms: 2
Width: 67' - 6"
Depth: 63' - 6"
Foundation: Basement

SEARCH ONLINE @ EPLANS.COM

Attention to detail and a touch of luxury create a home that showcases excellent taste and provides an efficient floor plan. From the raised foyer, a striking view is offered of the great room with its elegantly styled windows and views of the deck. Split bedrooms provide privacy for the master suite, where a sitting area is topped by an exciting ceiling. A garden bath with a walk-in closet and whirlpool tub pampers the homeowner. An optional finished basement adds a recreation room, exercise room, and a guest bedroom.

FIRST FLOOR

BASEMENT

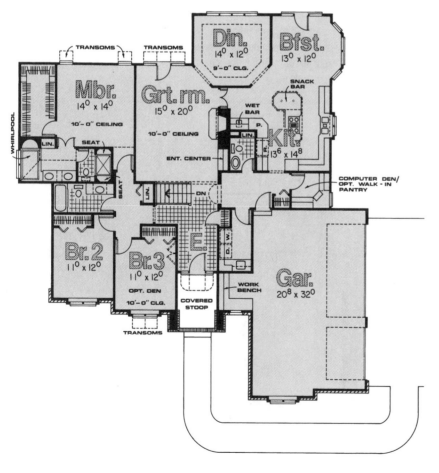

plan# HPK0400196

Style: Traditional
Square Footage: 2,186
Bedrooms: 3
Bathrooms: 2½
Width: 64' - 0"
Depth: 66' - 0"

SEARCH ONLINE @ EPLANS.COM

Brick columns and a tall, gabled entry create a prominent exterior with brick-and-siding accents. A bright 12-foot entry enjoys interior vistas of the expansive great room, which offers a fireplace with an extended hearth and opens to the formal dining room. The nearby gourmet island kitchen with a service bar and lots of wrapping counters is well integrated with the bayed breakfast and dining areas. A spacious and secluded master suite boasts a lavish whirlpool bath, a U-shaped walk-in closet, and 10-foot ceilings. The utility corridor leads to a laundry and to a convenient computer area, which could also be developed as an oversized walk-in pantry. A sunlit shop area highlights the three-car garage.

plan # HPK0400197

Style: Traditional
Square Footage: 2,120
Bedrooms: 3
Bathrooms: 3
Width: 62' - 0"
Depth: 62' - 6"
Foundation: Walkout Basement

SEARCH ONLINE @ EPLANS.COM

Arched-top windows act as graceful accents for this wonderful design. Inside, the floor plan is compact but commodious. The family room serves as the center of activity. It has a fireplace and connects to a lovely sunroom with rear-porch access. The formal dining room to the front of the plan is open to the entry foyer. A private den also opens off the foyer with double doors. It has its own private, cozy fireplace. The kitchen area opens to the sunroom, and it contains an island work counter. Bedrooms are split, with the master suite to the right side of the design and family bedrooms to the left. There are three full baths in this plan.

Quote One®

Cost to build? See page 333 to order complete cost estimate to build this house in your area!

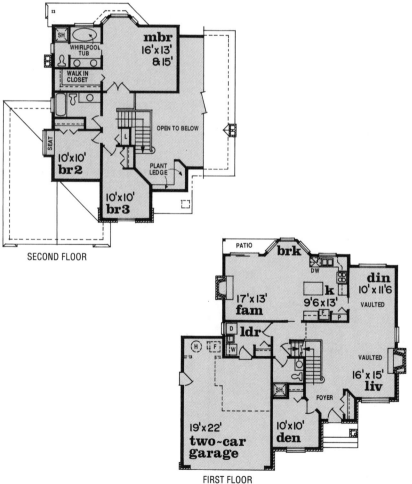

SECOND FLOOR

FIRST FLOOR

plan# HPK0400198

Style: Traditional
First Floor: 1,186 sq. ft.
Second Floor: 846 sq. ft.
Total: 2,032 sq. ft.
Bedrooms: 3
Bathrooms: 3
Width: 47' - 8"
Depth: 47' - 4"
Foundation: Crawlspace,
Basement

SEARCH ONLINE @ EPLANS.COM

Attention to detail is the key to this home's appeal. A private den and vaulted living room flank the two-story foyer. A center island adds efficiency to the kitchen, which flows easily into the family room and the breakfast bay. Double French doors open into the master suite, which offers a bay window overlooking the rear patio. Two other upstairs bedrooms share a bath; one provides a window seat. The laundry room exits to the two-car garage.

plan# HPK0400199

Style: Traditional
First Floor: 1,577 sq. ft.
Second Floor: 593 sq. ft.
Total: 2,170 sq. ft.
Bonus Space: 320 sq. ft.
Bedrooms: 3
Bathrooms: 2½
Width: 52' - 0"
Depth: 45' - 0"
Foundation: Crawlspace

SEARCH ONLINE @ EPLANS.COM

If you like drama in your design, but want a more moderately sized home, this plan will work for you. Not overly large, it contains many of the luxuries of much larger homes. Note the entry with arched window transom and solid brick pediment. The interior rooms start with a great room with fireplace and attached dining room. An L-shaped kitchen is nearby and features a walk-in pantry. The breakfast area has sliding glass doors to the rear deck. For privacy, the master suite is on the first floor. Here, you'll find a walk-in closet and bath with double sinks, whirlpool tub, and compartmented toilet. Two family suites—or three if you develop bonus space—share a full bath on the second floor. Suite 2 has a walk-in closet. Note the extra storage space in the garage.

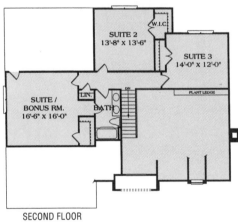

SECOND FLOOR

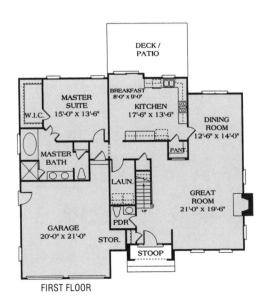

FIRST FLOOR

B. NATHAN

© 1990 Donald A. Gardner Architects, Inc.

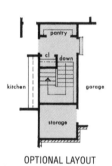

OPTIONAL LAYOUT

pantry

cl down

kitchen

garage

storage

plan⌗ HPK0400200

Style: French
Square Footage: 2,099
Bedrooms: 3
Bathrooms: 2
Width: 72' - 6"
Depth: 53' - 10"

SEARCH ONLINE @ EPLANS.COM

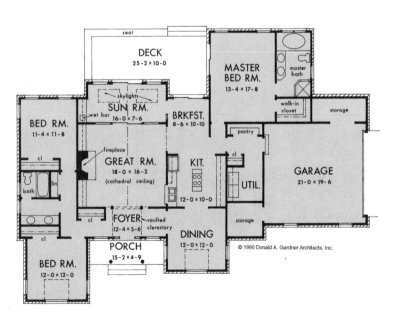

seat

DECK
25-2 × 10-0

skylights

SUN RM.
16-0 × 7-6

wet bar

MASTER BED RM.
13-4 × 17-8

master bath

walk-in closet

storage

BRKFST.
8-6 × 10-10

BED RM.
11-4 × 11-8

fireplace

pantry

GREAT RM.
18-0 × 16-2
(cathedral ceiling)

KIT.
12-0 × 10-0

cl

bath

lin

cl

UTIL.

GARAGE
21-0 × 19-6

FOYER
12-4 × 5-6

vaulted clerestory

storage

cl

PORCH
15-2 × 4-9

DINING
12-0 × 12-0

© 1990 Donald A. Gardner Architects, Inc.

BED RM.
12-0 × 12-0

This enchanting design incorporates the best in floor planning all on one amenity-filled level. Large arched windows and corner quoins lend a distinctly European flavor to the feeling of this brick-exterior home. A front porch framed by columns welcomes you inside to an inviting foyer. The central great room is the hub of the plan, from which all other rooms radiate. It is highlighted with a fireplace and cathedral ceiling. Nearby is a skylit sunroom with sliding glass doors to the rear deck and a built-in wet bar. The galley-style kitchen adjoins an attached breakfast room. The master suite is split from the family bedrooms and accesses the rear deck. The pampering master bath offers a whirlpool tub, separate shower, and twin-sink vanity. Family bedrooms on the opposite side of the house share a full hall bath. Extra storage space can be found in the two-car garage.

plan # HPK0400201

Style: Contemporary
Square Footage: 2,182
Basement: 1,229 sq. ft.
Bedrooms: 2
Bathrooms: 2
Width: 62' - 0"
Depth: 55' - 8"
Foundation: Basement

SEARCH ONLINE @ EPLANS.COM

An elegant traditional exterior, enhanced by stunning windows, provides expanding space. A study, off the foyer, opens discreetly to the formal dining room. A spacious great room shares the enjoyment of a see-through fireplace with the breakfast room. The master retreat features a walk-in closet, full bath with water closet and separate tub and shower. A family bedroom completes this level. The basement provides space for a secondary bedroom, family room, game room, and bath.

SECOND FLOOR

plan# HPK0400202

Style: Country Cottage
First Floor: 1,628 sq. ft.
Second Floor: 527 sq. ft.
Total: 2,155 sq. ft.
Bonus Space: 207 sq. ft.
Bedrooms: 3
Bathrooms: 2½
Width: 54' - 0"
Depth: 46' - 10"
Foundation: Basement, Slab, Crawlspace

SEARCH ONLINE @ EPLANS.COM

Multiple rooflines, charming stonework, and a covered entryway all combine to give this home plenty of curb appeal. Inside, the two-story foyer leads to either the formal dining room on the right or the spacious vaulted great room at the back. Here, a fireplace waits to warm cool evenings and a French door gives access to the rear yard. The large efficient kitchen offers plenty of counter and cabinet space and works well with the vaulted breakfast room and nearby vaulted keeping room. Sleeping quarters are split for privacy, with the deluxe master suite located on the first floor and two secondary bedrooms sharing a full bath on the second floor.

FIRST FLOOR

ORDER BLUEPRINTS 24 HOURS, 7 DAYS A WEEK, AT 1-800-521-6797

plan # HPK0400203

Style: Country Cottage
Square Footage: 2,282
Bonus Space: 629 sq. ft.
Bedrooms: 3
Bathrooms: 2½
Width: 60' - 0"
Depth: 75' - 4"
Foundation: Basement, Crawlspace

SEARCH ONLINE @ EPLANS.COM

Columns and keystone lintels lend a European aura to this stone-and-siding home. Arched openings and decorative columns define the formal dining room to the left of the foyer. A ribbon of windows with transoms above draws sunshine into the living room. The master suite opens from a short hallway and enjoys a tray ceiling and a vaulted bathroom with shelving, compartmented toilet, separate shower, and garden tub. Transoms abound in the open informal living areas of this home. A bay-windowed breakfast nook adjoins the kitchen with a central serving bar and the family room with a warming fireplace. Two additional bedrooms share a full bath to the left of the plan.

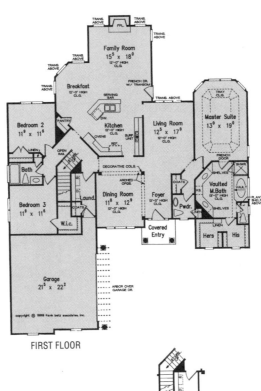

FIRST FLOOR

OPTIONAL LAYOUT

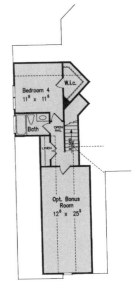

Box-bay windows give this exquisite two-story home its unique attraction. The dining room is entered through two archways as is the great room where a fireplace brings warmth to intimate gatherings. The U-shaped kitchen adjoins the morning room with sliding glass doors. An especially welcome feature upstairs is the computer loft, just steps away from the two family bedrooms. Also on this level is the master suite with His and Hers walk-in closets and a deluxe bath that pampers with a separate tub and shower and two-sink vanity. Through the laundry room the two-car garage can be entered from the kitchen.

plan# HPK0400204

Style: Traditional
First Floor: 1,025 sq. ft.
Second Floor: 1,036 sq. ft.
Total: 2,061 sq. ft.
Bedrooms: 3
Bathrooms: 2½
Width: 47' - 0"
Depth: 42' - 8"

SEARCH ONLINE @ EPLANS.COM

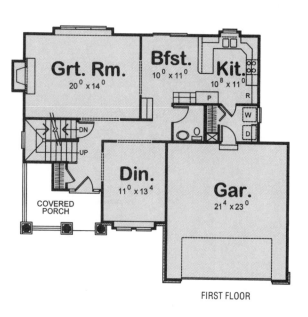

FIRST FLOOR

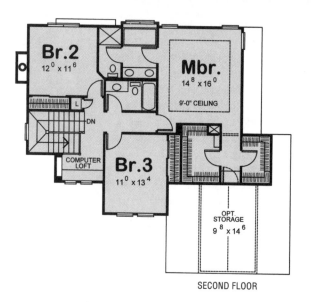

SECOND FLOOR

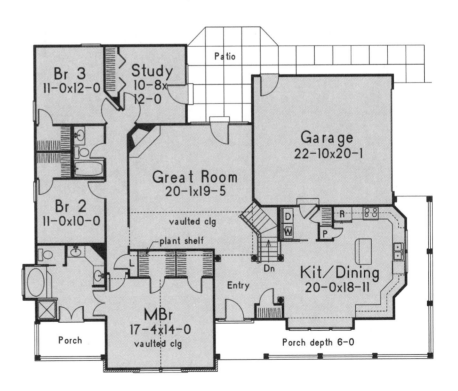

plan # HPK0400205

Style: Traditional
Square Footage: 2,029
Bedrooms: 3
Bathrooms: 2
Width: 61' - 0"
Depth: 51' - 0"
Foundation: Basement

SEARCH ONLINE @ EPLANS.COM

Stonework, gables, a roof dormer, and double porches create a country flavor in this home that fits hand-in-glove with many types of landscapes. The kitchen enjoys extravagant cabinetry and counter space in a bay, an island snack bar, a built-in pantry, and a cheery dining area. The large entry showcases beautiful wood columns and is also open to the vaulted great room, which features a corner fireplace. The master bedroom boasts His and Hers walk-in closets and double doors that lead to an opulent master bath and private porch. Two family bedrooms enjoy walk-in closets and share a full bath.

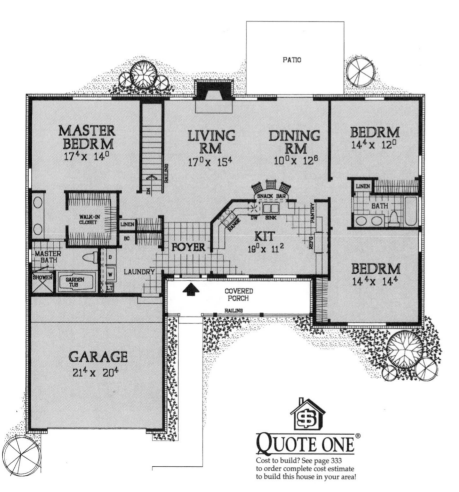

plan ⊕ HPK0400206

Style: Farmhouse
Square Footage: 2,076
Bedrooms: 3
Bathrooms: 2
Width: 64' - 8"
Depth: 54' - 7"
Foundation: Basement

SEARCH ONLINE @ EPLANS.COM

Multipane windows, mock shutters, and a covered front porch exhibit the charm of this home's facade. Inside, the foyer is flanked by a spacious, efficient kitchen to the right and a large, convenient laundry room to the left. The living room features a warming fireplace. To the right of the living room is the formal dining room; both rooms share a snack bar and direct access to the kitchen. Sleeping quarters are split, with two family bedrooms and a full bath on the right side of the plan and the deluxe master suite on the left. The private master bath offers such luxuries as a walk-in closet, a twin-sink vanity, a garden tub, and a separate shower.

Quote One®
Cost to build? See page 333
to order complete cost estimate
to build this house in your area!

plan# HPK0400207

Style: Traditional
Square Footage: 2,018
Bedrooms: 3
Bathrooms: 2
Width: 74' - 11"
Depth: 49' - 2"
Foundation: Crawlspace, Slab, Basement

SEARCH ONLINE @ EPLANS.COM

A Palladian window set into a front-facing gable highlights this country home. The dining room, on the right, includes accent columns and convenient kitchen service. The great room offers twin sets of French doors that access the rear porch. Meal preparation will be easy in the kitchen with a work island and cheerful light streaming in from the bay-windowed breakfast nook. The master suite is set to the rear and features a walk-in closet made for two, dual vanities, and a compartmented toilet. Two family bedrooms near the front of the plan share a full bath.

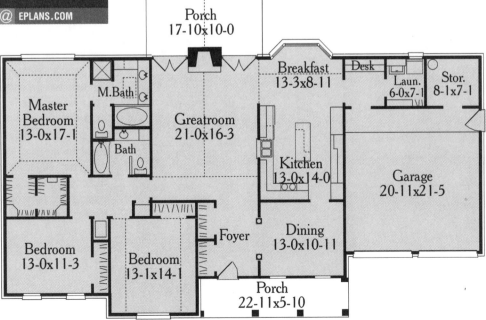

© 1989 Donald A. Gardner Architects, Inc.

B. NATHAN

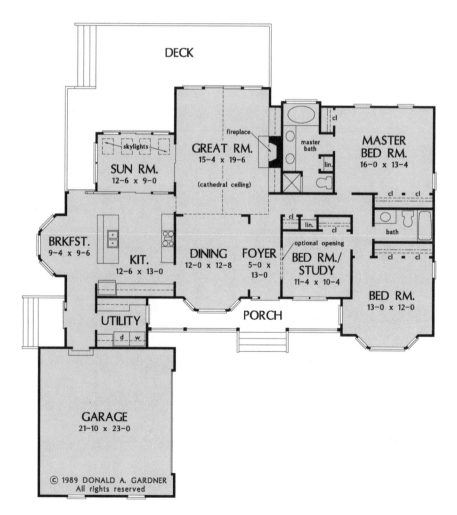

DECK

SUN RM.
12-6 x 9-0

skylights

GREAT RM.
15-4 x 19-6

(cathedral ceiling)

fireplace

master
bath

cl

lin.

MASTER
BED RM.
16-0 x 13-4

cl   cl

bath

BRKFST.
9-4 x 9-6

KIT.
12-6 x 13-0

DINING
12-0 x 12-8

FOYER
5-0 x
13-0

cl
lin.
cl

optional opening

BED RM./
STUDY
11-4 x 10-4

cl   cl

BED RM.
13-0 x 12-0

UTILITY

d   w

PORCH

GARAGE
21-10 x 23-0

plan # HPK0400208

Style: Country
Square Footage: 2,046
Bedrooms: 3
Bathrooms: 2
Width: 65' - 2"
Depth: 64' - 8"

SEARCH ONLINE @ EPLANS.COM

This three-bedroom country cottage projects an intriguing appearance with its bay windows, dormers, and L-shaped layout. The great room has a cathedral ceiling and an arched window above the exterior door leading to the expansive rear deck. The sunroom with skylights is accessible from the great room, kitchen, and deck for maximum exposure. The centrally located kitchen allows direct access to eating and living areas. Three bedrooms include a master suite and a bedroom that can be turned into a study.

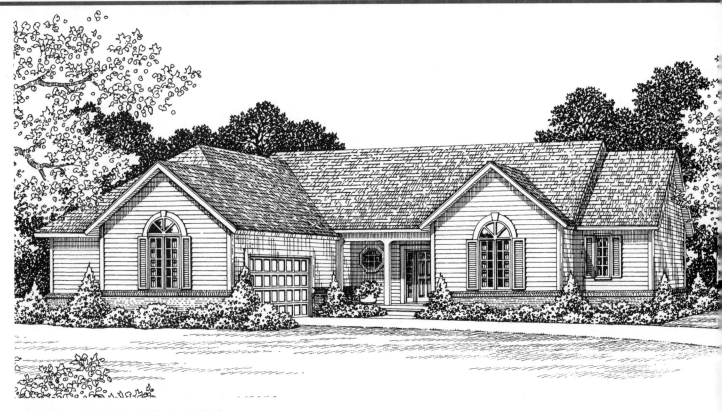

plan # HPK0400209

Style: Traditional L D
Square Footage: 2,098
Bedrooms: 3
Bathrooms: 2
Width: 64' - 0"
Depth: 69' - 8"
Foundation: Basement

SEARCH ONLINE @ EPLANS.COM

This is a fine home for a young family or for empty-nesters. The versatile bedroom/study offers room for growth or a quiet haven for reading. The U-shaped kitchen includes a handy nook with a snack bar and easy accessibility to the dining room or the gathering room—perfect for entertaining. The master suite includes its own private outdoor retreat, a walk-in closet, and an amenity-filled bathroom. An additional bedroom and a large laundry room with an adjacent, walk-in pantry complete the plan.

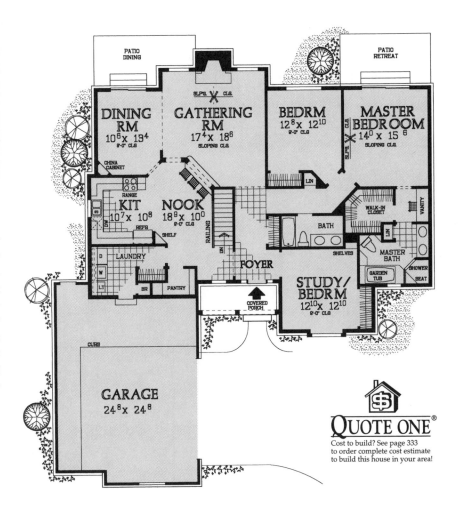

Quote One®
Cost to build? See page 333 to order complete cost estimate to build this house in your area!

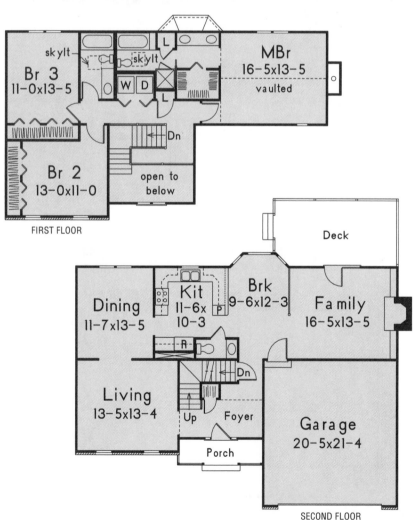

FIRST FLOOR

SECOND FLOOR

plan # HPK0400210

Style: Traditional
First Floor: 1,098 sq. ft.
Second Floor: 960 sq. ft.
Total: 2,058 sq. ft.
Bedrooms: 3
Bathrooms: 2½
Width: 50' - 0"
Depth: 36' - 0"
Foundation: Crawlspace, Slab, Basement

SEARCH ONLINE @ EPLANS.COM

Light pours in through many windows on this home's facade. The handsome two-story foyer with a balcony creates a spacious entrance area. The U-shaped kitchen provides easy serving access to the dining room and breakfast nook. A vaulted ceiling, private dressing area, and large walk-in closet complement the master bedroom. Skylights flood both the hall bath and master bath with natural light. A conveniently located second-floor laundry room resides near the bedrooms.

plan# HPK0400211

Style: Farmhouse
First Floor: 1,082 sq. ft.
Second Floor: 1,021 sq. ft.
Total: 2,103 sq. ft.
Bedrooms: 4
Bathrooms: 2½
Width: 50' - 0"
Depth: 40' - 0"

SEARCH ONLINE @ EPLANS.COM

A covered porch invites you into this country-style home. Handsome bookcases frame the fireplace in the spacious family room. Double doors off the entry provide the family room with added privacy. The kitchen features an island, a lazy Susan, and easy access to a walk-in laundry. The master bedroom features a boxed ceiling and separate entries to a walk-in closet and a pampering bath. The upstairs hall bath is compartmented, allowing maximum usage for today's busy family.

SECOND FLOOR

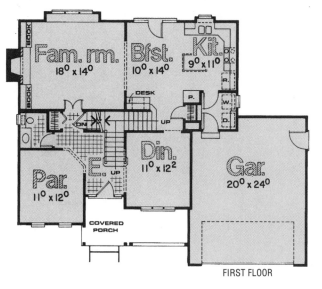

FIRST FLOOR

Symmetrically grand, this home features large windows which flood the interior with natural light. The massive sunken great room with a vaulted ceiling includes an exciting balcony overlook of the towering atrium window wall. The open breakfast nook and hearth room adjoin the kitchen. Four fireplaces throughout the house create an overall sense of warmth. A colonnade, a private entrance to the rear deck, and a sunken tub with a fireplace complement the master suite. Two family bedrooms share a dual-vanity bath between them.

plan # HPK0400212

Style: Traditional
First Floor: 1,112 sq. ft.
Second Floor: 1,070 sq. ft.
Total: 2,182 sq. ft.
Bedrooms: 3
Bathrooms: 3½
Width: 57' - 0"
Depth: 48' - 8"
Foundation: Basement

SEARCH ONLINE @ EPLANS.COM

FIRST FLOOR

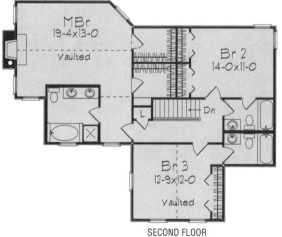

SECOND FLOOR

plan# HPK0400213

Style: Traditional
First Floor: 1,283 sq. ft.
Second Floor: 1,003 sq. ft.
Total: 2,286 sq. ft.
Bedrooms: 4
Bathrooms: 2½
Width: 64' - 0"
Depth: 34' - 0"
Foundation: Basement

SEARCH ONLINE @ EPLANS.COM

Fine architectural details make this home a show-place with its large windows, intricate brickwork, fine woodwork, and trim. The stunning two-story entry is decorated with an attractive wood railing and balustrades in the foyer. Conveniently, the wraparound kitchen features a window view and a planning center with a pantry. Upstairs, the master suite includes a sumptuous private bath and a walk-in closet. Three family bedrooms, one with a box-bay window, share a bath on this floor.

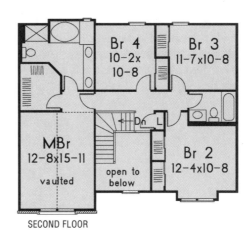

SECOND FLOOR

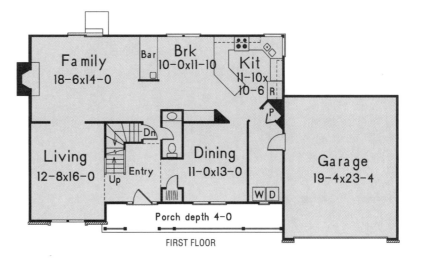

FIRST FLOOR

This lovely country design features a stunning wrapping porch and plenty of windows to provide the interior with natural light. The living room boasts a centered fireplace, which helps to define this spacious open area. A nine-foot ceiling on the first floor adds a sense of spaciousness and light. The casual living room leads outdoors to a rear porch. Upstairs, four bedrooms cluster around a central hall. The master suite sports a walk-in closet and a deluxe bath with an oval tub and a separate shower.

plan # HPK0400214

Style: Country Cottage
First Floor: 1,050 sq. ft.
Second Floor: 1,085 sq. ft.
Total: 2,135 sq. ft.
Bedrooms: 4
Bathrooms: 2½
Width: 50' - 8"
Depth: 39' - 4"
Foundation: Basement

SEARCH ONLINE @ EPLANS.COM

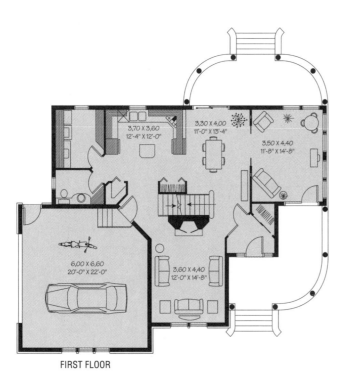

FIRST FLOOR

SECOND FLOOR

plan # HPK0400215

Style: Victorian
First Floor: 1,146 sq. ft.
Second Floor: 943 sq. ft.
Total: 2,089 sq. ft.
Bonus Space: 324 sq. ft.
Bedrooms: 3
Bathrooms: 2½
Width: 56' - 0"
Depth: 38' - 0"
Foundation: Basement

SEARCH ONLINE @ EPLANS.COM

This beautiful three-bedroom home boasts many attractive features. Two covered porches will entice you outside; inside, a special sunroom on the first floor brings the outdoors in. The foyer opens on the right to a comfortable family room that may be used as a home office. On the left, the living area is warmed by the sunroom and a cozy corner fireplace. A formal dining area lies adjacent to an efficient kitchen with a central island and breakfast nook overlooking the back porch. The second level offers two family bedrooms served by a full bath. A spacious master suite with a walk-in closet and luxurious bath completes the second floor.

FIRST FLOOR

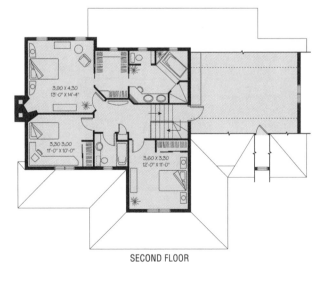

SECOND FLOOR

Although the details are authentic, the floor plan is much more contemporary than original Victorian houses. A front porch with gingerbread trim leads to a two-story foyer, island kitchen, and vaulted family room. Buyers of the original Victorians could only dream of a master suite like this house has. A spacious walk-in closet, full bath with spearate tub and shower complete the master bathroom. Two secondary bedrooms share a hall bath.

plan# HPK0400216

Style: Traditional
First Floor: 1,228 sq. ft.
Second Floor: 952 sq. ft.
Total: 2,180 sq. ft.
Bedrooms: 3
Bathrooms: 2½
Width: 48' - 0"
Depth: 40' - 0"
Foundation: Basement

SEARCH ONLINE @ EPLANS.COM

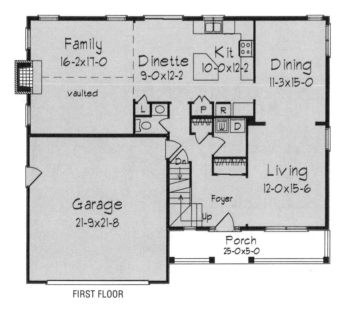

FIRST FLOOR

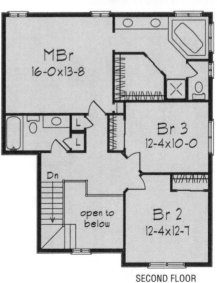

SECOND FLOOR

plan # HPK0400217

Style: Transitional
First Floor: 1,056 sq. ft.
Second Floor: 995 sq. ft.
Total: 2,051 sq. ft.
Bonus Space: 303 sq. ft.
Bedrooms: 3
Bathrooms: 2½
Width: 45' - 0"
Depth: 40' - 0"
Foundation: Slab, Crawlspace

SEARCH ONLINE @ EPLANS.COM

This delightful two-story home is a perfect place for raising a family. Three bedrooms upstairs, including a deluxe master suite, provide ample sleeping space. On the first level, the kitchen, informal dining area, and family room are linked in a way that offers significant flexibility in arranging the space. In the family room, at the end opposite the kitchen, a fireplace is a source of warmth. A half-bath is conveniently located nearby. Toward the front a formal dining area opens easily into a living room, an arrangement congenial to entertaining.

SECOND FLOOR

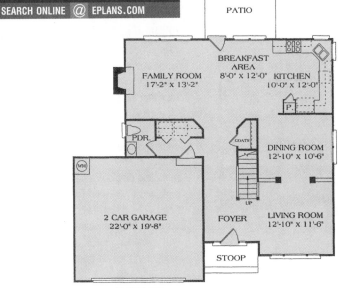

FIRST FLOOR

© 2003 Donald A. Gardner, Inc.

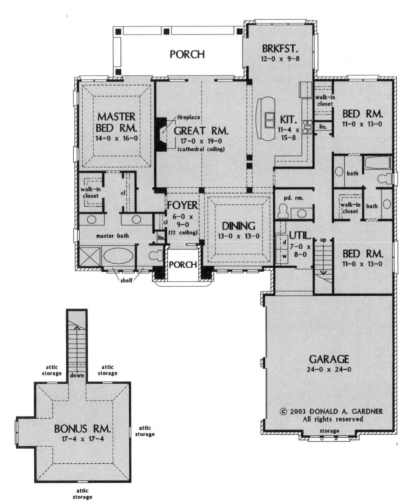

PORCH

BRKFST.
12-0 x 9-8

walk-in closet

MASTER BED RM.
14-0 x 16-0

fireplace

GREAT RM.
17-0 x 19-0
(cathedral ceiling)

KIT.
11-4 x 15-8

lin.

BED RM.
11-0 x 13-0

bath

walk-in closet

cl

walk-in closet

bath

FOYER
6-0 x 9-0
(12 ceiling)

cl

lin.

DINING
13-0 x 13-0

pd. rm.

master bath

UTIL.
7-0 x 8-0

d w

up

BED RM.
11-0 x 13-0

shelf

PORCH

GARAGE
24-0 x 24-0

© 2003 DONALD A. GARDNER
All rights reserved

storage

attic storage

down

attic storage

attic storage

BONUS RM.
17-4 x 17-4

attic storage

attic storage

plan # HPK0400218

Style: Traditional
Square Footage: 2,233
Bonus Space: 289 sq. ft.
Bedrooms: 3
Bathrooms: 2½
Width: 60' - 3"
Depth: 74' - 11"

SEARCH ONLINE @ EPLANS.COM

Crowned by a hipped roof, this traditional design boasts a low-maintenance brick exterior with attractive accents. Custom transoms top decorative windows and doors, ushering natural light inside. A single dormer caps the garage. Tray ceilings add elegance to the master bedroom and dining room, and the great room enjoys a cathedral ceiling and fireplace. The kitchen is open to the great room and breakfast nook and displays a handy island with a double sink and snack bar. Each secondary bedroom has a walk-in closet and private vanity. The master suite has twin vanities, a wardrobe closet, and a walk-in closet, along with French doors leading to the rear porch.

plan # HPK0400219

Style: Traditional
First Floor: 1,694 sq. ft.
Second Floor: 436 sq. ft.
Total: 2,130 sq. ft.
Bonus Space: 345 sq. ft.
Bedrooms: 4
Bathrooms: 3
Width: 54' - 0"
Depth: 53' - 8"

SEARCH ONLINE @ EPLANS.COM

This attractive four-bedroom house offers a touch of country with its covered front porch. The foyer, flanked by the dining room and the bedroom/study, leads to the spacious great room. Here, a fireplace and window wall enhance any gathering. The U-shaped kitchen features a window over the sink and a serving counter to the breakfast room. The dining room and breakfast room have cathedral ceilings with arched windows that fill the house with natural light. The master bedroom boasts a cathedral ceiling and a bath with a whirlpool tub, shower, and double-bowl vanity. Two family bedrooms reside upstairs.

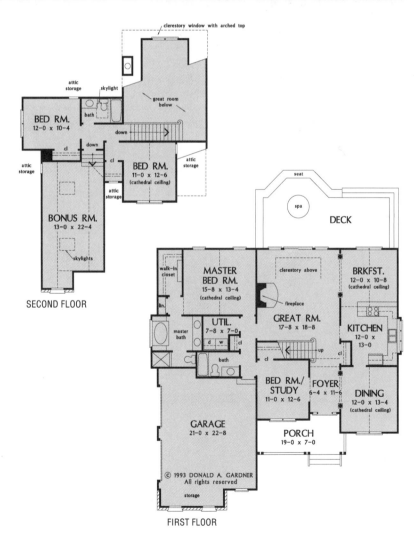

SECOND FLOOR

FIRST FLOOR

© 2002 Donald A. Gardner, Inc.

Elegant detail brings a sense of fresh refinement to this old-fashioned farmhouse. Gingerbread-style ornamentation on the gables combines with shutters and fanlight windows on the facade. Inside, the hearth-warmed great room—which accesses the rear porch—and open kitchen will be the center of family life. Dine in the bayed breakfast nook or the tray-ceilinged formal dining room. Two bedrooms share a bath on the left of the plan. A deluxe master suite, complete with a spacious bath and walk-in closet, takes up the right wing. A utility room and half-bath are convenient to both the kitchen and two-car garage. Bonus space upstairs awaits expansion.

plan # HPK0400220

Style: Traditional
Square Footage: 2,037
Bonus Space: 361 sq. ft.
Bedrooms: 3
Bathrooms: 2½
Width: 62' - 4"
Depth: 61' - 8"

SEARCH ONLINE @ EPLANS.COM

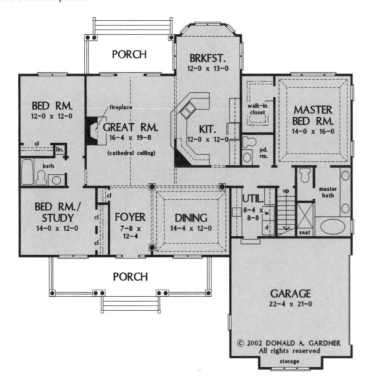

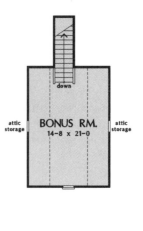

plan # HPK0400221

Style: Traditional
Square Footage: 2,151
Bedrooms: 3
Bathrooms: 2
Width: 76' - 8"
Depth: 40' - 0"

SEARCH ONLINE @ EPLANS.COM

A breezy front porch welcomes easy times while giving an appropriate introduction to the casual plan of this home. The entry opens to the formal dining room with the large great room and its magnificent fireplace flanked with transom windows directly ahead. The great room is open to the eat-in country kitchen that is complete with a work island, extra counter space, and access to the rear yard. The master bedroom has a private bath tucked behind double French doors. Two family bedrooms share a full hall bath. Plus, the plan includes a spacious home office that has a separate outside entrance.

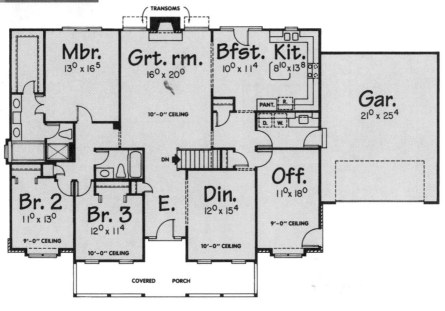

This grand two-story home proves that tried-and-true traditional style is still the best! Thoughtful planning brings formal living areas to the forefront and places open, casual living areas to the rear of the plan. Bedroom 4 serves as a multipurpose room, providing the flexibility desired by today's homeowner. The second floor is devoted to the relaxing master suite, two secondary bedrooms, a full hall bath, and a balcony overlook.

plan# HPK0400222

Style: **Colonial**
First Floor: **1,135 sq. ft.**
Second Floor: **917 sq. ft.**
Total: **2,052 sq. ft.**
Bonus Space: **216 sq. ft.**
Bedrooms: **4**
Bathrooms: **3**
Width: **52' - 4"**
Depth: **37' - 6"**
Foundation: **Slab, Crawlspace, Basement**

SEARCH ONLINE @ EPLANS.COM

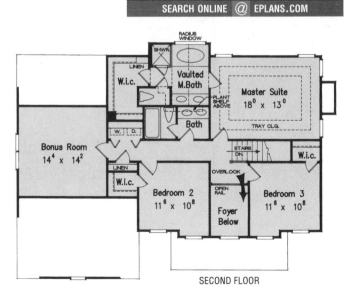

FIRST FLOOR

SECOND FLOOR

plan # HPK0400223

Style: Williamsburg
First Floor: 1,132 sq. ft.
Second Floor: 1,064 sq. ft.
Total: 2,196 sq. ft.
Bonus Space: 316 sq. ft.
Bedrooms: 4
Bathrooms: 2½
Width: 69' - 0"
Depth: 28' - 4"
Foundation: Basement

SEARCH ONLINE @ EPLANS.COM

The classic look of this traditional two-story home skillfully uses exterior trim and detailing to create an impressive curb appeal. The popular floor plan offers formal and informal spaces; the flow of the kitchen, breakfast area, and family room allows for comfortable family living. A deluxe master bedroom suite pampers the home-owner with a whirlpool tub, a dual-sink vanity, and dressing area. A spacious bonus room above the garage offers the possibility of a home office, additional storage, or a private retreat.

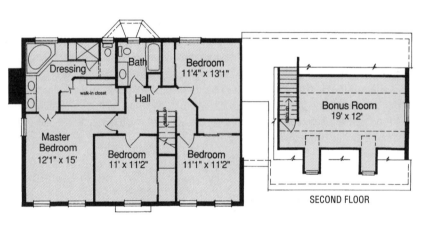

SECOND FLOOR

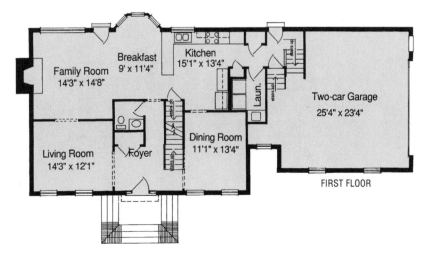

FIRST FLOOR

A gambrel roof provides volume and authenticity to this charming Cape Cod reproduction. Dormers front and rear pierce the roof to allow in plenty of natural light. The shutter-trimmed front door opens to a central foyer that leads to all areas of the house. Family and guests will all delight in the massive corner fireplace in the living room. A beamed ceiling contributes to the rustic atmosphere. Mealtime options include a dining room, breakfast room, and snack bar. The U-shaped kitchen easily serves them all. With both a covered porch and a patio, outdoor dining is another possibility. A front study has built-in bookshelves and would make a fine home office. Upstairs, three bedrooms include a master suite with a dressing room and twin vanities.

plan # HPK0400224

Style: Cape Cod   L D
First Floor: 1,122 sq. ft.
Second Floor: 884 sq. ft.
Total: 2,006 sq. ft.
Bedrooms: 3
Bathrooms: 2½
Width: 53' - 8"
Depth: 39' - 4"
Foundation: Basement

SEARCH ONLINE @ EPLANS.COM

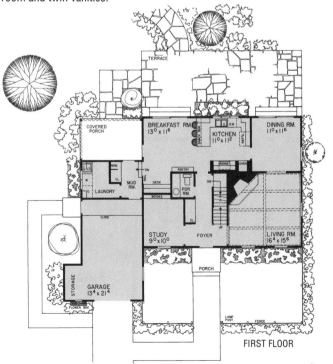

FIRST FLOOR

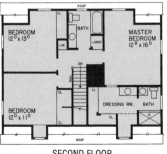

SECOND FLOOR

The unique charm of this farmhouse begins with a flight of steps and a welcoming, covered front porch. Just inside, the foyer leads to the formal dining room on the left—with easy access to the kitchen—and straight ahead to the great room. Here, a warming fireplace and built-in entertainment center are balanced by access to the rear screened porch. The first-floor master suite provides plenty of privacy; upstairs, two family bedrooms share a full bath. The lower level offers space for a fourth bedroom, a recreation room, and a garage.

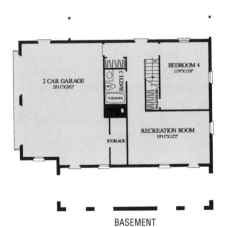

BASEMENT

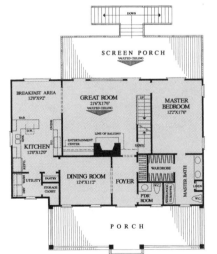

FIRST FLOOR

SECOND FLOOR

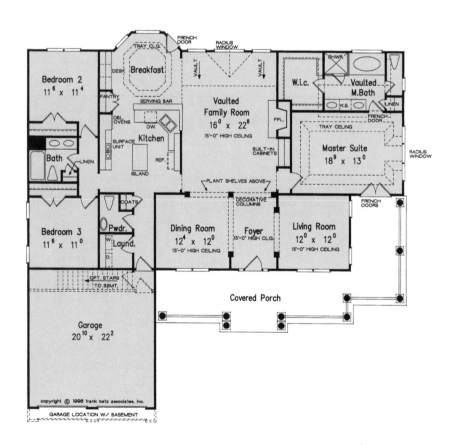

plan # HPK0400226

Style: Country Cottage
Square Footage: 2,170
Bedrooms: 3
Bathrooms: 2½
Width: 63' - 6"
Depth: 61' - 0"
Foundation: Crawlspace, Basement

SEARCH ONLINE @ EPLANS.COM

Twin dormers frame an impressive entrance to this fine three-bedroom home. The covered front porch leads to a foyer flanked by formal living and dining rooms. The spacious family room—complete with a warming fireplace and built-ins—opens to the breakfast bay. The well-positioned kitchen, with an island, easily serves the formal and informal areas. The master suite has a tray ceiling in the sleeping area and a vaulted ceiling in the bath. The other two bedrooms flank a full bath with a double-bowl vanity.

plan # HPK0400227

Style: Country Cottage
First Floor: 1,743 sq. ft.
Second Floor: 555 sq. ft.
Total: 2,298 sq. ft.
Bonus Space: 350 sq. ft.
Bedrooms: 4
Bathrooms: 3
Width: 77' - 11"
Depth: 53' - 2"

SEARCH ONLINE @ EPLANS.COM

A lovely arch-top window and a wraparound porch set off this country exterior. Inside, formal rooms open off the foyer, which leads to a spacious great room. This living area provides a fireplace and access to a screened porch with a cathedral ceiling. Bay windows allow natural light into the breakfast area and formal dining room. The master suite features a spacious bath and access to a private area of the rear porch. Two second-floor bedrooms share a bath and a balcony hall that offers an overlook to the great room.

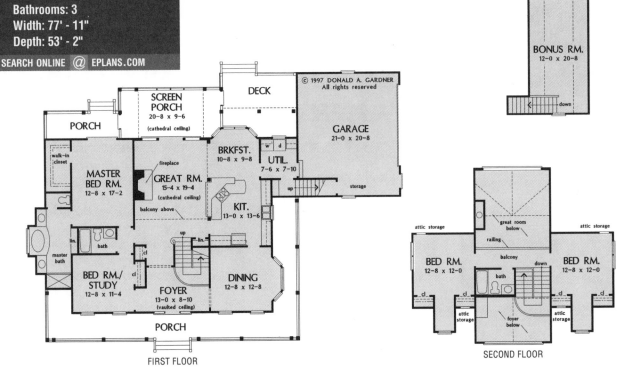

FIRST FLOOR

SECOND FLOOR

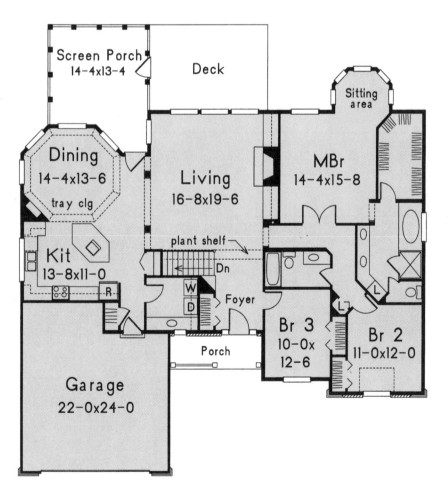

Screen Porch
14-4x13-4

Deck

Dining
14-4x13-6
tray clg

Living
16-8x19-6

Sitting area

MBr
14-4x15-8

Kit
13-8x11-0

plant shelf

Foyer

Dn

W
D

Br 3
10-0x
12-6

Br 2
11-0x12-0

Porch

Garage
22-0x24-0

plan# HPK0400228

Style: Contemporary
Square Footage: 2,003
Bedrooms: 3
Bathrooms: 2
Width: 60' - 0"
Depth: 57' - 0"
Foundation: Basement

SEARCH ONLINE @ EPLANS.COM

A covered porch and dormers bring great curb appeal to the exterior of this extremely livable home. A traditional exterior contrasts with a modern interior that boasts many amenities and features. The rear-facing living room will delight with a plant shelf, central fireplace, and access to a deck and screened porch. Twin columns set apart the stunning octagonal dining room, which boasts a tray ceiling. The adjacent kitchen with an island countertop is open to family gathering areas for ease of entertaining. The sleeping wing includes two family bedrooms and a luxurious master suite. Special features here include an octagonal sitting area, a walk-in closet, and a bath with twin vanities and a garden tub.

plan# HPK0400229

Style: **Farmhouse**
First Floor: **1,618 sq. ft.**
Second Floor: **570 sq. ft.**
Total: **2,188 sq. ft.**
Bonus Space: **495 sq. ft.**
Bedrooms: **3**
Bathrooms: **2½**
Width: **87' - 0"**
Depth: **57' - 0"**

SEARCH ONLINE @ EPLANS.COM

The foyer and great room in this magnificent farmhouse have Palladian window clerestories to allow natural light to enter, illuminating the whole house. The spacious great room boasts a fireplace, cabinets, and bookshelves. The second-floor balcony overlooks the great room. The kitchen with a cooking island is conveniently located between the dining room and the breakfast room with an open view of the great room. A generous master bedroom has plenty of closet space as well as an expansive master bath. A bonus room over the garage allows for expansion.

QUOTE ONE®

Cost to build? See page 333
to order complete cost estimate
to build this house in your area!

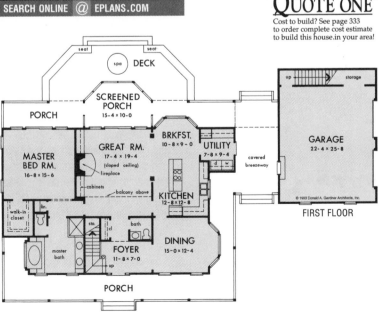

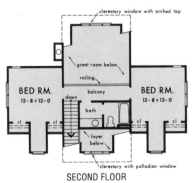

plan# HPK0400230

Style: Farmhouse
Square Footage: 2,078
Bedrooms: 4
Bathrooms: 2
Width: 75' - 0"
Depth: 47' - 10"
Foundation: Slab

SEARCH ONLINE @ EPLANS.COM

Colonial style meets farmhouse charm in this plan, furnishing old-fashioned charisma with a flourish. From the entry, double doors open to the country dining room and a large island kitchen. Nearby, the spacious great room takes center stage and is warmed by a fireplace flanked by large windows. Tucked behind the three-car garage, the secluded master suite features a vaulted ceiling in the bedroom. The master bath contains a relaxing tub, double-bowl vanity, separate shower, and compartmented toilet. Beyond the bath is a huge walk-in closet with two built-in chests. Three family bedrooms—one doubles as a study or home office—a full bath, and a utility room complete the plan.

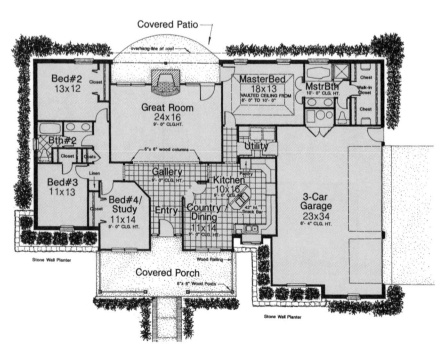

plan # HPK0400231

Style: Country
First Floor: 1,618 sq. ft.
Second Floor: 570 sq. ft.
Total: 2,188 sq. ft.
Bonus Space: 495 sq. ft.
Bedrooms: 3
Bathrooms: 2½
Width: 54' - 0"
Depth: 49' - 0"

SEARCH ONLINE @ EPLANS.COM

A two-story great room and two-story foyer, both with dormer windows, welcome natural light into this graceful country classic. A wraparound porch underscores the plan's down-home appeal. The large kitchen, featuring a center cooking island and large breakfast area, opens to the great room for easy entertaining. Columns punctuate the interior spaces, and a separate dining room provides a formal touch to the plan. The master suite, privately situated on the first floor, has a dual-sink vanity, garden tub, and separate shower. The partially detached garage features a large bonus room.

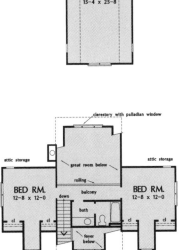

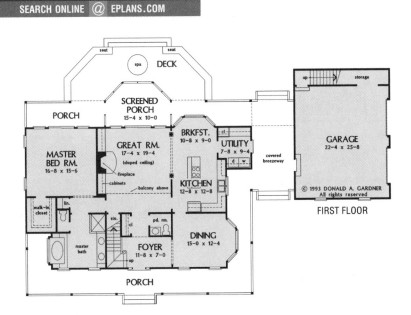

FIRST FLOOR

SECOND FLOOR

Symmetry and Southern charm combine to make this home a family favorite. Inside, natural light is a cheerful addition. Nine-foot ceilings bring height and grandeur to every room—the living room ceiling tops off at a soaring 11 feet! The U-shaped kitchen features a bonus side counter for extra workspace and easily serves the breakfast and dining rooms. Separated for privacy, the master suite is a joy, with a spa-style bath and His and Hers walk-in closets. Two more bedrooms are located to the far right. A bonus room would be a perfect home office, guest room, or nursery. Future space upstairs awaits your imagination.

plan # HPK0400232

Style: Traditional
Square Footage: 2,122
Bonus Space: 965 sq. ft.
Bedrooms: 3
Bathrooms: 2½
Width: 69' - 0"
Depth: 67' - 10"
Foundation: Crawlspace, Slab, Basement

SEARCH ONLINE @ EPLANS.COM

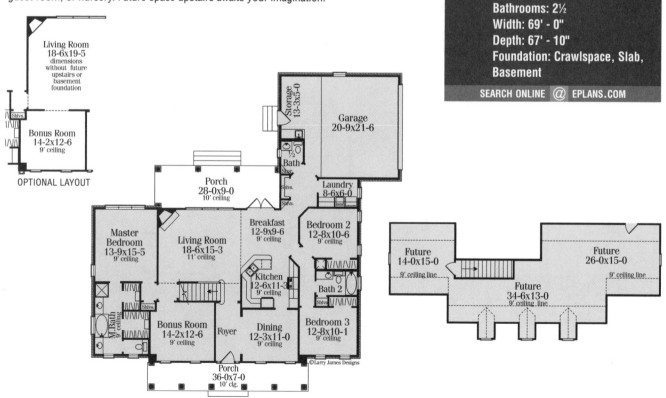

© 1994 Donald A. Gardner Architects, Inc.

B. NATHAN

plan # HPK0400233

Style: Farmhouse
Square Footage: 2,207
Bonus Space: 435 sq. ft.
Bedrooms: 4
Bathrooms: 2½
Width: 76' - 1"
Depth: 50' - 0"

SEARCH ONLINE @ EPLANS.COM

This quaint four-bedroom home with front and rear porches reinforces its beauty with arched windows and dormers. The pillared dining room opens on the right, and a study that could double as a guest room is available on the left. Straight ahead lies the massive great room with its cathedral ceiling, enchanting fireplace, and access to the private rear porch. Within steps of the dining room is the efficient kitchen and the sunny breakfast nook. The master suite enjoys a cathedral ceiling, rear-deck access, and a master bath with a skylit whirlpool tub. Three additional bedrooms located at the opposite end of the house share a full bath.

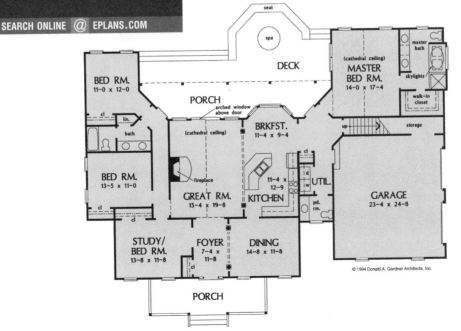

© 1994 Donald A. Gardner Architects, Inc.

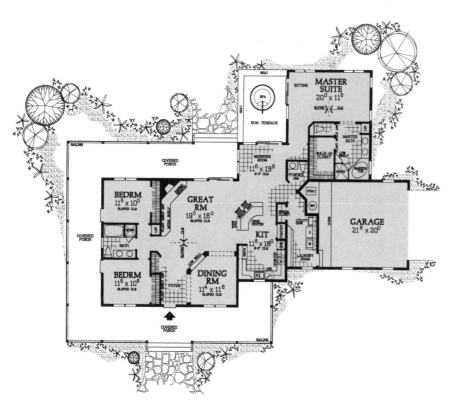

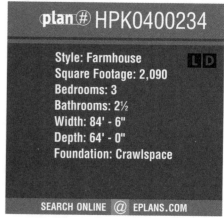

plan # HPK0400234

Style: Farmhouse L D
Square Footage: 2,090
Bedrooms: 3
Bathrooms: 2½
Width: 84' - 6"
Depth: 64' - 0"
Foundation: Crawlspace

SEARCH ONLINE @ EPLANS.COM

This classic farmhouse enjoys a wraparound porch that's perfect for enjoyment of the outdoors. To the rear of the plan, a sun terrace with a spa opens from the master suite and the morning room. A grand great room offers a sloped ceiling and a corner fireplace with a raised hearth. The formal dining room is defined by a low wall and graceful archways set off by decorative columns. The tiled kitchen has a centered island counter with a snack bar and adjoins a laundry area. Two family bedrooms reside to the side of the plan, and each enjoys private access to the covered porch. A secluded master suite nestles in its own wing and features a sitting area with access to the rear terrace and spa.

© 1994 Donald A. Gardner Architects, Inc.   B. NATHAN.

plan# HPK0400235

Style: Farmhouse
Square Footage: 2,136
Bonus Space: 405 sq. ft.
Bedrooms: 3
Bathrooms: 2½
Width: 76' - 4"
Depth: 64' - 4"

SEARCH ONLINE @ EPLANS.COM

An expansive front porch, three dormers, and a score of windows all add to the charm and character of this country home. The spacious great room features built-in cabinets, a fireplace, and a cathedral ceiling that continues into the adjoining screened porch. An island kitchen is conveniently grouped with the great room, the dining room, and the skylit breakfast area for the cook who enjoys conversation while preparing meals. The master suite features a cathedral ceiling, a large walk-in closet, and a relaxing private bath with a skylit whirlpool tub and separate shower. Two secondary bedrooms share a full bath.

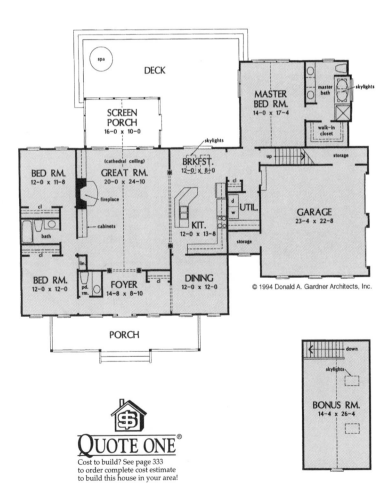

© 1994 Donald A. Gardner Architects, Inc.

QUOTE ONE®
Cost to build? See page 333
to order complete cost estimate
to build this house in your area!

A wonderful wraparound covered porch at the front and sides of this house and the open deck with a spa at the back provide plenty of outside living area. Inside, the spacious great room is appointed with a fireplace, cathedral ceiling, and clerestory with an arched window. The kitchen is centrally located for maximum flexibility in layout and features a food-preparation island for convenience. In addition to the master bedroom, with access to the sunroom, there are two second-level bedrooms that share a full bath.

plan # HPK0400236

Style: Farmhouse
First Floor: 1,651 sq. ft.
Second Floor: 567 sq. ft.
Total: 2,218 sq. ft.
Bedrooms: 3
Bathrooms: 2½
Width: 55' - 0"
Depth: 42' - 4"

SEARCH ONLINE @ EPLANS.COM

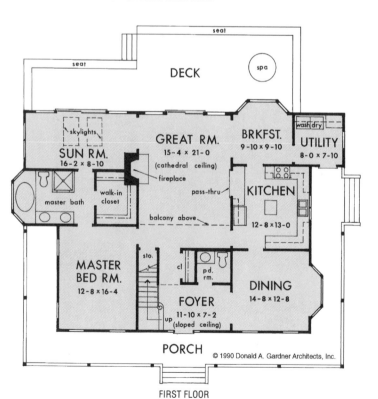

DECK

spa

seat

seat

seat

skylights

SUN RM.
16-2 x 8-10

GREAT RM.
15-4 x 21-0
(cathedral ceiling)

fireplace

pass-thru

BRKFST.
9-10 x 9-10

wash dry

UTILITY
8-0 x 7-10

KITCHEN
12-8 x 13-0

walk-in closet

master bath

balcony above

MASTER BED RM.
12-8 x 16-4

sto.

cl

pd. rm.

DINING
14-8 x 12-8

FOYER
11-10 x 7-2
(sloped ceiling)

up

PORCH

© 1990 Donald A. Gardner Architects, Inc.

FIRST FLOOR

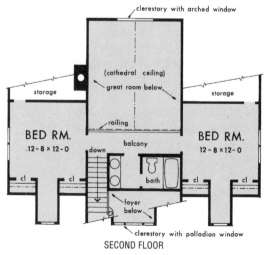

clerestory with arched window

(cathedral ceiling)

great room below

storage

storage

railing

BED RM.
12-8 x 12-0

BED RM.
12-8 x 12-0

balcony

down

cl

cl

bath

cl

cl

foyer below

clerestory with palladian window

SECOND FLOOR

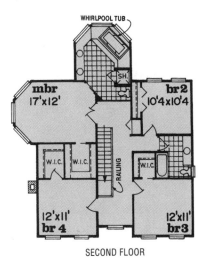

Graced by a wraparound veranda, multipaned shutters, and decorative wood trim, this four-bedroom design is as attractive as it is comfortable. Large bay windows and high ceilings throughout the first level further enhance the charm. The living room, with a masonry fireplace, extends to the bayed dining area. Eating or serving bars on the counter and center preparation island make easy work of mealtimes. Upstairs are the bayed master suite and three additional family bedrooms.

plan # HPK0400237

Style: Farmhouse
First Floor: 1,193 sq. ft.
Second Floor: 1,188 sq. ft.
Total: 2,381 sq. ft.
Bedrooms: 4
Bathrooms: 2½
Width: 62' - 0"
Depth: 47' - 0"
Foundation: Crawlspace, Basement

SEARCH ONLINE @ EPLANS.COM

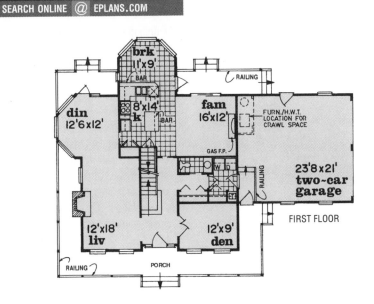

SECOND FLOOR

FIRST FLOOR

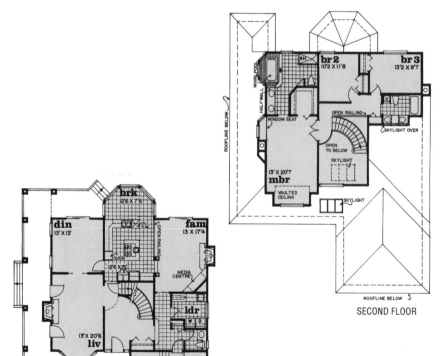

SECOND FLOOR

FIRST FLOOR

plan# HPK0400238

Style: Traditional
First Floor: 1,446 sq. ft.
Second Floor: 1,047 sq. ft.
Total: 2,493 sq. ft.
Bedrooms: 3
Bathrooms: 2½
Width: 47' - 0"
Depth: 65' - 0"
Foundation: Basement

SEARCH ONLINE @ EPLANS.COM

This unique design is bedecked with a veranda that wraps around two sides of the house. The skylit foyer contains a curved staircase to the second floor. On the left are the living room with fireplace and bay window and the dining room with sliding glass doors to the veranda. Double doors from the living room access the veranda. A family room at the other end of the plan holds a corner media center and a fireplace. Sliding glass doors open to the rear yard. In between is an island kitchen with breakfast bay. The bedrooms upstairs include a master suite with walk-in closet, vaulted alcove, and private bath with whirlpool tub. Family bedrooms share a full bath that has a double-sink vanity.

plan # HPK0400239

Style: SW Contemporary
First Floor: 1,463 sq. ft.
Second Floor: 872 sq. ft.
Total: 2,335 sq. ft.
Bedrooms: 3
Bathrooms: 3
Width: 44' - 0"
Depth: 58' - 10"
Foundation: Crawlspace, Basement

SEARCH ONLINE @ EPLANS.COM

ALTERNATE EXTERIOR

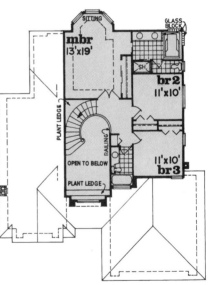

SECOND FLOOR

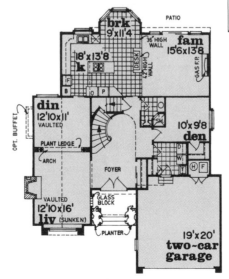

FIRST FLOOR

Two different facades are available for this home: a California stucco or a traditional brick-and-siding version. The interior plan begins with a vaulted foyer hosting a sweeping curved staircase spilling into a sunken living room with a masonry fireplace and vaulted ceiling. The kitchen features a pantry, center cooking island, built-in desk, and sunny breakfast bay. A den with a walk-in closet and nearby bath can easily double as a guest room. The master suite on the second floor boasts a drop ceiling, bayed sitting area, and lavish bath. The family bedrooms share a full bath.

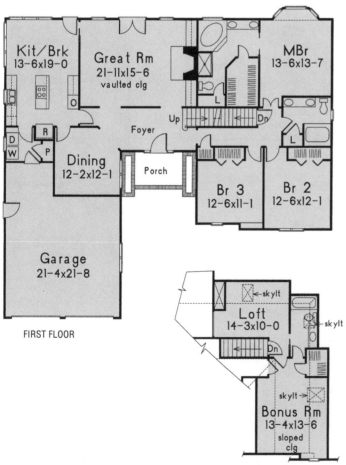

FIRST FLOOR

Loft
14-3x10-0

Bonus Rm
13-4x13-6
sloped
clg

SECOND FLOOR

plan# HPK0400240

Style: Traditional
First Floor: 1,965 sq. ft.
Second Floor: 503 sq. ft.
Total: 2,468 sq. ft.
Bedrooms: 3
Bathrooms: 3
Width: 62' - 0"
Depth: 54' - 0"
Foundation: Basement,
Crawlspace

SEARCH ONLINE @ EPLANS.COM

Three first-floor bedrooms, a skylit loft, and extra space upstairs for a fourth bedroom or a study are all housed in this modest plan. The posh master suite includes a separate shower and tub and a twin-sink vanity. The great room enjoys a fireplace and French-door access to the backyard; the well-organized kitchen boasts an island counter. An elegant dining room, easily served from the kitchen, is just to the right of the foyer. A two-car garage completes this plan.

plan# HPK0400241

Style: Country Cottage
Square Footage: 1,159 / 1,159
Bedrooms: 3 / 3
Bathrooms: 2 / 2
Width: 80' - 0"
Depth: 42' - 8"
Foundation: Basement

SEARCH ONLINE @ EPLANS.COM

This peaceful suburban duplex features a traditional rustic look, which blends easily into any countryside setting. The units mirror each other starting with quaint front covered porches, single-car garages, and a family-efficient floor plan. Each plan features a petite kitchen area connecting to a dining room, overlooking a patio—perfect for outdoor grilling. The vaulted great room is warmed by a fireplace and has a spacious feel. A staircase in the foyer leads to an optional basement plan. Bedrooms 2 and 3 share a full hall bath; the master suite enjoys a walk-in closet and a private bath.

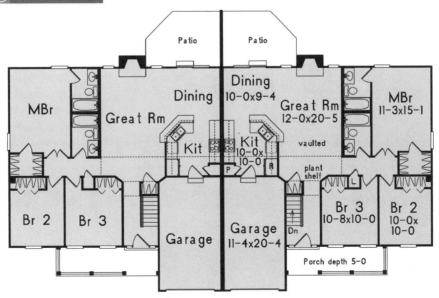

FIRST FLOOR

BASEMENT

plan# HPK0400242

Style: Traditional
Square Footage: 2,349
Basement: 850 sq. ft.
Bedrooms: 3
Bathrooms: 2½
Width: 79' - 4"
Depth: 59' - 6"
Foundation: Basement

SEARCH ONLINE @ EPLANS.COM

Sunbursts over the entryway and front windows add sophistication to this home. The mix of stone and siding adds a versatile feel to this pleasant home. The rear of this home offers plenty of natural lighting as well as porch space. The grand-scale kitchen features bay-shaped cabinetry overlooking an atrium with a two-story window wall. A second atrium dominates the master suite, which boasts a bayed sitting area and a luxurious bath with a whirlpool tub. The lower level contains a study, family room, and unfinished space for future expansion.

plan# HPK0400243

Style: Contemporary
Square Footage: 2,408
Bonus Space: 1,100 sq. ft.
Bedrooms: 4
Bathrooms: 2
Width: 75' - 8"
Depth: 52' - 6"
Foundation: Basement

SEARCH ONLINE @ EPLANS.COM

Contemporary and Mediterranean influences shape the spirit and inner spaces of this new-age home. An arched entrance and front covered porch welcome you inside to the formal dining room and great room. The relaxing kitchen/breakfast area is reserved for more intimate and casual occasions. The master suite provides a walk-in closet and private bath. Bedrooms 2 and 3 share a hall bath. Bedroom 4 makes the perfect guest suite. A family room, sitting area, wet bar, office, and additional bath reside in the basement.

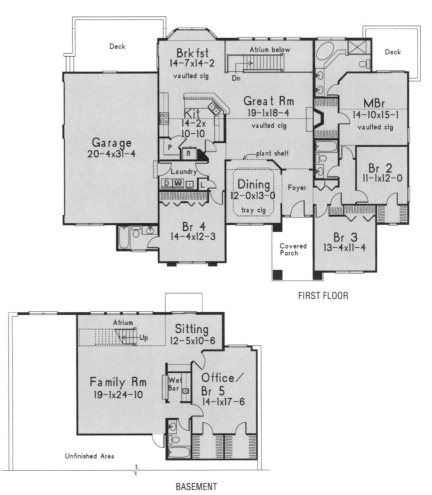

FIRST FLOOR

BASEMENT

719

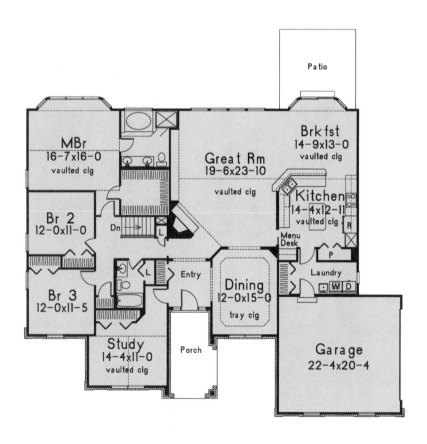

Patio

MBr
16-7x16-0
vaulted clg

Brkfst
14-9x13-0
vaulted clg

Great Rm
19-6x23-10

vaulted clg

Kitchen
14-4x12-11
vaulted clg

Br 2
12-0x11-0

Dn

L

Menu
Desk

R

P

Entry

Laundry

W D

Br 3
12-0x11-5

L

Dining
12-0x15-0

tray clg

Study
14-4x11-0
vaulted clg

Porch

Garage
22-4x20-4

plan # HPK0400244

Style: Traditional
Square Footage: 2,483
Bedrooms: 3
Bathrooms: 2
Width: 69' - 0"
Depth: 53' - 8"
Foundation: Basement

SEARCH ONLINE @ EPLANS.COM

This elegant traditional home is distinguished by its brick exterior and arched entryway with keystone accent. The entryway opens on the right to a formal dining room with an attractive tray ceiling. On the left, a private study—or make it a fourth bedroom—boasts a vaulted ceiling and a picture window with sunburst transom. Family living space includes a vaulted great room with a corner fireplace and a gourmet kitchen with an adjacent breakfast room. Special features in the kitchen include a breakfast bar, center island, menu desk, and pantry. The fabulous master suite enjoys a bay window, large bath, walk-in closet, and vaulted ceiling. Two family bedrooms sharing a full hall bath complete the plan. An unfinished basement provides room for future expansion.

plan# HPK0400245

Style: Country Cottage
Square Footage: 2,366
Bedrooms: 3
Bathrooms: 2
Width: 61' - 10"
Depth: 62' - 6"
Foundation: Crawlspace, Slab

SEARCH ONLINE @ EPLANS.COM

Cedar shingles and brick give this home the flavor of a country cottage. Inside, an up-to-date floor plan includes all of today's amenities. Nine-foot ceilings throughout give the plan a spacious feel. The dining room is defined by elegant arched openings flanked by columns. A corner fireplace serves the great room with panache. The kitchen features lots of counter and cabinet space along with a walk-in pantry and a snack bar. The master suite provides a nearby nursery/study as well as a lavish bath and walk-in closet. Two secondary bedrooms share a hall bath. The optional second floor includes space for an additional bedroom, bath, and large storage area over the garage.

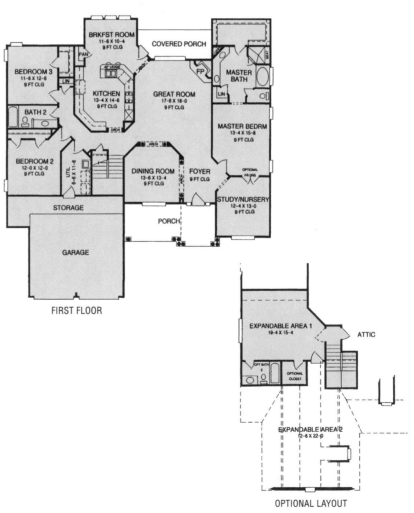

FIRST FLOOR

OPTIONAL LAYOUT

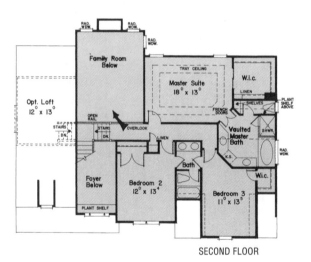

SECOND FLOOR

plan # HPK0400246

Style: Victorian
First Floor: 1,415 sq. ft.
Second Floor: 1,015 sq. ft.
Total: 2,430 sq. ft.
Bonus Space: 169 sq. ft.
Bedrooms: 4
Bathrooms: 3½
Width: 54' - 0"
Depth: 43' - 4"
Foundation: Basement, Crawlspace

SEARCH ONLINE @ EPLANS.COM

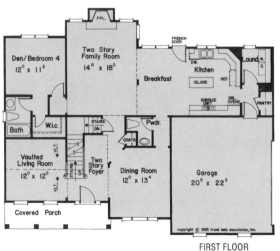

FIRST FLOOR

This striking design is reminiscent of the grand homes of the past century. Its wood siding and covered porch are complemented by shuttered windows and a glass-paneled entry. Historic design is updated in the floor plan to include a vaulted living room, a two-story family room, and a den that doubles as a guest suite on the first floor. Second-floor bedrooms feature a master suite with tray ceiling and vaulted bath. An optional loft on the second floor may be finished as a study area.

plan# HPK0400247

Style: Country Cottage
First Floor: 1,716 sq. ft.
Second Floor: 618 sq. ft.
Total: 2,334 sq. ft.
Bedrooms: 3
Bathrooms: 3
Width: 47' - 0"
Depth: 50' - 0"
Foundation: Crawlspace

SEARCH ONLINE @ EPLANS.COM

This country farmhouse enjoys special features such as gables, dormers, plenty of windows, and a covered front porch. Columns adorn the home throughout for an extra touch of elegance. The formal dining room enjoys a tray ceiling and is open to the kitchen, which enjoys access to either a utility room or the breakfast nook with a bay window. The massive great room enjoys a vaulted ceiling, a cozy fireplace, and built-ins—French doors tie this room to a vaulted rear porch. On the left of this home is a study/office along with the sumptuous master suite. The second floor holds two family bedrooms—both with walk-in closets and built-in desks—sharing a full bath.

SECOND FLOOR

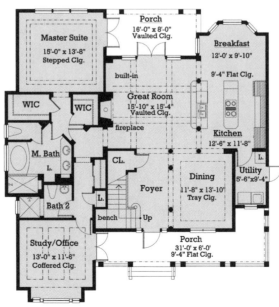

FIRST FLOOR

SECOND FLOOR

FIRST FLOOR

plan# HPK0400248

Style: Farmhouse
First Floor: 1,670 sq. ft.
Second Floor: 763 sq. ft.
Total: 2,433 sq. ft.
Bedrooms: 3
Bathrooms: 2½
Width: 53' - 0"
Depth: 54' - 0"
Foundation: Crawlspace

SEARCH ONLINE @ EPLANS.COM

Pillars line the front of a fine covered porch on this attractive two-story home. Craftsman architecture is represented by a smattering of shingles on the second story and the shelter of an overhanging roofline. Inside, a formal dining room has easy access to the efficient kitchen as well as to the front porch. A spacious gathering room features a fireplace, access to the rear patio/deck and shares a snack bar with the kitchen and breakfast room. Located on the first floor for privacy, the master suite is sure to please with its many amenities, which include a large walk-in closet, plenty of windows, a detailed ceiling, and a sumptuous bath. Upstairs, two suites share a full bath as well as a large loft—perfect for a study area, computer space, or play area. A two-car garage easily shelters the family fleet.

plan# HPK0400249

Style: Farmhouse
First Floor: 1,710 sq. ft.
Second Floor: 618 sq. ft.
Total: 2,328 sq. ft.
Bedrooms: 3
Bathrooms: 3
Width: 47' - 0"
Depth: 50' - 0"
Foundation: Crawlspace

SEARCH ONLINE @ EPLANS.COM

SECOND FLOOR

FIRST FLOOR

Here's a new American farmhouse that's just right for any neighborhood—in town or far away. A perfect interior starts with an open foyer and interior vistas through a fabulous great room. A fireplace anchors the living space, and a beamed, vaulted ceiling adds volume. Decorative columns open the central interior to the gourmet kitchen and breakfast area, which boasts a bay window. The master wing includes a study that easily converts to a home office. Upstairs, the secondary bedrooms feature built-in desks and walk-in closets.

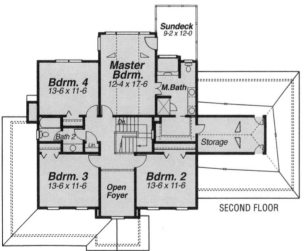

Sundeck
9-2 x 12-0

Master Bdrm.
12-4 x 17-6

M.Bath

Bdrm. 4
13-6 x 11-6

Bath 2

Lin

Dn

Storage

Bdrm. 3
13-6 x 11-6

Open Foyer

Bdrm. 2
13-6 x 11-6

SECOND FLOOR

plan

Style: Farmhouse
First Floor: 1,250 sq. ft.
Second Floor: 1,166 sq. ft.
Total: 2,416 sq. ft.
Bedrooms: 4
Bathrooms: 2½
Width: 64' - 0"
Depth: 52' - 0"
Foundation: Basement

SEARCH ONLINE @ EPLANS.COM

With its classic features, this home is reminiscent of Main Street, USA. The two-story foyer is flanked by the formal living and dining rooms, and the stairs are tucked back in the center of the house. Columns create a separation from the family room to the breakfast area, keeping that open feeling across the entire rear of the house. Corner windows in the kitchen look into the side yard and rear screened porch. The porch leads to the rear deck, which also ties into the side porch, creating outdoor living on three sides of the house. As you ascend the staircase to the second floor, you will pass a lighted panel of stained glass on the landing, creating the illusion of a window wall. The second floor features four bedrooms and a compartmented hall bath.

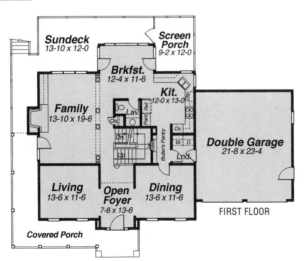

Sundeck
13-10 x 12-0

Screen Porch
9-2 x 12-0

Brkfst.
12-4 x 11-6

Kit.
12-0 x 13-0

Family
13-10 x 19-6

Lav

Pant. Ref.

Butler's Pantry

Ov

Dn

W/D

Up

Lnd.

Double Garage
21-8 x 23-4

Living
13-6 x 11-6

Open Foyer
7-8 x 13-6

Dining
13-6 x 11-6

FIRST FLOOR

Covered Porch

plan # HPK0400251

Style: Farmhouse
First Floor: 1,710 sq. ft.
Second Floor: 618 sq. ft.
Total: 2,328 sq. ft.
Bedrooms: 3
Bathrooms: 3
Width: 47' - 0"
Depth: 50' - 0"
Foundation: Crawlspace

SEARCH ONLINE @ EPLANS.COM

Decorative details complement this home's country facade, and pedimented arches and a covered porch add sophistication. The foyer leads to the vaulted great room where a fireplace awaits. Both the magnificent master suite and the great room showcase French doors to the rear vaulted porch. The breakfast bay sheds sunlight onto the spacious kitchen. An elegant coffered ceiling and three-window bay dress up the front study (or make it into an office). Two bedrooms, both with walk-in closets, share the second level with a bath and an equipment room.

SECOND FLOOR

FIRST FLOOR

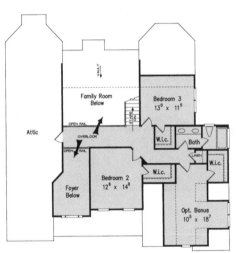

SECOND FLOOR

plan# HPK0400252

Style: Traditional
First Floor: 1,797 sq. ft.
Second Floor: 654 sq. ft.
Total: 2,451 sq. ft.
Bonus Space: 266 sq. ft.
Bedrooms: 3
Bathrooms: 2½
Width: 54' - 0"
Depth: 54' - 10"
Foundation: Crawlspace,
Basement

SEARCH ONLINE @ EPLANS.COM

Capstones and brick accents add a touch of class to the charm and comfort of this American dream home. A vaulted breakfast bay brings the outdoors in and fills a sophisticated gourmet kitchen with natural light. The spacious family room enjoys radius windows and a French door to the back property; a private formal living room opens off the foyer. A centered fireplace flanked by windows dresses up the master suite, which also features a vaulted private bath with a whirlpool tub. The second-floor bedrooms are connected by a balcony hall that overlooks the family room and the foyer.

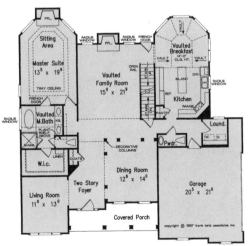

FIRST FLOOR

plan # HPK0400253

Style: Traditional
First Floor: 1,720 sq. ft.
Second Floor: 724 sq. ft.
Total: 2,444 sq. ft.
Bonus Space: 212 sq. ft.
Bedrooms: 4
Bathrooms: 3
Width: 58' - 0"
Depth: 47' - 0"
Foundation: Crawlspace, Basement

SEARCH ONLINE @ EPLANS.COM

Columns announce the front covered porch and entry of this comfortable home. An open arrangement of the interior allows vistas that extend from the two-story foyer to the rear property. A fireplace and two sets of radius windows define the vaulted great room, which allows passage to the casual breakfast area. The well-organized kitchen offers a serving bar, planning desk, and an ample pantry. To the rear of the plan, a flex room offers the possibility of a guest suite or home office. The master suite offers a compartmented bath, separate vanities, and a walk-in closet. Upstairs, two secondary bedrooms share a gallery hall that ends in a computer nook.

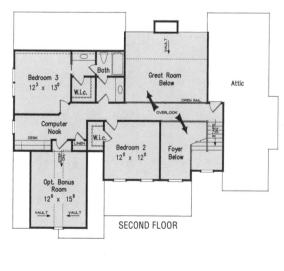

SECOND FLOOR

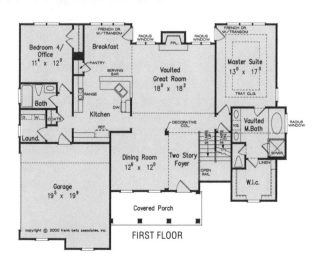

FIRST FLOOR

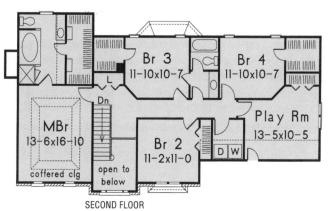

SECOND FLOOR

Br 3
11-10x10-7

Br 4
11-10x10-7

MBr
13-6x16-10

coffered clg

Dn

open to below

Br 2
11-2x11-0

Play Rm
13-5x10-5

D W

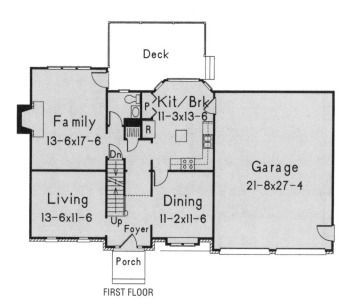

FIRST FLOOR

Deck

Family
13-6x17-6

Kit/Brk
11-3x13-6

Garage
21-8x27-4

Living
13-6x11-6

Dining
11-2x11-6

Up Foyer

Dn

Porch

plan # HPK0400254

Style: Traditional
First Floor: 972 sq. ft.
Second Floor: 1,364 sq. ft.
Total: 2,336 sq. ft.
Bedrooms: 4
Bathrooms: 2½
Width: 56' - 0"
Depth: 32' - 0"
Foundation: Basement

SEARCH ONLINE @ EPLANS.COM

Four upstairs bedrooms and a playroom make this the right plan for a growing family. The formal dining area and living room flank the foyer on the main level making entertaining truly gracious and enjoyable. The spacious family room is warmed by a fireplace and opens to the rear deck. The kitchen and breakfast bay enjoy views overlooking the deck into the backyard. A half-bath is conveniently near. The two-car garage has two side entries, one into the kitchen.

plan # HPK0400255

Style: Contemporary
First Floor: 1,861 sq. ft.
Second Floor: 598 sq. ft.
Total: 2,459 sq. ft.
Bedrooms: 4
Bathrooms: 2½
Width: 0' - 0"
Depth: 0' - 0"
Foundation: Basement

SEARCH ONLINE @ EPLANS.COM

Vaulted ceilings highlight the interior of this classy two-story home. Nearly every room on the main level has one—the living and family rooms, breakfast bay, and two-story foyer. Other special features include a first-floor master bedroom with a private study and an island kitchen with a walk-in pantry. Near the deluxe master suite, a study is available for quiet times. Upstairs, three family bedrooms share a bath. Between the main living areas and the garage, a laundry and half-bath are conveniently placed.

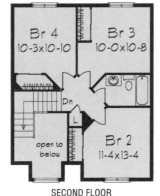

SECOND FLOOR

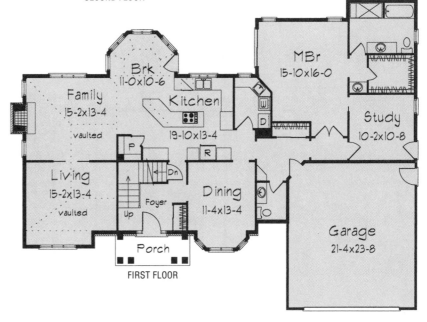

FIRST FLOOR

Two sets of staircases conveniently carry traffic from one floor to the other in this elegant two-story plan. The family room, breakfast area, and kitchen are organized to have wide open spaces between them, allowing for greater flexibility in organizing these areas. A walk-in pantry will make the family chef's eyes sparkle. The front living room enjoys a vaulted ceiling and a sunken floor; the formal dining room is across the foyer. Four bedrooms are located upstairs, including a resplendent master suite, with a lavish, amenity-filled bath.

plan# HPK0400256

Style: Traditional
First Floor: 1,291 sq. ft.
Second Floor: 1,045 sq. ft.
Total: 2,336 sq. ft.
Bedrooms: 4
Bathrooms: 2½
Width: 49' - 0"
Depth: 42' - 0"
Foundation: Basement

SEARCH ONLINE @ EPLANS.COM

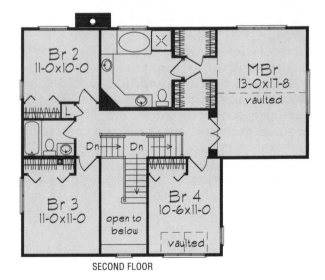

FIRST FLOOR

SECOND FLOOR

plan # HPK0400257

Style: French
First Floor: 1,530 sq. ft.
Second Floor: 968 sq. ft.
Total: 2,498 sq. ft.
Bonus Space: 326 sq. ft.
Bedrooms: 3
Bathrooms: 2½
Width: 40' - 0"
Depth: 66' - 4"
Foundation: Basement, Slab, Crawlspace

SEARCH ONLINE @ EPLANS.COM

The timeless influence of the French Quarter is exemplified in this home designed for riverfront living. The double French-door entry opens into a large living room/dining room area separated by a double archway. A railed balcony with a loft on the second floor overlooks the living room. A pass-through between the kitchen and dining room also provides seating at a bar for informal dining. The spacious master bedroom at the rear includes a sitting area and a roomy bath with a large walk-in closet. Two additional bedrooms, a bath, and a bonus area for an office or game room are located upstairs.

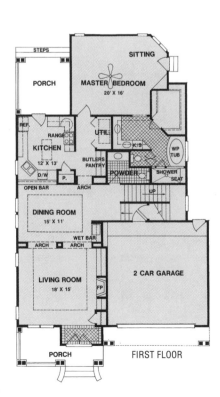

FIRST FLOOR

SECOND FLOOR

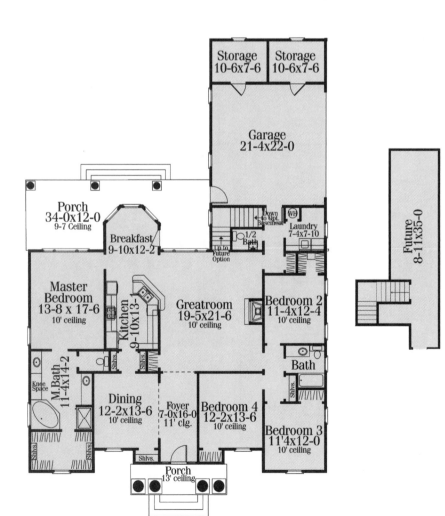

Storage 10-6x7-6

Storage 10-6x7-6

Garage 21-4x22-0

Porch 34-0x12-0
9-7 Ceiling

Breakfast 9-10x12-2

Down to Opt. Basement

WH

1/2 Bath

Laundry 7-4x7-10

Future 8-11x35-0

Up to Future Option

Master Bedroom 13-8 x 17-6
10' ceiling

Kitchen 9-10x13-1

Shlvs.

Shlvs.

Greatroom 19-5x21-6
10' ceiling

Bedroom 2 11-4x12-4
10' ceiling

M.Bath 11-4x14-2

Knee Space

Bath

Dining 12-2x13-6
10' ceiling

Foyer 7-0x16-0
11' clg.

Bedroom 4 12-2x13-6
10' ceiling

Bedroom 3 11'4x12-0
10' ceiling

Shlvs.

Shlvs.

Shlvs.

Porch
13' ceiling

plan # HPK0400258

Style: Gothic Revival
Square Footage: 2,402
Bonus Space: 294 sq. ft.
Bedrooms: 4
Bathrooms: 2½
Width: 56' - 6"
Depth: 82' - 0"
Foundation: Crawlspace, Slab, Basement

SEARCH ONLINE @ EPLANS.COM

Pillars and shuttered windows grace the facade of this handsome home. Space is well organized for casual and comfortable family living and for memorable social events. The formal dining room is just to the left as guests enter and is served from the kitchen through a butler's pantry. Straight ahead from the foyer the spacious great room enjoys a fireplace at one end and is connected to the kitchen by a counter/bar at the opposite end. The stylish breakfast bay projects out over the covered rear porch. Four bedrooms, including an unforgettable master suite, are also located on the first level.

plan # HPK0400259

Style: Traditional
Square Footage: 2,409
Bonus Space: 709 sq. ft.
Bedrooms: 3
Bathrooms: 2½
Width: 85' - 8"
Depth: 68' - 4"
Foundation: Crawlspace, Slab, Basement

SEARCH ONLINE @ EPLANS.COM

The great room of this home provides a large masonry fireplace. Built-ins are included on one wall for entertainment equipment and books. The master suite is located to the rear of the house and has a luxury bath that includes large walk-in closets. The kitchen, equipped with a snack bar, walk-in pantry, and desk, is well designed for the busy cook. From the kitchen area, the staircase rises to an expandable second floor. With a future bedroom, game room, and bath upstairs, this home will fit the needs of a growing family.

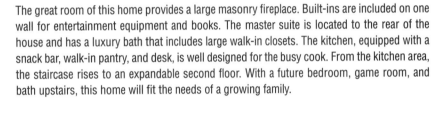

QUOTE ONE®

Cost to build? See page 333 to order complete cost estimate to build this house in your area!

FIRST FLOOR

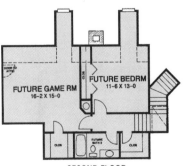

SECOND FLOOR

Grand, welcoming, and cozy—these are the words that describe this two-story brick house. The first floor consists of a family room with an 18-foot ceiling, a dramatic breakfast nook, a deck, and a guest bedroom with a full bath. Family sleeping quarters are located upstairs. Here you'll find a glorious master suite; it includes His and Hers walk-in closets and a bath with a spa tub, shower, and double-bowl vanity. Bedrooms 3 and 4 share a full compartmented bath. The home is completed with a two-car garage.

plan # HPK0400260

Style: Colonial
First Floor: 1,270 sq. ft.
Second Floor: 1,070 sq. ft.
Total: 2,340 sq. ft.
Bedrooms: 4
Bathrooms: 3½
Width: 53' - 0"
Depth: 44' - 0"
Foundation: Walkout Basement

SEARCH ONLINE @ EPLANS.COM

DECK
11'-0" x 28'-0"

BREAKFAST
9'-8" x 9'-8"

FAMILY ROOM
18'-10" x 13'-10"

KITCHEN
12'-0" x 9'-10"

LNDRY
5'-6" x 7'-10"

GUEST BEDROOM
12'-4" x 10'-4"

BATH #2
8'-8" x 5'-0"

UP

DN

POWDER

FOYER
6'-4" X 12'-0"

DINING ROOM
11'-8" x 11'-10"

TWO-CAR GARAGE
20'-4" x 20'-4"

LIVING ROOM
9'-10" X 14'-0"

PORCH

FIRST FLOOR

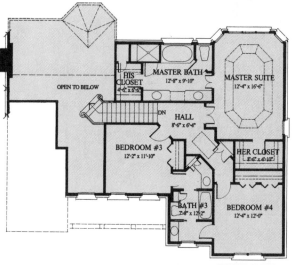

HIS CLOSET
4'-4" x 6'-8"

MASTER BATH
12'-8" x 9'-10"

MASTER SUITE
12'-4" x 16'-6"

OPEN TO BELOW

DN

HALL
8'-6" x 6'-4"

BEDROOM #3
12'-2" x 11'-10"

HER CLOSET
8'-6" x 4'-10"

BATH #3
7'-8" x 12'-2"

BEDROOM #4
12'-4" x 12'-0"

SECOND FLOOR

plan # HPK0400261

Style: Colonial
First Floor: 1,252 sq. ft.
Second Floor: 1,209 sq. ft.
Total: 2,461 sq. ft.
Bedrooms: 4
Bathrooms: 2½
Width: 60' - 6"
Depth: 38' - 9"
Foundation: Basement, Slab, Crawlspace

SEARCH ONLINE @ EPLANS.COM

This Colonial home offers a historically correct exterior design with an updated interior for modern living. The foyer is flanked by the living and dining rooms; the more intimate family room is found in the rear where a fireplace brings warmth and atmosphere. The U-shaped kitchen adjoins the sunny breakfast bay in the rear. The two-car garage is accessed from the kitchen via the utility room for added convenience. The grand staircase in the foyer rises to three family bedrooms, a full bath, and a luxurious master suite.

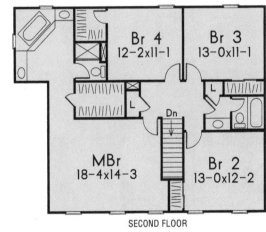

Br 4
12-2x11-1

Br 3
13-0x11-1

Dn

MBr
18-4x14-3

Br 2
13-0x12-2

SECOND FLOOR

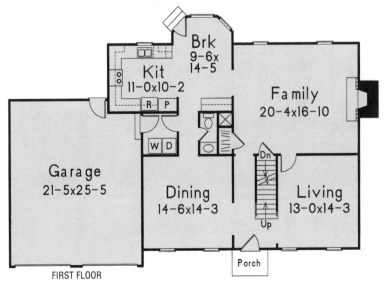

Brk
9-6x
14-5

Kit
11-0x10-2

Family
20-4x16-10

Garage
21-5x25-5

Dn

Dining
14-6x14-3

Living
13-0x14-3

Up

Porch

FIRST FLOOR

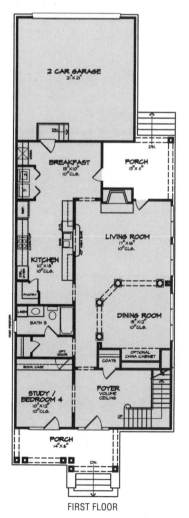

FIRST FLOOR

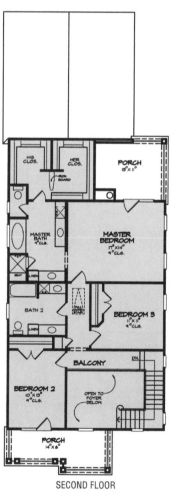

SECOND FLOOR

plan# HPK0400262

Style: Traditional
First Floor: 1,311 sq. ft.
Second Floor: 1,136 sq. ft.
Total: 2,447 sq. ft.
Bedrooms: 4
Bathrooms: 3
Width: 29' - 10"
Depth: 79' - 4"
Foundation: Crawlspace

SEARCH ONLINE @ EPLANS.COM

The two front porches of this appealing home can be accessed by French doors through the study and the upper bedroom. The dining room offers built-in cabinetry that's perfect for storing china. The breakfast room and living room, with fireplace, open onto a back porch. The second-floor balcony overlooks the generous foyer. The master suite has His and Hers closets, a separate shower and tub, two vanities, and an adjacent porch, proving that luxury does not have to be sacrificed in a narrow-lot home.

plan # HPK0400263

Style: French
Square Footage: 2,416
Bedrooms: 4
Bathrooms: 3
Width: 58' - 0"
Depth: 71' - 6"
Foundation: Crawlspace, Basement

SEARCH ONLINE @ EPLANS.COM

Arches and quoins lend a quaint appearance to this 21st-Century country home and harmonize with a thoroughly up-to-date interior. Decorative columns define formal rooms, which enjoy the soaring interior vistas of the vaulted family room, with wide views of the outdoors through radius windows. The lavish master suite boasts two walk-in closets, a windowed whirlpool tub, and a knee-space vanity. Three family bedrooms share a full bath. A curved serving bar makes kitchen service to the keeping and family rooms simple.

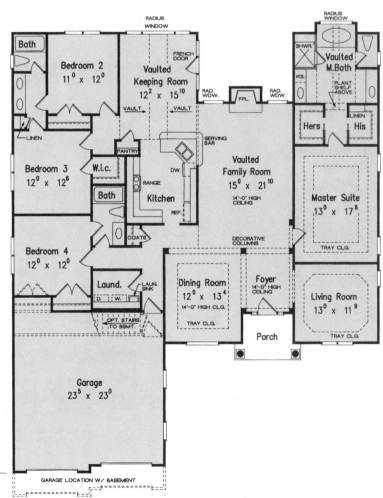

© William E. Poole Designs, Inc.

Graceful rooflines and front-porch columns speak to the elegance this wonderful home offers, inside and out. A magnificent master suite with a gigantic walk-in closet and a private bath that includes a shower and whirlpool tub ensures relaxing comfort. Upstairs, three more bedrooms and space for a future recreation room can be found. The main living areas on the main level are organized for both casual comfort and formal get-togethers. The island counter in the kitchen conveniently houses a sink, the dishwasher, and a serving bar. The two-story family room enjoys a media center, fireplace, and entry to the rear terrace (or make it a deck).

plan # HPK0400264

Style: Craftsman
First Floor: 1,627 sq. ft.
Second Floor: 783 sq. ft.
Total: 2,410 sq. ft.
Bonus Space: 418 sq. ft.
Bedrooms: 4
Bathrooms: 2½
Width: 46' - 0"
Depth: 58' - 0"
Foundation: Crawlspace

SEARCH ONLINE @ EPLANS.COM

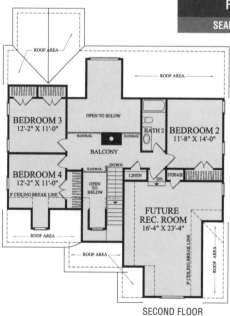

ORDER BLUEPRINTS 24 HOURS, 7 DAYS A WEEK, AT 1-800-521-6797

plan# HPK0400265

Style: Country Cottage
First Floor: 1,627 sq. ft.
Second Floor: 783 sq. ft.
Total: 2,410 sq. ft.
Bonus Space: 418 sq. ft.
Bedrooms: 4
Bathrooms: 2½
Width: 46' - 0"
Depth: 58' - 6"
Foundation: Crawlspace

SEARCH ONLINE @ EPLANS.COM

This "little jewel" of a home emanates a warmth and joy not soon forgotten. The two-story foyer leads to the formal living room, defined by graceful columns. A formal dining room opens off from the living room, making entertaining a breeze. A family room at the back features a fireplace and works well with the kitchen and breakfast areas. A lavish master suite is secluded on the first floor; three family bedrooms reside upstairs.

SECOND FLOOR

FIRST FLOOR

This stucco home with careful details and all the most-wanted amenities will delight at every turn. Open planning defines the dining room with a cathedral ceiling and a single column. The two-story great room has a cathedral ceiling and a brick extended-hearth fireplace. From here, expansive rear views continue to the sunny breakfast nook. An angled galley kitchen is made for gourmet meals. Two left-wing bedrooms share a full bath. In the right wing, the master suite revels in a cathedral bath and a bumped-out Roman tub. His and Hers closets are a wonderful convenience.

plan # HPK0400266

Style: European Cottage
First Floor: 2,094 sq. ft.
Second Floor: 264 sq. ft.
Total: 2,358 sq. ft.
Bedrooms: 3
Bathrooms: 2½
Width: 65' - 6"
Depth: 62' - 7"
Foundation: Basement, Crawlspace, Slab

SEARCH ONLINE @ EPLANS.COM

FIRST FLOOR

SECOND FLOOR

ORDER BLUEPRINTS 24 HOURS, 7 DAYS A WEEK, AT 1-800-521-6797

plan# HPK0400267

Style: Traditional
Square Footage: 2,423
Bedrooms: 3
Bathrooms: 2½
Width: 71' - 8"
Depth: 70' - 0"
Foundation: Basement

SEARCH ONLINE @ EPLANS.COM

For the son or daughter who has just moved back or wants more independence; for the in-laws who just moved in; or for the budding entrepreneur, the room at the front of this home, with a large closet, private bath, and separate outside entrance, makes a great bedroom suite or home office. This spacious plan includes three bedrooms—one a lavish master suite—and considerable living room. The country-style kitchen offers lots of elbowroom for preparing gourmet meals. The dining room appears to be part of the great room, but is clearly defined by its stepped ceiling. French doors from the great room open to the rear deck.

This elegant European-style home easily accommodates formal entertaining, with a foyer that opens to a living room on the left and a dining room on the right. Introduce your guests to the warmth of the family room with its cozy fireplace and expansive views. The first floor also makes room for a guest bedroom and a full bath. The second floor holds three additional bedrooms. The master suite, with His and Hers closets, is sure to delight.

plan # HPK0400268

Style: Norman
First Floor: 1,270 sq. ft.
Second Floor: 1,070 sq. ft.
Total: 2,340 sq. ft.
Bedrooms: 4
Bathrooms: 3½
Width: 50' - 0"
Depth: 44' - 0"
Foundation: Walkout Basement

SEARCH ONLINE @ EPLANS.COM

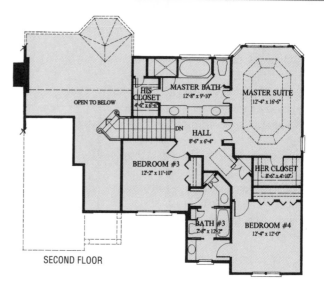

FIRST FLOOR

SECOND FLOOR

plan # HPK0400269

Style: French
First Floor: 1,180 sq. ft.
Second Floor: 1,205 sq. ft.
Total: 2,385 sq. ft.
Bonus Space: 210 sq. ft.
Bedrooms: 3
Bathrooms: 2½
Width: 46' - 0"
Depth: 51' - 6"
Foundation: Walkout Basement

SEARCH ONLINE @ EPLANS.COM

Exceptional detail and quality are the hallmarks of this classic European-styled design. Step down to the formal living area or enjoy formal dining to the left of the foyer. The family room with a fireplace and the kitchen with a sunny, bayed breakfast nook offer a superb casual counterbalance. The second floor accommodates three bedrooms—one a spacious master suite. The master bath, with a corner tub, a separate shower, dual vanities, and a compartmented water closet, completes this relaxing retreat. An unfinished upstairs bedroom and bath provide opportunities for future expansion.

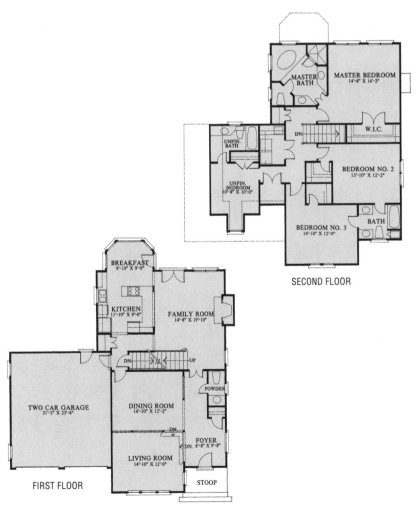

SECOND FLOOR

FIRST FLOOR

A smart floor plan resides behind this stone-and-brick facade. Inside, the great room occupies the central part of the home, adjacent to the island kitchen and breakfast area. It opens to the covered rear patio. The vaulted ceiling in the master bedroom creates an open feel, and the master bath provides convenience with a dual-sink vanity, and an oversized walk-in closet. Two additional bedrooms, a guest room/study, and two full baths are available for family members or visitors.

plan# HPK0400270

Style: European Cottage
Square Footage: 2,352
Bedrooms: 4
Bathrooms: 3
Width: 77' - 6"
Depth: 53' - 2"
Foundation: Crawlspace, Slab

SEARCH ONLINE @ EPLANS.COM

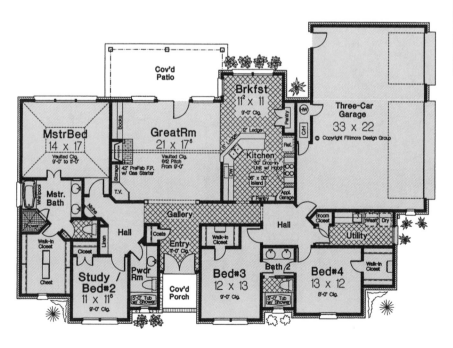

plan# HPK0400271

Style: European Cottage
First Floor: 1,231 sq. ft.
Second Floor: 1,154 sq. ft.
Total: 2,385 sq. ft.
Bonus Space: 277 sq. ft.
Bedrooms: 3
Bathrooms: 2½
Width: 46' - 0"
Depth: 50' - 6"
Foundation: Walkout Basement

SEARCH ONLINE @ EPLANS.COM

All the Old World elements of gables, dormer windows, stone work, multilevel roof, and spires combine to create this charming cottage. The main focal point of the foyer is the large formal dining room with its beautiful triple window combination. The family room features a beamed ceiling, fireplace, and covenient back staircase. The breakfast area has a bay window and a door to the back deck, ideal for outdoor entertaining. The master suite has extended space with its own bay sitting area, roomy bath with whirlpool tub, and spacious closet. Other bedrooms share a bath. There is also a bonus room over the garage.

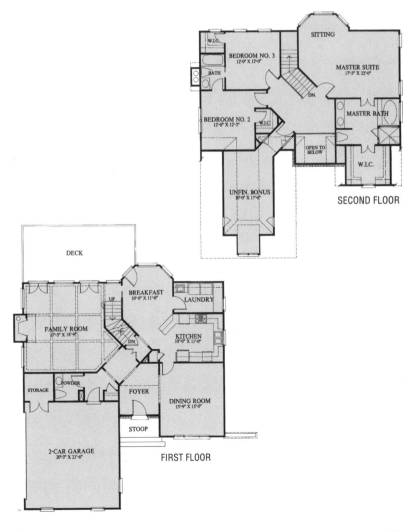

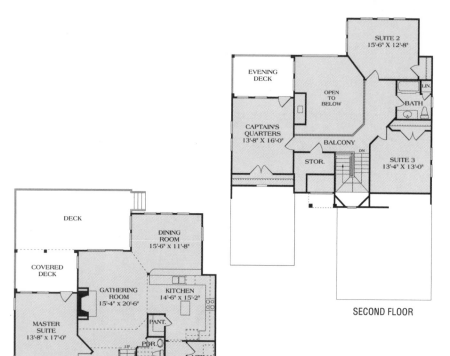

SECOND FLOOR

SUITE 2
15'-6" X 12'-8"

EVENING
DECK

OPEN
TO
BELOW

LIN.

BATH

CAPTAIN'S
QUARTERS
13'-8" X 16'-0"

BALCONY

DN

STOR.

SUITE 3
13'-4" X 13'-0"

FIRST FLOOR

DECK

DINING
ROOM
15'-6" x 11'-8"

COVERED
DECK

GATHERING
ROOM
15'-4" X 20'-6"

KITCHEN
14'-6" X 15'-2"

MASTER
SUITE
13'-8" x 17'-0"

PANT.

PDR.

UTIL.

FOYER

W.I.C.

W.I.C.

PORTICO

MASTER
BATH

GARAGE
20'-4" x 22'-4"

plan ⊕ HPK0400272

Style: Transitional
First Floor: 1,494 sq. ft.
Second Floor: 954 sq. ft.
Total: 2,448 sq. ft.
Bedrooms: 3
Bathrooms: 2½
Width: 45' - 0"
Depth: 60' - 2"
Foundation: Crawlspace

SEARCH ONLINE @ EPLANS.COM

With hints of Cape Cod and a dash of country, this unique home makes a perfect vacation retreat or a comfortable full-time home. The foyer leads into the welcoming two-story gathering room, graced with a fireplace and sliding glass doors to the deck. The island kitchen is open to the gathering room, for effortless entertaining, and serves the dining room with the help of a snack bar. The master suite is located on this level and enjoys deck access, dual amenities, and a lavish bath with a tub set in a flower-box window. Two bedrooms share a full bath upstairs, joined by the "captain's quarters" that would provide a great home office or guest room (with a private evening deck). Extra storage is a thoughtful touch.

plan # HPK0400273

Style: SW Contemporary
First Floor: 1,520 sq. ft.
Second Floor: 929 sq. ft.
Total: 2,449 sq. ft.
Bedrooms: 3
Bathrooms: 3
Width: 47' - 0"
Depth: 56' - 6"
Foundation: Basement, Crawlspace

SEARCH ONLINE @ EPLANS.COM

A recessed entry with double doors introduces this lovely plan. Vaulted ceilings throughout the foyer, living room, dining room, and kitchen add a sense of spaciousness and allow for plant ledges. A peninsula fireplace separates the dining room and living room. The family room has another fireplace, flanked by shelves to serve as an entertainment center. A private den sits adjacent to the family room. The master bedroom and the two family bedrooms reside on the upper level.

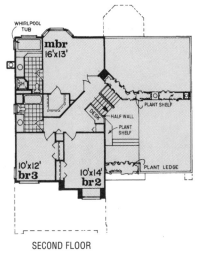

SECOND FLOOR

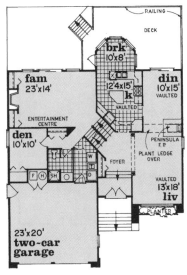

FIRST FLOOR

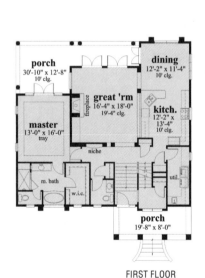

porch
30'-10" x 12'-8"
10' clg.

dining
12'-2" x 11'-4"
10' clg.

great 'rm
16'-4" x 18'-0"
19'-4" clg.

fireplace

kitch.
12'-2" x
13'-4"
10' clg.

master
13'-0" x 16'-0"
tray

niche

m. bath

w.i.c.

util.

porch
19'-8" x 8'-0"

FIRST FLOOR

open deck
30'-10" x 12'-8"

porch
8' clg.

porch
8' clg.

bedroom
12'-2" x 14'-0"
tray

open

bath

bedroom
13'-2" x 12'-0"
tray

w.i.c.

bath

loft
10'-4" x 11'-4"
8' clg.

open

SECOND FLOOR

storage/ bonus
29'-6" x 39'-0"

garage
24'-0" x 25'-6"

BASEMENT

plan # HPK0400274

Style: Tidewater
First Floor: 1,492 sq. ft.
Second Floor: 854 sq. ft.
Total: 2,346 sq. ft.
Bedrooms: 3
Bathrooms: 3½
Width: 44' - 0"
Depth: 48' - 0"
Foundation: Basement

SEARCH ONLINE @ EPLANS.COM

The staircase leading to a columned front porch lends a touch of grandeur to this residence. The great room is made inviting with a fireplace and twin sets of double doors opening to a wrap-around porch that's also accessed by the master suite. This spacious suite features luxurious extras like His and Hers sinks, a separate garden tub and shower, and a huge walk-in closet. The kitchen provides plenty of counter space and overlooks the formal dining room. Upstairs, two additional bedrooms open up to a second-floor porch and have their own private baths and walk-in closets.

plan # HPK0400305

Style: Tidewater
First Floor: 1,266 sq. ft.
Second Floor: 1,324 sq. ft.
Total: 2,590 sq. ft.
Bedrooms: 3
Bathrooms: 2½
Width: 34'-0"
Depth: 63'-2"
Foundation: Crawlspace

SEARCH ONLINE @ EPLANS.COM

This Floridian-style home boasts an impressive balcony that is sure to catch the eye. A large veranda borders two sides of the home. The entry leads into a long foyer, which runs from the entrance to the rear of the design. The coffered great room enjoys a fireplace, built-in cabinetry and French doors to the veranda; the dining room also accesses the veranda. The island kitchen leads into a bayed nook, perfect for Sunday morning breakfasting. The second floor is home to two family bedrooms, both with access to the deck, a study and a luxurious master suite. A vaulted sitting area, full bath and deck access are just some of the highlights of the master suite.

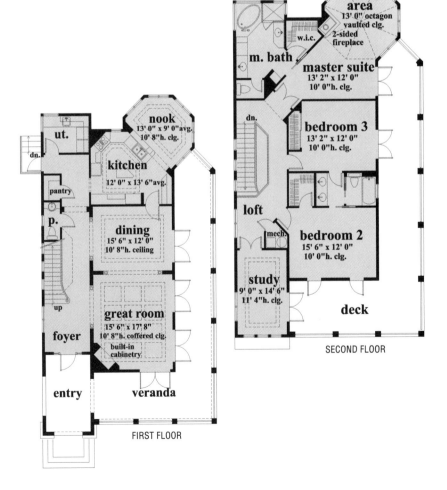

SECOND FLOOR

veranda

sitting
9' 4"h. clg.

master suite
17' 0" x 17' 0" avg.
10' 4"h. tray clg.

vaulted ceiling
open to
below

overlook

dn.

w.i.c.

linen

m. bath

mech.

FIRST FLOOR

dn.

veranda

window seat

bedroom 3
11' 8" x 12' 4"
9' 4"h. clg.

nook
11' 0" x 8' 0"
9' 4"h. clg.

built-in
cabinetry

great room
19' 6" x 19' 0"
2-story ceiling
fireplace

kitchen

linen

ut.

up

study
11' 0" x 13' 6"
14' 0"h. clg.

up

foyer

dining
11' 0" x 13' 6"
14' 0"h. clg.

bedroom 2
11' 8" x 10' 6"
9' 4"h. clg.

entry porch
32' 0" x 8' 6"
14' 0"h. ceiling

dn.

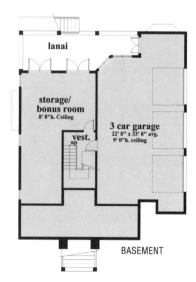

BASEMENT

lanai

storage/
bonus room
8' 8"h. Ceiling

vest.

up

3 car garage
22' 8" x 33' 8" avg.
9' 0"h. ceiling

plan# HPK0400275

Style: Italianate
First Floor: 1,671 sq. ft.
Second Floor: 846 sq. ft.
Total: 2,517 sq. ft.
Bedrooms: 3
Bathrooms: 2
Width: 44' - 0"
Depth: 55' - 0"
Foundation: Basement

SEARCH ONLINE @ EPLANS.COM

This magnificent villa boasts a beautiful stucco exterior framing a spectacular entry. The heart of the home is served by a well-crafted kitchen with wrapping counter space and an island cooktop counter. The breakfast nook enjoys a view of the veranda and beyond, and brings natural light to the casual eating space. Archways supported by columns separate the dining room from the great room, which boasts a fireplace and built-in cabinetry. On the upper level, the master suite features a sitting area and a private veranda. The master bath provides a knee-space vanity, whirlpool tub, and walk-in closet.

plan# HPK0400276

Style: Italianate
First Floor: 1,266 sq. ft.
Second Floor: 1,324 sq. ft.
Total: 2,590 sq. ft.
Bedrooms: 3
Bathrooms: 2½
Width: 34' - 0"
Depth: 63' - 2"
Foundation: Slab

SEARCH ONLINE @ EPLANS.COM

This modern take on the Italian villa boasts plenty of indoor/outdoor flow. Four sets of double doors wrap around the great room and dining area and open to the stunning veranda. The great room is enhanced by a coffered ceiling and built-in cabinetry, and the entire first floor is bathed in sunlight from a wall of glass doors overlooking the veranda. The dining room connects to a gourmet island kitchen. Upstairs, a beautiful deck wraps gracefully around the family bedrooms. The master suite is a skylit haven enhanced by a sitting bay, which features a vaulted octagonal ceiling and a cozy two-sided fireplace. Private double doors access the sundeck from the master suite, the secondary bedrooms, and the study.

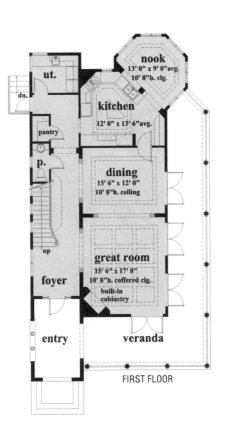

FIRST FLOOR

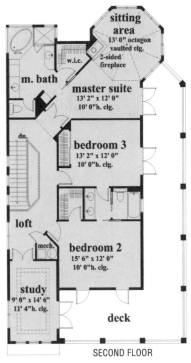

SECOND FLOOR

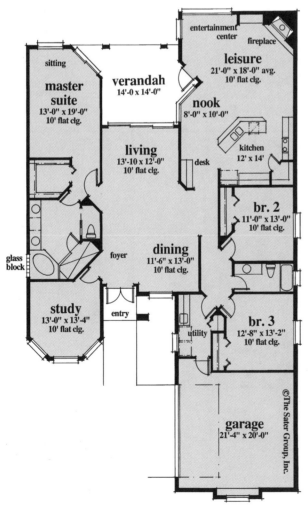

plan # HPK0400277

Style: Floridian
Square Footage: 2,562
Bedrooms: 3
Bathrooms: 2
Width: 49' - 10"
Depth: 84' - 0"
Foundation: Slab

SEARCH ONLINE @ EPLANS.COM

The turret study and raised entry add interest to the front exterior. The double-door entry opens up to the dining room on the right and the formal living room ahead. The informal living wing features a large kitchen, nook for casual meals, and leisure room area complete with a corner fireplace and entertainment center. The opulent master suite has a sitting area and extensive glass doors and windows. It pampers with a corner tub and a shower large enough for two. A very special place is the front study set into the sunlit turret.

plan # HPK0400278

Style: Traditional
First Floor: 1,796 sq. ft.
Second Floor: 771 sq. ft.
Total: 2,567 sq. ft.
Bonus Space: 220 sq. ft.
Bedrooms: 4
Bathrooms: 3½
Width: 50' - 0"
Depth: 57' - 4"
Foundation: Slab

SEARCH ONLINE @ EPLANS.COM

This contemporary Mediterranean home features a vibrant octagonal entry, formal living and dining rooms, gourmet kitchen with adjoining nook and laundry facilities, and a first-floor master suite. A spacious family room opens to the breakfast nook and has a fireplace flanked by a built-in entertainment center. Upstairs, three family bedrooms, two full baths, and an optional bonus room complete the floor plan.

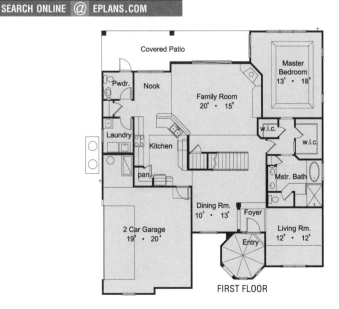

FIRST FLOOR

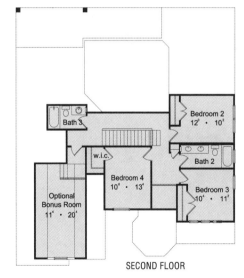

SECOND FLOOR

SECOND FLOOR

FIRST FLOOR

plan # HPK0400279

Style: Country Cottage
First Floor: 1,805 sq. ft.
Second Floor: 952 sq. ft.
Total: 2,757 sq. ft.
Bonus Space: 475 sq. ft.
Bedrooms: 4
Bathrooms: 3½
Width: 48' - 10"
Depth: 64' - 10"
Foundation: Crawlspace, Basement

SEARCH ONLINE @ EPLANS.COM

The European allure of this stunning two-story home will be the delight of the neighborhood. With the living room to the right, the foyer leads to the family room with a magnificent view of the outdoors. The island kitchen is thoughtfully situated between the sunny breakfast area and the formal dining room, which opens to the side terrace. The master suite finds privacy on the first floor; the three family bedrooms share two full baths on the second floor.

plan# HPK0400280

Style: European Cottage
First Floor: 1,763 sq. ft.
Second Floor: 947 sq. ft.
Total: 2,710 sq. ft.
Bedrooms: 3
Bathrooms: 2½
Width: 50' - 0"
Depth: 75' - 4"
Foundation: Walkout Basement

SEARCH ONLINE @ EPLANS.COM

A special feature of this classy home is the second-floor media room and adjoining exercise area. Convenient to two upstairs bedrooms and a full bath, the media room is a great place for family computers and a fax machine. On the main level a gourmet kitchen provides a snack counter and a walk-in pantry. Double doors open to a gallery hall that leads to the formal dining room—an enchanting retreat for chandelier-lit evenings—that provides a breathtaking view of the front yard. A classic great room is warmed by a cozy fireplace and brightened by a wall of windows. The outdoor living area is spacious enough for grand events. The master suite is brightened by sweeping views of the backyard and a romantic fireplace just for two.

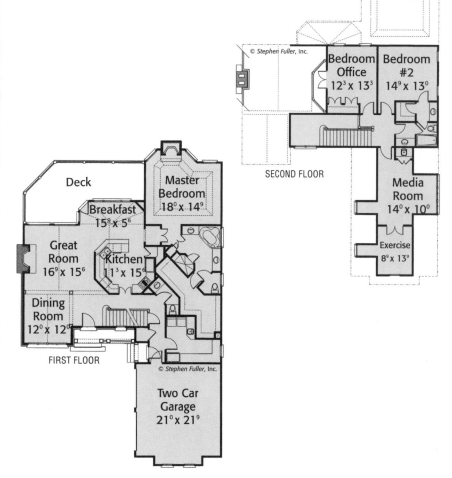

The heart of this home is the highly functional kitchen located between the vaulted great room and charming hearth room. A handy island increases work space, making meal preparation easier. A large pantry adds to the already abundant storage space. The kitchen overlooks an expansive rear deck, which opens to a covered screened porch and to the family room. The gorgeous master suite comes with His and Hers walk-in closets and a private bath with a posh corner tub. Three more bedrooms and two baths are situated upstairs.

plan# HPK0400281

Style: Contemporary
First Floor: 1,742 sq. ft.
Second Floor: 855 sq. ft.
Total: 2,597 sq. ft.
Bedrooms: 4
Bathrooms: 3½
Width: 62' - 4"
Depth: 48' - 0"
Foundation: Basement

SEARCH ONLINE @ EPLANS.COM

FIRST FLOOR

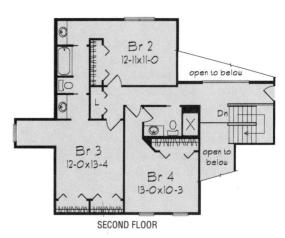

SECOND FLOOR

plan # HPK0400282

Style: European Cottage
First Floor: 1,395 sq. ft.
Second Floor: 1,210 sq. ft.
Total: 2,605 sq. ft.
Bonus Space: 225 sq. ft.
Bedrooms: 3
Bathrooms: 2½
Width: 47' - 0"
Depth: 49' - 6"
Foundation: Basement

SEARCH ONLINE @ EPLANS.COM

QUOTE ONE®

Cost to build? See page 333
to order complete cost estimate
to build this house in your area!

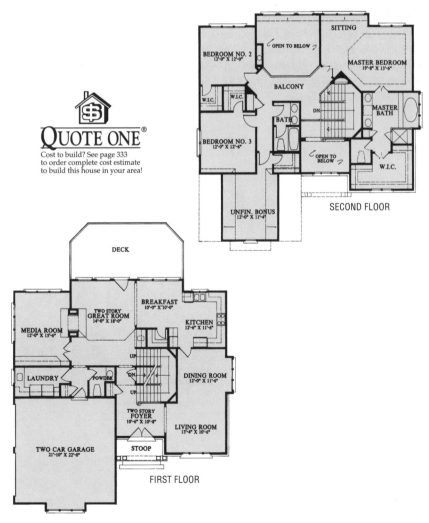

The well-balanced use of stucco and stone combined with box-bay window treatments and a covered entry make this English Country home especially inviting. The two-story foyer opens on the right to formal living and dining rooms, bright with natural light. A spacious U-shaped kitchen adjoins a breakfast nook with views of the outdoors. This area flows nicely into the two-story great room, which offers a through-fireplace to the media room. A plush retreat awaits the homeowner upstairs with a master suite that offers a quiet, windowed sitting area with views to the rear grounds. Two family bedrooms share a full bath and a balcony hall that has a dramatic view of the great room below.

A dramatic two-story foyer opens to a bayed dining room and magnificent great room with an 18-foot ceiling, grand fireplace, and Palladian windows. The kitchen works smoothly with the breakfast area and the great and dining rooms. The master suite boasts a vaulted ceiling and a private bath set into an unusual-shaped window bay. A garden tub and separate shower highlight the many amenities. Upstairs, three more bedrooms and a bath offer sleeping quarters to family members and guests.

plan # HPK0400283

Style: Traditional
First Floor: 1,774 sq. ft.
Second Floor: 850 sq. ft.
Total: 2,624 sq. ft.
Bedrooms: 4
Bathrooms: 2½
Width: 70' - 8"
Depth: 46' - 4"
Foundation: Basement

SEARCH ONLINE @ EPLANS.COM

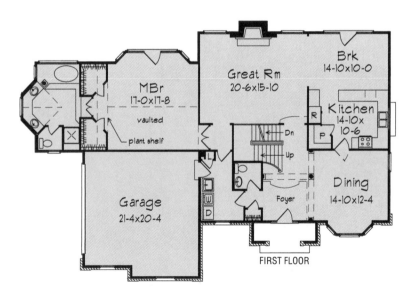

FIRST FLOOR

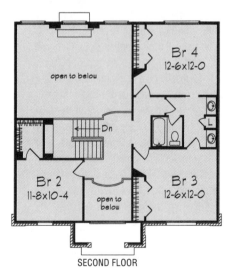

SECOND FLOOR

plan # HPK0400284

Style: Traditional
First Floor: 1,230 sq. ft.
Second Floor: 1,496 sq. ft.
Total: 2,726 sq. ft.
Bedrooms: 4
Bathrooms: 3½
Width: 60' - 0"
Depth: 34' - 6"
Foundation: Crawlspace, Slab, Basement

SEARCH ONLINE @ EPLANS.COM

Arch-top and multipane window treatments give the exterior of this four-bedroom, two-story home an unmistakable elegance. Inside, the floor plan is equally appealing. Note the bay windows in the formal dining room and living area, visible from the entrance foyer. The large family room has a fireplace and opens to the food-preparation area via an angled breakfast bar. A spacious, sunlit breakfast area adjoins the kitchen, which features a nearby walk-in pantry and internal access to the garage. The second-floor master suite is highlighted by a tray ceiling, walk-in closet, and luxurious master bath including a large tub, shower, and dual vanities. A separate bedroom suite and two family bedrooms sharing a full bath complete the second floor with a conveniently placed upstairs laundry.

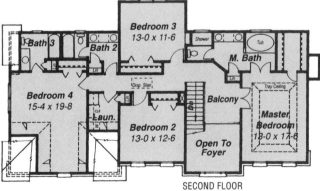

SECOND FLOOR

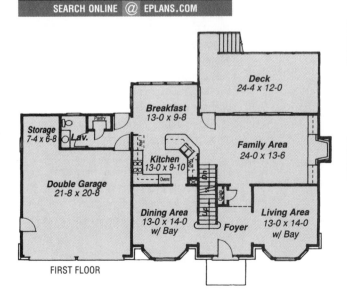

FIRST FLOOR

plan# HPK0400285

Style: Traditional
Square Footage: 2,723
Bedrooms: 3
Bathrooms: 2½
Width: 79' - 4"
Depth: 66' - 6"
Foundation: Basement

SEARCH ONLINE @ EPLANS.COM

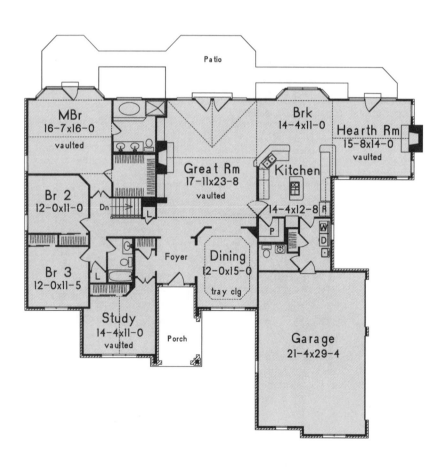

The arched entry and windows on the front facade promise something grand inside—and you won't be disappointed. A sense of spaciousness and excitement flows from the different ceiling styles used throughout the plan. This is most dramatic between the great room with a soaring vaulted ceiling and the adjacent dining room with a tray ceiling. Also intriguing are the bays in the master suite and the breakfast nook, which overlook the expansive rear patio. The kitchen, especially the walk-in pantry, is a chef's dream come true. Three bedrooms and a study are all found on the first floor with the main living areas.

plan# HPK0400286

Style: Traditional
First Floor: 1,977 sq. ft.
Second Floor: 524 sq. ft.
Total: 2,501 sq. ft.
Bedrooms: 4
Bathrooms: 2½
Width: 64' - 0"
Depth: 47' - 8"
Foundation: Slab, Crawlspace, Basement

SEARCH ONLINE @ EPLANS.COM

The traditional brick exterior of this house does not hint at the drama inside. Not only does the great room have a vaulted ceiling, but the kitchen and breakfast area have a two-story ceiling. The dining room boasts a bay window and an entry to the rear covered deck. Three bedrooms, including an amenity-loaded master suite, are all found on the first floor. A staircase leads to a second-floor balcony with a commanding view of the open first floor.

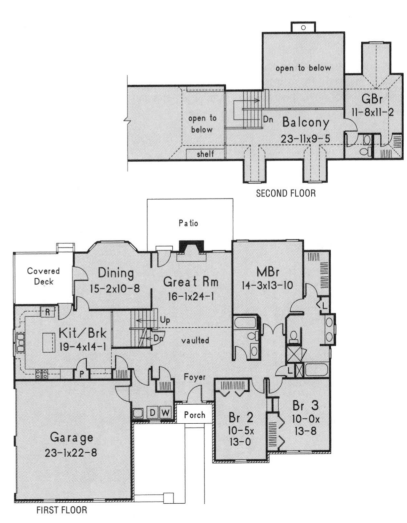

SECOND FLOOR

FIRST FLOOR

With an attractive mix of traditional and contemporary accents, this stunning design is sure to be a family favorite. Inside, vaulted living and dining rooms flank the foyer. A fireplace warms the formal living room. Located at the rear of the plan, the casual family room is vaulted and shares a see-through fireplace with the breakfast nook. The gourmet kitchen connects to the formal dining room. The master suite features its own bath with a walk-in closet and private access to the rear patio. Three additional family bedrooms are located on the opposite side of the home. A laundry room connects to the garage.

plan # HPK0400287

Style: Contemporary
Square Footage: 2,520
Bedrooms: 4
Bathrooms: 2½
Width: 80' - 0"
Depth: 58' - 8"
Foundation: Slab, Crawlspace, Basement

SEARCH ONLINE @ EPLANS.COM

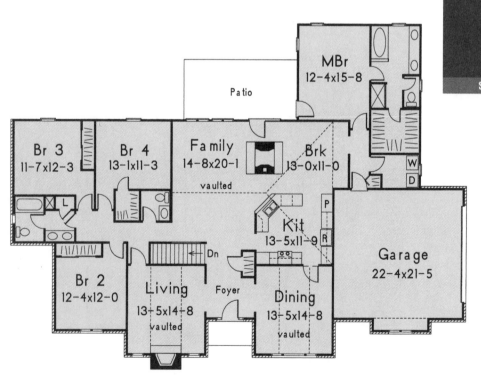

plan# HPK0400288

Style: Adam Style
First Floor: 1,540 sq. ft.
Second Floor: 1,051 sq. ft.
Total: 2,591 sq. ft.
Bedrooms: 4
Bathrooms: 3
Width: 62' - 4"
Depth: 48' - 10"
Foundation: Crawlspace

SEARCH ONLINE @ EPLANS.COM

This extraordinary four-bedroom home will bring years of enjoyment and comfort to your family. For openers, the immense kitchen works well with the breakfast nook and the cozy keeping room to provide a wonderful family focus. For entertaining, the front dining and living rooms lead into a grand room. The window seat in the two-story foyer is a nice touch. One bedroom is on the main level, and the others, including the master suite, are upstairs. A laundry room and storage space are also found on this level.

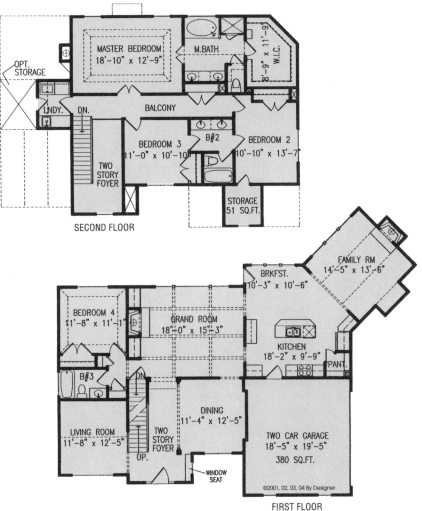

Muntin windows and gentle arches decorate the exterior of this traditional home. Living spaces consist of a formal dining room, a kitchen with an adjacent breakfast bay, and a great room with access to the rear veranda. A private study or guest suite in the rear left corner of the plan offers its own door to the veranda. The master suite enjoys a spacious bath with twin vanities, a dressing area, and two walk-in closets. A gallery hall on the second floor leads to a computer loft with built-ins for books and software.

plan # HPK0400289

Style: Farmhouse
First Floor: 1,676 sq. ft.
Second Floor: 851 sq. ft.
Total: 2,527 sq. ft.
Bedrooms: 5
Bathrooms: 2½
Width: 55' - 0"
Depth: 50' - 0"
Foundation: Slab

SEARCH ONLINE @ EPLANS.COM

FIRST FLOOR

SECOND FLOOR

plan# HPK0400290

Style: Traditional
Square Footage: 2,758
Bedrooms: 4
Bathrooms: 2½
Width: 72' - 0"
Depth: 68' - 0"
Foundation: Basement

SEARCH ONLINE @ EPLANS.COM

This home is highlighted by its exterior of combined elegant stone and siding. Inside, three dormers draw in natural light. The vaulted great room excels with a fireplace, wet bar, plant shelves, and skylights. The fabulous master suite also enjoys a fireplace, large bath, walk-in closet, and vaulted ceiling. A trendsetting kitchen and breakfast nook adjoin a spacious screened porch. The convenient office near the kitchen is perfect for a computer room, hobby area, or fifth bedroom.

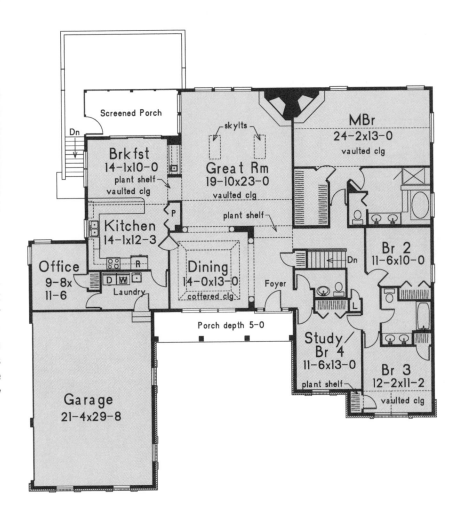

On the first floor of this cozy home the foyer opens to a columned dining room on the left and to a great room with a fireplace straight ahead. In the kitchen, an angled cooktop facilitates meal preparation. A laundry room is close to the two-car garage where storage closets are an added bonus. The master bedroom pampers with dual walk-in closets and a private bath with a double-bowl vanity, separate shower, and compartmented toilet. Tucked upstairs, two secondary bedrooms share a full bath, and the attic provides plenty of storage for all the family treasures.

plan# HPK0400291

Style: Victorian
First Floor: 1,859 sq. ft.
Second Floor: 645 sq. ft.
Total: 2,504 sq. ft.
Bedrooms: 3
Bathrooms: 2½
Width: 49' - 9"
Depth: 74' - 3"
Foundation: Walkout Basement

SEARCH ONLINE @ EPLANS.COM

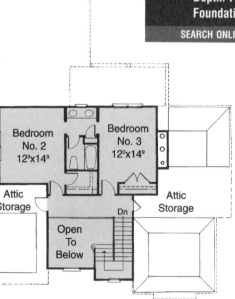

Two Car Garage
21³x21³

Storage

Porch

Kitchen
17⁶x11⁹

Great Room
17⁶x16⁹

Dining Room
12⁹x15⁹

Foyer

Up

Dn

Master Bedroom
16³x14⁹

Porch

FIRST FLOOR

Bedroom No. 2
12³x14⁹

Bedroom No. 3
12⁰x14⁹

Attic Storage

Open To Below

Dn

Attic Storage

SECOND FLOOR

plan# HPK0400292

Style: Farmhouse
First Floor: 1,921 sq. ft.
Second Floor: 716 sq. ft.
Total: 2,637 sq. ft.
Bedrooms: 3
Bathrooms: 2½
Width: 50' - 0"
Depth: 77' - 0"
Foundation: Walkout Basement

SEARCH ONLINE @ EPLANS.COM

Gracious living takes off in this delightful two-story home. A columned front porch offers passage to the foyer. To the right, a well-proportioned living room combines with a rear-facing dining room to offer fine formal living patterns. An angled kitchen easily serves the dining room as well as the informal areas. Sleeping accommodations begin with a private master suite located at the front. It enjoys a smartly zoned bath with dual walk-in closets, a double-bowl vanity, compartmented toilet, and separate tub and shower. Upstairs, two family bedrooms share a sectioned bath.

FIRST FLOOR

SECOND FLOOR

This rustic stone and siding exterior with Craftsman influences includes a multitude of windows flooding the interior with natural light. The foyer opens to the great room, which is complete with three sets of French doors and a two-sided fireplace. The master suite offers an expansive private bath, two large walk-in closets, a bay window, and a tray ceiling. The dining room, kitchen, and utility room make an efficient trio.

plan# HPK0400293

Style: Bungalow
First Floor: 1,798 sq. ft.
Second Floor: 900 sq. ft.
Total: 2,698 sq. ft.
Bedrooms: 3
Bathrooms: 3
Width: 54' - 0"
Depth: 57' - 0"
Foundation: Crawlspace

SEARCH ONLINE @ EPLANS.COM

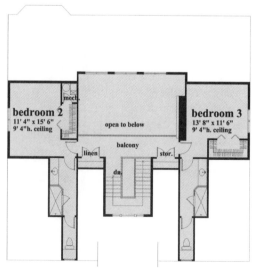

FIRST FLOOR

master suite
14' 0" x 15' 0"
11' 4"h. ceiling

porch

w.i.c.   w.i.c.

great room
22' 0" x 13' 0"
2-story ceiling

built-in cabinetry

2-sided fireplace

dining
13' 6" x 13' 6"
10' 0"h. clg.

up

study
12' 0" x 13' 0"
10' 0"h. clg.

foyer

kitchen
12' 0" x 13' 0"
10' 0"h. clg.

ut.

dn.

entry porch

SECOND FLOOR

bedroom 2
11' 4" x 15' 6"
9' 4"h. ceiling

mech.

open to below

balcony

linen

stor.

dn.

bedroom 3
13' 8" x 11' 6"
9' 4"h. ceiling

© William E. Poole Designs, Inc.

plan # HPK0400294

Style: Victorian
First Floor: 1,809 sq. ft.
Second Floor: 944 sq. ft.
Total: 2,753 sq. ft.
Bonus Space: 440 sq. ft.
Bedrooms: 4
Bathrooms: 3½
Width: 54' - 4"
Depth: 59' - 0"
Foundation: Basement, Crawlspace

SEARCH ONLINE @ EPLANS.COM

This charming Victorian cottage brings to mind the simpler days of yesteryear and artfully blends in the amenities of today. Enter from a covered porch to find an open foyer. The living room is on the right and flows easily into the dining room for effortless entertaining. The kitchen is appointed with a serving bar to the two-story bayed breakfast nook, which leads into the hearth-warmed family room. The master suite completes this level with a fabulous spa bath and plenty of closet space. The upper level hosts three bedrooms that share a quiet sitting room and access to an expansive recreation room.

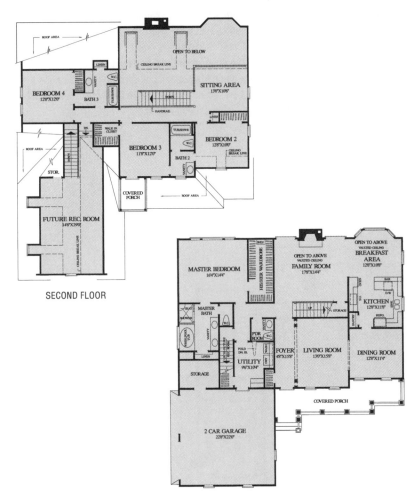

SECOND FLOOR

FIRST FLOOR

© Stephen Fuller, Inc.

This beautiful brick design displays fine family livability in over 2,600 square feet. The wrap-around porch welcomes family and friends to inside living areas. The great room sports an elegant ceiling, a fireplace, and built-ins. The kitchen displays good traffic patterning. An island cooktop will please the house gourmet. The dining room features double doors that open out onto the porch. In the master bedroom, a pampering bath includes a whirlpool tub and separate vanities. A walk-in closet is located at the back of the bath. Two family bedrooms upstairs enjoy peace and quiet and a full hall bath with natural illumination.

plan # HPK0400295

Style: Georgian
First Floor: 1,787 sq. ft.
Second Floor: 851 sq. ft.
Total: 2,638 sq. ft.
Bonus Space: 189 sq. ft.
Bedrooms: 3
Bathrooms: 2½
Width: 51' - 3"
Depth: 70' - 6"
Foundation: Walkout Basement

SEARCH ONLINE @ EPLANS.COM

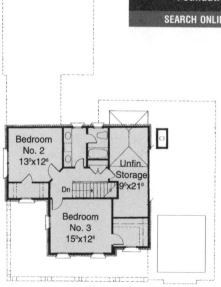

FIRST FLOOR

SECOND FLOOR

ORDER BLUEPRINTS 24 HOURS, 7 DAYS A WEEK, AT 1-800-521-6797

plan ⊕ HPK0400296

Style: Traditional
First Floor: 1,436 sq. ft.
Second Floor: 1,069 sq. ft.
Total: 2,505 sq. ft.
Bedrooms: 3
Bathrooms: 2½
Width: 70' - 0"
Depth: 40' - 0"
Foundation: Crawlspace, Basement

SEARCH ONLINE @ EPLANS.COM

The brick quoins draw attention to the cabin feeling of this home's facade, making it a perfect home for wooded areas. The covered front porch extends to the middle of the home, allowing for plenty of space to lounge outside. The open family room features a fireplace and connects to the breakfast nook where French doors lead to the rear patio. Upstairs, a deluxe raised tub and an immense walk-in closet grace the master suite.

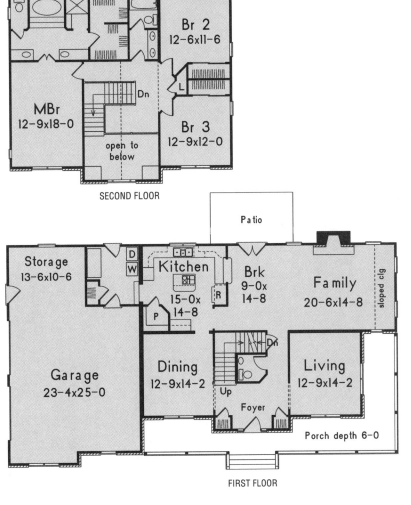

plan # HPK0400297

Style: Georgian
First Floor: 2,025 sq. ft.
Second Floor: 688 sq. ft.
Total: 2,713 sq. ft.
Bedrooms: 3
Bathrooms: 2½
Width: 53' - 9"
Depth: 74' - 3"
Foundation: Walkout Basement

SEARCH ONLINE @ EPLANS.COM

This 1½-story home reflects the Colonial archi-tecture of the South with its columned entry and shutters. Enter the formal dining room from the right of the foyer through a columned entrance. Entertaining is simple with nearby access to a kitchen with an island prep area. The adjoining breakfast room provides passage to a covered side porch. A fireplace warms the great room. Privacy takes precedence in the first-floor mas-ter suite, containing dual walk-in closets, a relax-ing tub, a corner shower and separate vanities. Upstairs, Bedrooms 2 and 3 share a full bath. Space for attic storage or a future bedroom and bath is furnished to develop as needed.

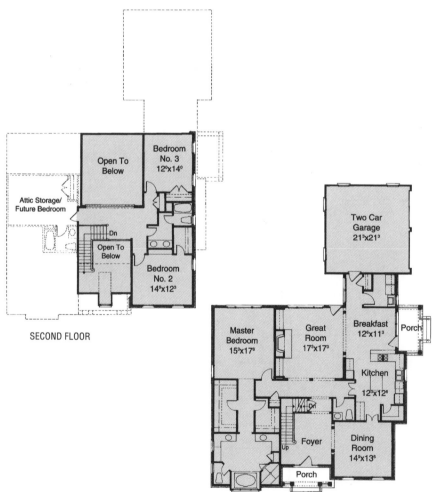

SECOND FLOOR

FIRST FLOOR

plan # HPK0400298

Style: Contemporary
First Floor: 1,337 sq. ft.
Second Floor: 1,174 sq. ft.
Total: 2,511 sq. ft.
Bedrooms: 4
Bathrooms: 2½
Width: 68' - 0"
Depth: 38' - 0"
Foundation: Crawlspace,
Basement, Slab

SEARCH ONLINE @ EPLANS.COM

Based on traditional farmhouse architecture, this variation has contemporary overtones. The home's focal point is a uniquely designed front porch that makes an unforgettable first impression. Once inside, the layout is more conventional with formal rooms, inviting casual spaces, great detailing, and plenty of storage. The dropped ceiling in the living room adds interest, just as the bay window in the family room brightens that area. Four bedrooms offer sleeping quarters upstairs; one is a master suite with a private bath.

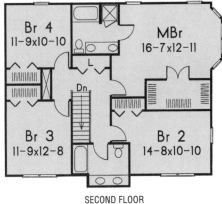

SECOND FLOOR

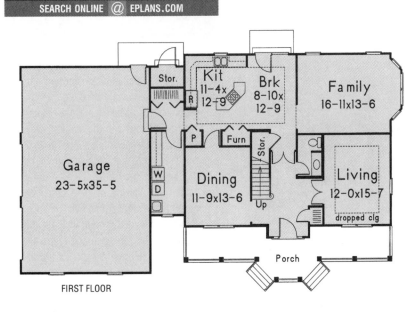

FIRST FLOOR

© William E. Poole Designs, Inc.

SECOND FLOOR

FIRST FLOOR

plan# HPK0400299

Style: **Country Cottage**
First Floor: **1,598 sq. ft.**
Second Floor: **932 sq. ft.**
Total: **2,530 sq. ft.**
Bonus Space: **415 sq. ft.**
Bedrooms: **4**
Bathrooms: **3½**
Width: **55' - 8"**
Depth: **61' - 0"**
Foundation: **Crawlspace,
Basement**

SEARCH ONLINE @ EPLANS.COM

Come home to comfort in this country classic! A covered porch, pedimented dormers, and a delightful weather vane atop the garage denote down-home charm, while family life reigns within. Enjoy the fireplace in the soaring two-story great room, which opens to a sunny bayed breakfast nook. The adjacent kitchen, with its curved counter, leads to the formal dining room at the front of the plan. The master suite, complete with an enormous private bath and walk-in closet, is convenient to the utility room, which features a roomy closet. Upstairs, two bedrooms share a bath and a computer workstation; a fourth bedroom has its own bath. A balcony overlook gazes down on the first floor.

plan # HPK0400300

Style: Southern Colonial
First Floor: 1,273 sq. ft.
Second Floor: 1,358 sq. ft.
Total: 2,631 sq. ft.
Bedrooms: 4
Bathrooms: 3½
Width: 54' - 10"
Depth: 48' - 6"
Foundation: Crawlspace

SEARCH ONLINE @ EPLANS.COM

This two-story home suits the needs of each household member. Family gatherings won't be crowded in the spacious family room, which is adjacent to the kitchen and the breakfast area. Just beyond the foyer, the dining and living rooms view the front yard. The master suite features its own full bath with dual vanities, a whirlpool tub, and separate shower. Three family bedrooms are available upstairs—one with a walk-in closet—and two full hall baths. Extra storage space is found in the two-car garage.

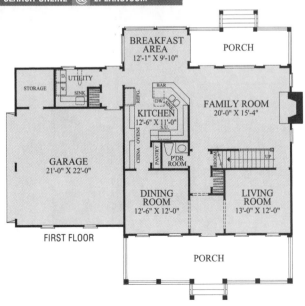

FIRST FLOOR

SECOND FLOOR

© William E. Poole Designs, Inc.

Fine living is guaranteed in this stately Early American home. The front living and dining rooms are laid out side-by-side for gracious entertaining, and service from the huge country-style kitchen will be convenient and smooth. To the left of the kitchen, the ceiling in the great room soars two stories above the hearth-warmed room. The first-floor master suite with a sumptuous bath is considerably separated from the three family bedrooms located upstairs. Also on the second floor is space for a future recreation room.

plan # HPK0400301

Style: Colonial
First Floor: 1,816 sq. ft.
Second Floor: 968 sq. ft.
Total: 2,784 sq. ft.
Bonus Space: 402 sq. ft.
Bedrooms: 4
Bathrooms: 3½
Width: 54' - 6"
Depth: 52' - 8"
Foundation: Crawlspace

SEARCH ONLINE @ EPLANS.COM

FIRST FLOOR

SECOND FLOOR

plan # HPK0400302

Style: Country Cottage
First Floor: 1,733 sq. ft.
Second Floor: 950 sq. ft.
Total: 2,683 sq. ft.
Bedrooms: 5
Bathrooms: 3½
Width: 54' - 0"
Depth: 46' - 0"
Foundation: Slab, Basement

SEARCH ONLINE @ EPLANS.COM

The long front porch with stately columns radiate the charm of earlier eras in American history. Yet, the interior will wow you with its modernity. A two-story foyer brings you into the dining room on the left and the spacious grand room straight ahead. This room opens to the well-equipped and up-to-date kitchen, which enjoys a sunlit breakfast nook. A delightful master suite with tasteful amenities is also on the main level. Above, four more bedrooms and two more baths offer family members and guests outstanding comfort.

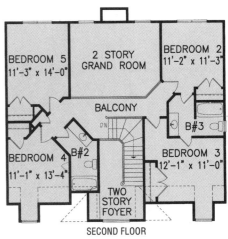

SECOND FLOOR

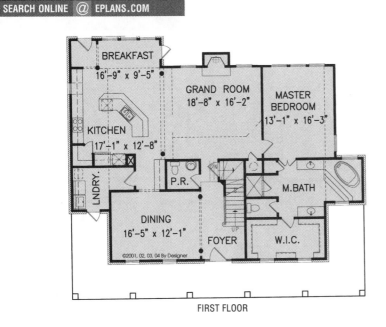

FIRST FLOOR

Country Victoriana embellishes this beautiful home. Perfect for a corner lot, this home begs for porch swings and lemonade. Inside, extra-high ceilings expand the space, as a thoughtful floor plan invites family and friends. The two-story great room enjoys a warming fireplace and wonderful rear views. The country kitchen has a preparation island and easily serves the sunny bayed nook and the formal dining room. To the far left, a bedroom serves as a perfect guest room; to the far right, a turret houses a private den. Upstairs, two bedrooms (one in a turret) share a full bath and ample bonus space. The master suite opens through French doors to reveal a grand bedroom and a sumptuous bath with a bumped-out spa tub.

plan# HPK0400303

Style: Farmhouse
First Floor: 1,464 sq. ft.
Second Floor: 1,054 sq. ft.
Total: 2,518 sq. ft.
Bonus Space: 332 sq. ft.
Bedrooms: 4
Bathrooms: 3
Width: 59' - 0"
Depth: 51' - 6"
Foundation: Crawlspace

SEARCH ONLINE @ EPLANS.COM

FIRST FLOOR

SECOND FLOOR

Build it Smart:
Home-Building
Reference Guide

How to get exactly what you want in a home

Building a home is an inherently complicated process. There's no way to wave a magic wand and make a brand-new home appear, but it doesn't have to be difficult. In fact, armed with the right information, building your new home could be one of the most exciting and rewarding projects you'll ever undertake.

That's the goal of Build it Smart's Home-Building Reference Guide. With helpful advice on everything from selecting a home plan to your final walk-through, you'll turn to this guide throughout the building process.

Along the way, we've kept an eye on the topics that home-builders have told us are important to them — including ways to make your new home more affordable, and how to find professionals you trust. They all combine to work towards the same goal: giving you the home of your dreams.

This attractive four-bedroom home, Design HPK00141 (page 145), is just under 2,000 square feet.

Make the big decisions —like style and size— first, then narrow down your home plan search from there.

THE BIG STEPS

There are countless little steps in the home-building process, but there are some big ones to get you started. We'll help with advice for each of these stages on the following pages.

☑ **Find a Plan**
Building your dream home begins with finding the right plan for you and your family.

☑ **Find a Lot**
In many cases you'll have a lot before you shop for a plan. Either way, as they always tell you in real estate, location is everything.

☑ **Find Financing**
Home-building financing has some crucial differences from a conventional mortgage, so you should learn as much as you can about the process before you begin.

☑ **Find a Builder**
The most important player in your home-building adventure, finding a builder you trust can be the key to success. ■

FIND THE RIGHT PLAN

For most of us, building a home is a once-in-a-lifetime endeavor. Consequently, finding the right home plan is crucial. You probably have some notions of the type of design you want to build. Plenty of major options await—two-story versus one-story, traditional rather than contemporary, an outdoor porch or maybe a sunroom. However, putting those ideas together and considering the hundreds of other details that will make your home perfect can be daunting. Here are some of the basic elements you need to ponder to help you make wise decisions as you search.

One way to help define what you would like to have in your new home is to list the pluses and minuses of homes you've lived in before. You already know what you liked about those houses, so put it down on paper to help sort out your criteria and come to some conclusions. We've developed a short questionnaire on the following pages that will help you begin, or build upon your initial thoughts.

Facade Options

Remember that the facade, shown in the rendering of the home plan, may be flexible. Today's siding materials often make it possible to choose a home plan

showing horizontal wood siding that can be built with brick siding.

Selecting a roof type is a major decision, and one that will go hand-in-hand with the style of home you choose. While flat roofs are fine in warm, mild climates, they simply won't hold up in snow country. In many areas, there are specific roofing codes to accommodate snow loads and high winds. If you suspect this may be the case in your building area, familiarize yourself with the code before you choose a plan.

You also will face decisions about foundation choices. Some plans are designed with a specific foundation (basement, crawlspace, slab, or pier) but may be converted by a qualified professional to suit your needs.

Finally, get acquainted with some basics on reading floor plans so you can understand the home completely. It may even be a good idea to buy a set of study plans (a single set of the full working drawings) for a design you are considering, so that you can check out the home in greater detail. The floor plans show all levels for the home, including a finished basement if it is part of the design. Rooms should be clearly defined as bedrooms, bathrooms, living areas, utility areas, and bonus spaces. Closets, cabinets and other built-ins, windows and doors (interior and exterior), stairways, and other pertinent features should be distinctly marked. The plan's overall width and depth (at its widest and deepest points) should be indicated somewhere near the floor plans.

QUESTIONS AND ANSWERS

You have countless considerations when you sit down to search for a home plan, and with so many possibilities available, picking the right one can be a daunting task.

How can you best determine what type of home you want? In trying to balance your needs and desires, we've put together a few questions to consider as you begin the process of narrowing your search.

Questions to Consider

1. Where do you plan to build your new home? What's the climate like?

2. What style homes are prevalent in your region?

3. How much time do you spend outdoors? Will you want a porch, patio, or deck?

4. Would you like one or two levels? Do you mind climbing stairs?

5. When entertaining, do you prefer more formal, separate rooms or more open, casual spaces?

6. What is your favorite vacation spot? Are there elements from another region or country that could influence your decision on what type of home to build?

7. Do you have or plan to have any children?

8. Do you have pets?

9. Do you work from home or need a home office?

10. Will you have elderly parents living with you?

11. Will you need to incorporate any universal design elements?

12. What kinds of extra features—such as storage spaces or a fireplace—should be included?

Understanding Your Answers

1. **Location:** If you're planning on building your new home in a region that typically gets a lot of snow, then you need to be prepared for that. A Mediterranean-style house would not be appropriate in Minnesota or Maine. You'd need to consider a design with a steeper-pitched roof, such as a Victorian, Cape Cod, or Colonial. Likewise, if your new home will be built in warmer climates, you may consider a Southern-style home with large, wraparound porches or sunrooms.

2. **Neighborhood:** What style home is predominant in the neighborhood where you'll build? While it's not necessary to have your home replicate all the other homes, it should at least complement them. Building a Victorian home on the beach in Florida would look a bit out of place. Let your neighbors serve as your guide.

3. **Outdoor Options:** If you and your family love spending time outside—either eating a meal or just visiting with each other—then plan your space accordingly. There are all kinds of options for you to consider when choosing a home plan. Many Mediterranean home plans call for verandas or lanais, and porches are a common feature on farmhouses and Victorian plans.

4. **Number of Stories:** Perhaps climbing stairs doesn't bother you now, but will it in the future? If you're spending the time and money to build your dream home, chances are you're planning on staying in it for a while.

You'll save money down the road if you consider what features you'll want in your home in the long run. If you want to avoid stairs altogether, consider building a ranch-style home. If you love the style of more traditional multilevel homes, like Colonial or Victorian, but don't want to deal with the stairs on a daily basis, consider plans with master suites on the first floor.

5. **Entertainment:** Depending on how often you entertain at home—and what sort of entertaining you typically do—you'll want your home plan to reflect those interests. If you prefer more traditional, formal affairs,

FIVE TIPS TO FOLLOW THROUGHOUT THE PROCESS

■ **Ask questions.** If there's any part of the process that you don't understand, ask. Make sure that you choose a contractor who you feel comfortable turning to for answers—and make sure they feel comfortable with answering your questions along the way.

■ **Get references.** Don't hire a person or service to work on your home without checking with references first. A few quick phone calls could save you headaches down the road.

■ **Sign on the dotted line.** Have a clear, signed agreement before any work is done on your home.

■ **Plan ahead and stay organized.** Knowing what you want ahead of time will help keep the process moving and save you money—change orders are the biggest reason for cost increases. Keeping all the information organized will help you navigate the process as well.

■ **Stand your ground.** Don't be a pushover for architects who want more than you can afford, or builders who want to eliminate items from your wish list. If it's something you want, stick with your convictions.

you'll want to choose a plan with both a formal dining room and living room, which are especially common in Victorian, Colonial, and Federalist plans. Perhaps more casual gatherings are the norm in your home. If so, you'll likely want an open floor plan, where the great room adjoins the kitchen and guests can easily mingle with the host or hostess.

6. **Vacation spot:** Take into account your favorite travel destination when planning your new home. What is it about that spot that you like so much? Do you prefer Southern France or the Swiss Alps? New England or

SEARCH ENGINE

Here are four ways to make your search for the perfect home plan easier:

☑ **Write it Down**
Putting your answers to our 12 questions on paper can help keep you focused during your search.

☑ **Cut and Paste**
Read home-improvement magazines and the home section of your local newspaper. Keep a scrapbook of the ideas you like.

☑ **Ask Around**
Talk to friends who have built and see what they love —or what they would change—about their home.

☑ **Drive Time**
Getting in the car—or better yet, taking a walk—to look at houses can help you decide what you're looking for, and possibly give you new ideas. ■

the Southwest? Perhaps there's a way to bring a bit of that place you love so much into your home—by seeking plans boasting architectural elements from another region. Again, you'll want to consider what your neighbors' homes look like before building a Southwestern home in a town full of Cape Cods. But wouldn't it be great to come home to a place every day that reminds you of a special town or country many miles away?

7. Children: Having kids plays a huge factor in the type and size of home you choose to build. Aside from the obvious question of how many bedrooms and baths you'll need to include, you must consider other factors, too. Will you want to include a gameroom? Or perhaps an island snack bar in the kitchen? And, if you've got young children, you may not want a master suite on the opposite end of the home.

8. Pets: Like children, whether or not you have a pet can play a role in the type of home plan you ultimately choose. If you've got a big black lab or a golden retriever, a plan containing a mudroom may be more important to you than that extra half bath on the first floor. Or perhaps French doors separating the breakfast nook and the patio out back would be a nice feature, so you can easily let your pet outdoors.

9. Office Space: Whether you telecommute on a regular basis or just have the occasional assignment to finish up at home, you'll need to determine how important it is to include space for a home office or study. If you only need the computer to check your e-mail, setting it up in the kitchen or the family room may work just fine. But if you need a space that will be quiet and minimize distractions, plan ahead. The home plan you like might not specifically call for an office or study, but if it has either an extra bedroom or bonus room, either could be converted to accommodate your needs.

10. Elderly Parents: As the general population lives longer, it's more common for elderly parents to be a consideration in new homes. A plan with a bedroom and full bath on the home's first level to accommodate their needs may be just right for you.

11. Universal Design: Whether you've got an elderly parent or someone with special needs in your family, incorporating universal design elements at the build-

ing stage is much less expensive than adding them later. Adding a handrail in the bath tub or lowering the kitchen counters are just a few ideas to consider. You know your lifestyle (and those of your loved ones) best, and you know the ways to make their everyday chores easier. Why not think ahead and plan for this from the project's outset?

12. Extra Features: Regardless of the style home you want or the location where you plan to build, coming up with a list of special features to include is an important step. Perhaps you have visions of a fireplace or cathedral ceilings adorning your great room, or ample storage spaces throughout the house. With so many stock home plan options available and Hanley Wood HomePlanners Customization Service, there's no reason you can't have it all.

BENEFITS OF STOCK PLANS

The home-building process is filled with decisions, from selecting a builder for your dream home to the materials and appliances that will fill the space.

The decision-making actually begins earlier than that—with your home plan. Your first major choice may be whether you should work with an architect to create a custom home or to use a stock home plan like those found in this book.

Stock home plans offer incredible value for relatively low costs. While a custom architect or designer may charge as much as $10,000 for a full set of working drawings to design the home of your choice, you can most likely get everything you're dreaming of in a stock home plan for less than $2,000. And additional services and products are available to help you understand the building process more completely, adjust your plans with customization, simplify the bidding process with general contractors, and finish your home with a professional landscape or deck design.

Build with Confidence

Besides the cost factor, there is a built-in confidence factor. Builders have come to trust stock plans. They know the plans have been checked and tested and, in most cases, are ready for permitting right out of the package, as most are designed to conform to national uniform building codes. This saves the

ABOVE: The interior of your new home should begin to really take shape around the 12-week point.

builders time and money—which translates to savings for you as well.

There is a wide variety of stock plans available. Buying from a reputable stock plan company guarantees that you'll receive working drawings from the best architects and designers in the business—experienced professionals whose designs have been built hundreds of times. These design experts hail from all over the United States and Canada with each bringing a distinctive regional flavor to the designs.

You'll be able to personalize the plans to fit your dreams, by working with the designer or architect (or your own personal design professional) to make changes to the plans, before building begins. Your general contractor can even accomplish some simple changes. It's like getting a custom home without the custom price. However, because there is such a huge variety of stock plans available today, you'll probably find the perfect plan for you and your family without having to make any changes at all.

MORTGAGE INFORMATION

Finding the money to build a new home differs from taking out a conventional mortgage on an existing home, because to build a home, you essentially need three loans: one for the land, one for the construction phase, and one for the permanent financing of the home after it is built.

But the process is not nearly as difficult to navigate as it may seem, as many lenders combine these three

MORTGAGE TERMS

- **Adjustable-Rate Mortgage (ARM):** This loan type allows the lender to adjust the interest rate during the term of the loan. Usually changes are based on market conditions and determined by an index. Most have a rate change and lifetime cap.
- **Annual Percentage Rate (APR):** A standard format developed by the federal government to provide an effective interest rate for comparison shopping of loans. Some closing costs are factored into the APR. Actual monthly payments are based on the periodic interest rate, not the APR.
- **Appraised Value:** This is the property's fair-market value, based on an appraiser's knowledge and an analysis of the property, which takes into account home values in the area.
- **Assessed Value:** The valuation is determined by a public tax assessor for taxation purposes.
- **Balloon Mortgage:** This is a short-term fixed-rate loan with smaller payments for a certain period of time and one large payment for the entire balance due at the end of the loan term.
- **Conventional Mortgage:** A mortgage that is not insured or guaranteed by a government agency.
- **Convertible ARM:** An adjustable-rate mortgage (ARM) that allows a borrower to convert their mortgage to a fixed-rate loan for the remainder of the loan term if certain conditions are met.
- **Escrow:** Funds paid by one party to another to hold until a specific date when the funds are released to a designated individual.
- **Fixed-Rate Mortgage:** A mortgage in which the monthly principal and interest payments remain the same throughout the life of the loan. The most common mortgage terms are 30 and 15 years.
- **Initial Interest Rate:** The original, starting interest rate at the time of closing. This rate can change in the future in an adjustable-rate mortgage.
- **Lender Fees:** Fees that are kept by the lender to cover some of their expenses and meet their profitability goals. Typically fees such as origination fees, discount points, processing/administration fees, underwriting fees, and document preparation fees are lender fees.
- **P&I:** This is the monthly principal and interest payment required when repaying a mortgage in accordance with its terms.
- **PITI:** Principal (P), Interest (I), Taxes (T), and Insurance (I) is a reference to the total monthly payment required to repay a mortgage in accordance with its term, as well as monthly escrow payments for taxes and insurance.
- **Points:** Fees that are collected by the lender in exchange for a lower interest rate. Commonly called discount points, each point is equal to 1 percent of the loan amount.

loans into two or even one loan. Here is some basic information about the process to get you started:

Buying land: Most lenders are cautious about lending money on raw land because it can often be difficult to resell in case of default. Those that will lend may want a large down payment—20 percent or

SIGNS OF A GOOD BUILDER

You have to call references and do your homework to find a good builder. But here are some tell-tale signs to watch for if you visit a job site:

☑ They should have a sign identifying the company.

☑ The site should be clean and orderly, without scraps and trash lying around.

☑ If you tour a model or a completed home, check the finish work. Open and close doors, windows, and cabinets, and make sure they all line up correctly.

☑ Inspect drywall carefully. Don't expect it to be completely perfect, but you shouldn't notice sags in the ceiling or waves and bumps in walls.

☑ Check the drainage outside the house. Good builders take special care to move water away from the foundation. ∎

more — with a high interest rate. It might be best to pay cash, if you can.

Building the home: In order to build, you'll need a construction loan, which isn't offered by all lenders. Those that do will require blueprints and specifications, appropriate permits, and a licensed bonded contractor before they will consider lending for construction. This type of loan allows the contractor to make draws on the total amount of money as each phase of construction is completed. The lender may want to inspect the property to insure that the work has been done.

Permanent financing: Once the home is completed, construction financing ends – which means that loan must be paid off. Usually this happens with a permanent loan, the same way any real property is refinanced.

Bringing it Together

When each of these three loans is accomplished separately, there are three closings and all of the attendant closing costs, legal fees, and taxes. Combination financing, which ties together all or at least two of the loans, minimizes these costs and paperwork.

One unique approach is a rollover loan, which allows money for the purchase of land, construction of the home, and permanent financing all in one package. You need to qualify only once and pay only one set of closing costs. Or you may be able to tie only the construction and permanent loans together, if you've already purchased the land or intend to pay cash for it. In some cases, you may be able to use the equity in the land as a down payment for a construction-to-permanent loan.

Every lender is different in their approach to construction-to-permanent loans. To get the best rates and the most appropriate lending plan, shop around and compare. The Web is a good place to start investigating some of the various options and get an idea of what kind of terms you can expect.

FINDING A BUILDER

Ordering take-out may be easy as picking up the phone book, but getting what you want from your builder requires a little more homework. Nevertheless, it's not hard — just follow these seven simple steps to selecting the right builder for your project. Then use that phone book to order a large pizza on the first night in your dream house.

Chances are you have a vision for your perfect home. The challenge now: find a builder who will embrace that vision and, most importantly, help make it a reality.

Seven Simple Steps

Luckily, it's not a matter of chance. Follow these seven steps and you're much more likely to end up with your dream house — instead of a headache.

1. Ask for referrals from everyone you know — friends, acquaintances, business associates, etc. Learn about their experiences, and ask to see the builder's work. Ask whether the house was completed on time, came in on budget, and met all their needs.

2. Contact professional associations like the local builders' association or the Chamber of Commerce. Talk to people who keep tabs on the building industry, and who are qualified to give you names of trustworthy, reliable builders. Local lumberyard managers and building supply outlets can also provide advice, including which builders may have had trouble with payments or materials. Call the Better Business Bureau, which can tell you if complaints were filed on any builders you are considering (although it is not at liberty to tell you whether those complaints were resolved).

3. Visit neighborhoods you like, or new developments, and ask people who are tending their gardens or washing their cars about their experiences. Find out if they are happy with their new homes, and whether or not they would enthusiastically recommend their builder. New homeowners are generally thrilled to share the excitement of building a new home with others. Model homes offer good opportunities to judge workmanship and the quality of materials and products that the builder deems appropriate.

4. Evaluate the level of on-site supervision provided by the builder. "A builder should be able to guarantee an end product, and the people he hires should conduct themselves properly and be well trained," says Dan Giddings, a New York-based builder. "A good builder will know how to manage his people whether or not he spends all day on site. Ultimately, he should be held accountable for any problems, and most importantly, he should be instantly accessible should problems or delays arise."

5. Once you've compiled a list of several builders, be sure each one is a member of a professional organization. Narrow the list to five candidates, and request an interview with each one at their office.

This wraparound porch adds significant living space to Design HPK0400010 (see page 14 for details).

Ask for a sample copy of a contract. Find out how long they have been in business, and ask for a list of clients you can contact to arrange for a tour of their homes. Always ask to see the completed work. Tell them your needs, your time frame, and your budget. Discuss warranties and ask for bank references to ensure that your builder is in good financial standing.

Try to determine not only whether each builder is a good match for you, but whether you are a good match for them. If the builder regularly constructs million-dollar homes, and you want to spend $200,000, you may be better off with someone else. Pay special attention to your comfort level during the meeting—do you feel as if you can communicate easily and successfully convey your wants and concerns to the builder?

6. Ask for a written estimate from the top three candidates. You'll need to compare bids on an apples-to-apples basis, so give them copies of your plans and materials list. Expect some builders to charge fees to prepare an estimate (which will probably be waived if they are awarded the project). The process takes time; do not

KEY PLAYERS IN THE PROCESS

■ **Architect:** If you select a plan like those in this book, the architect's work has already been done. If you decide to create a completely custom home, you will meet with an architect and they will create the blueprints from scratch, based on extensive meetings with you about what you are looking for.

■ **General Contractors:** Your general contractor, or builder, is the single most important person in the process. They are the point person for all construction at the site, coordinating schedules and (hopefully) keeping the project moving on time. Depending on the size of the building company you work with, there may be a site superintendent (or supervisor or foreman) who is in charge of your project.

■ **Sub-Contractors:** Sub-contractors, or subs, are specialists who will work on particular elements of your project under the direction of your general contractor. Examples include electricians, plumbers, framers, and painters.

■ **Interior Designers:** An interior designer, while not necessary to the home-building process, can help you make the most of your space once you move in. Get them involved early and they can help you plan for how you will use the different rooms before the builder gets started.

A hillside lot can be a great opportunity to build a plan with a finished basement.

LOCATION, **LOCATION**

Finding the right neighborhood to build has a lot of similarities to shopping for a house, but a few differences. Here are some considerations to keep in mind as you look:

☑ Quality of schools

☑ Property taxes

☑ Association or government building fees

☑ Zoning laws

☑ Water and sewer systems

☑ Environmental restrictions

☑ Proximity to shops, services, and transportation

☑ Your potential neighbors ∎

be surprised if your bids are not ready for several weeks.

7. Analyze the completed bids not only in terms of final cost, but also for attention to detail and thorough preparation. And remember, don't select the lowest bidder unless you are sure he is capable of delivering a high-quality product, on time. After all, you'll be counting on this builder to make your dreams come true.

PLANNING FOR YOUR SITE

Sloping lots, wetlands acreage, and narrow-width sites are all buildable, with the right home plan. Sloping lots, for example, can even offer advantages, from the cost of the land to the fact that they generally offer great views and cool breezes.

Tough lots can be tamed by a hillside plan designed to fit a slope to the front, back, or side, as needed by the lot. You might consider a plan with a drive-under garage or a finished basement that makes perfect use of a sloping lot.

Wetlands or other areas prone to swampy ground or high water, even for part of the year, may be accommodated by building a home with a pier foundation. These foundations raise the main body of the home up and away from soggy sites and are often in accordance with local laws protecting wetlands areas. In dry seasons, the area formed by the piers under the house provides great storage for a boat or other seaside perks.

If your lot is unusually narrow, there are hundreds of plans available with a slender footprint; some as little as 25 feet in width that have great livability. Another option is choosing a plan that is fairly wide—but not very deep—and turning it to fit the lot. With some plans, it may be possible to adapt them to a narrow lot by tucking the garage to the rear, thus narrowing the footprint.

Set Your Sites

Proper "siting" of a home means situating it on your lot to take full advantage of (or protect your home from) sun exposure and prevailing winds, while also maximizing great views and ease of access.

Home siting takes into account grade changes on the lot, available views, orientation to the sun, prevailing winds, and existing vegetation. Your builder should be able to help you with a site plan for placing your home optimally on your lot. Some local building departments require such a document before they will approve plans and issue permits. If your plan doesn't completely meet site requirements, the builder may be able to suggest modifications that will make it more workable.

A big part of correct siting involves considering the specific climatic conditions in your building area. Correctly orienting your home on the building site will keep your home comfortable, while saving on heating and cooling bills. In hot climates, for example, locate the

living areas in your home on the north or east side of the plan, reserving the south and west sides for non-living space, such as garages or storage areas.

Homes built in temperate climates should emphasize sun exposure in the cool months and shade in the summer, while reducing the impact of winter wind and increasing the flow of summer breezes. Here living areas should be on the south and west sides of the home, with non-living areas on the northeast.

Cold climates require that homes be arranged to gather the most sun exposure. That's why living areas are best placed on the south and west sides of the home, reserving the northeast side for non-living spaces. Choose a plan with a steeply pitched roof that can be placed on the windward side of the lot to deflect winter winds. If possible, minimize windows on the north side of the home and protect against wind intrusion with courtyard walls or recessed entries on the windward side.

HOW TO CUSTOMIZE YOUR HOME PLAN

The home building process is different for everyone—some people know exactly what kind of plan they'd like to build from the get-go, and others must search numerous plans to see what strikes their fancy. Regardless of which category you fall into, one thing's certain: Hanley Wood HomePlanners has the largest selection of stock home plans available today. Keep in mind, too, that any plan can be customized to meet your specific needs and desires.

Even if you don't find the perfect plan in this book or on ePlans.com, maybe there's a design that would be perfect with a few alterations. Either way, getting the home you want—your way—is not only possible, but it's easily within reach.

The HomePlanners team of architectural professionals and customization experts use state-of-the-art technology and CAD drafting services. These cutting-edge tools make it possible to modify,

AVERAGE MODIFICATIONS PRICE GUIDELINES

Categories	Average Cost (from—to)
Adding or removing living space (square footage)	Quote required
Adding or removing a garage	$400-$680
Garage: Front entry to side load or vice versa	Starting at $300
Adding a screened porch	$280-$600
Adding a bonus room in the attic	$450-$780
Changing a full basement to crawlspace or vice versa	Starting at $220
Changing a full basement to slab or vice versa	Starting at $260
Changing exterior building material	Starting at $200
Changing roof lines	$360-$630
Adjusting ceiling height	$280-$500
Adding, moving, or removing an exterior opening	$55 per opening
Adding or removing a fireplace	$90-$200
Modifying a nonbearing wall or room	$55 per room
Changing exterior walls from 2"x4" to 2"x6"	Starting at $200
Redesigning a bathroom or kitchen	$120-$280
Reverse plan right reading	Quote required
Adapting plans for local building code requirements	Quote required
Engineering stamping only	$450 / any state
Any other engineering services	Quote required
Adjust plan for handicapped accessibility	Quote required
Interactive illustrations (choices of exterior materials)	Quote required
Metric conversion of home plan	$400

Note: Any home plan can be customized to accommodate your desired changes. The average prices specified above are provided only as examples for the most commonly requested changes and are subject to change without notice. Prices for changes will vary according to the number of modifications requested, plan size, style, and method of design used by the original designer. To obtain a detailed cost estimate, please call 1-800-526-4667.

redesign, and renovate existing stock home plans quickly and efficiently. This easy-to-use service provides an affordable alternative to hiring an architect to customize the plans—an endeavor that can cost thousands of dollars.

The Customization Service is not only cost-efficient, but it allows you to:

■ save time by avoiding face-to-face design meetings,

■ communicate design and home plan changes faster and more efficiently,

■ speed up project turnaround time,

■ save money without sacrificing quality, and

CUSTOM BLEND

Customizing a stock home plan is easier than you might think. Here are five examples of the simple types of changes that the HomePlanners Customization Service can help you make:

☑ Your lot may be wide enough for you to turn your front-loading garage into a side-loading garage, a simple change that will add curb appeal.

☑ Want to enjoy a warm fire in your master bedroom? Adding a fireplace may be possible, depending on the location of your master suite.

☑ Customization experts can often turn a half bath to a full bath, or vice versa, if needed.

☑ Add a closet to a home office to give it the added flexibility of an additional bedroom— or just extra out-of-the-way storage space.

☑ If you love a home's layout, but the style doesn't fit your taste, you can change the exterior and roofline to your liking. ∎

■ transform stock home plans to suit your unique style.

The modifications made to the home plan are categorized as either major or minor changes. Major modifications typically refer to a room addition or roofline change; minor ones usually involve adding windows or moving doors. The Average Modifications Pricing Guide offers some general ideas about cost. For a more detailed estimate, we suggest a phone consultation with HomePlanners' residential design specialists regarding your specific requests.

Five Simple Steps to Customization

Customizing your home plan has never been easier. Once you decide which plan is right for you, follow the steps outlined below:

1. Purchase the reproducible master for the chosen home plan.

2. Pay the $50 consultation fee and HomePlanners will send you a customization change form via e-mail or fax. Complete and return the form, outlining the changes and revisions you want the customization specialists to make. (Note: If you decide to use the customization service, the $50 consultation fee will be applied to the total cost of the modifications.)

3. The customization specialists will review your design changes to determine if they're major or minor and to ensure that the integrity of your home's structure is maintained. A detailed cost estimate will be sent out within 48 hours or two business days of receipt of your custom changes.

4. After you review and approve the estimate, return a signed copy and the customization specialists will complete the plan.

5. The customized plan will be completed in two to three weeks following the approval of any preliminary designs. You'll receive either five sets or a reproducible master of your modified design, plus a detailed materials list and any other options you select.

HomePlanners Customization Service can add a bay window to your plan to maximize views and natural light.

With a process this easy and affordable, we've made building your clients' dream home hassle-free. Once you find the home plan that most closely fits your clients' needs and desires, give HomePlanners a call to set that dream in motion.

BUILDING AN ENERGY-FRIENDLY HOME

Chances are, as you plan your new home, your mind is filled with plans and possibilities: gables, dormers, wraparound porches, elegant foyers, and a grand master bath replete with luxurious amenities. With all that in mind, who could blame you if tightly sealed air ducts and insulation weren't the first things that popped into your head?

On the other hand, what if incorporating these, and other, energy-efficient design elements into your new home could save hundreds, perhaps thousands, of dollars per year? It's true. It has never been easier, or more advantageous, to design an energy-efficient home. What's more, the time and effort you invest now will pay you back in a home that offers greater comfort, lower maintenance, and higher resale value.

Not sure where to begin? Here is a comprehensive checklist with the very latest information for you to consider when planning your own "energy-smart" home. From the design phase all the way through to selecting appliances and lighting, we'll show you how to save energy—and money—every step of the way. And think about this: Along with doing your part to conserve natural resources, you might even save enough on utilities to splurge on those granite countertops!

Energy-Wise Design

Evaluate the building site to take advantage of climate and seasonal changes. Is the home positioned on the lot to take maximum advantage of natural sunlight, cooling breezes, and temperature changes?

Consider surrounding topography: Nestling the home among sheltering hills, existing vegetation, and surrounding shade trees may create a natural buffer zone, as well as keep heating and cooling costs down.

Insulate the foundation: To prevent energy loss, your home's foundation should be as well insulated as your living spaces. Using thermal mass materials, like concrete, brick, or packed earth, will keep your home warmer in the winter and cooler in the summer.

Head upstairs: If you're planning a two-story

GENERAL TIMELINE FOR BUILDING A HOME

The specific time frame for each home-building process can vary widely depending on the size of your home, the size of your builder, and even the weather. But this general outline provides a look at the procession of tasks involved in most projects.

Weeks 1-4: Site work, excavation, foundation
Weeks 4-5: Rough framing
Week 6: Windows and exterior doors
Week 6: Decking and sheathing
Weeks 6-7: Rough plumbing
Weeks 7-8: Rough electrical
Week 7: Roofing
Week 8: Exterior paint
Weeks 8-9: Rough HVAC
Week 9: Insulation
Weeks 10-11: Exterior siding
Week 12: Flooring and underlayment
Weeks 13-15: Interior wall finishing
Week 15: Interior trim and doors
Week 16: Cabinetry
Weeks 16-18: Interior paint
Week 19: Countertops, vinyl and tile floors
Weeks 20-22: Plumbing, heating, and electrical trim; appliances
Week 23: Carpeting
Weeks 23-24: Cleanup, landscaping, and final inspection

home, consider locating bedrooms on the first level and living areas on the second. Aesthetically, you'll benefit by more light, better views, and varied ceiling heights. Plus, downstairs sleeping areas will naturally remain comfortably cooler.

The Thermal Envelope

A home's "thermal envelope" shields the living space from the outdoors. The tighter the envelope, or "seal," the more efficiently your home will operate and the greater your energy savings. The overall design, building techniques, and quality of construction of your home will determine how tightly it is sealed from the elements. Specific areas to address with your builder include:

Air leakage: Takes place when air enters or leaves the home through gaps between framing materials, plumbing and wiring holes, or around improperly installed doors and windows. Ask your contractor what

Expensive windows may seem like a luxury in the planning stage, but can be among the best ways to save on heating and cooling bills down the road.

CONSERVE AND SAVE

With the greater demand for energy efficiency throughout the marketplace, the selection of energy efficient products is better than ever. In addition to the typical big-ticket items, like furnaces and refrigerators, Energy Star offers suggestions on other products like:

☑ **Light**
The right bulbs can significantly reduce energy bills and time spent changing them. Smart lighting systems also can be controlled from afar, or feature automatic shutoff.

☑ **Toilets and Faucets**
Low-flow toilets and faucets can save water and energy.

☑ **Home Electronics**
Home audio systems, televisions, and even cordless phones can be designed to save energy.

☑ **Office Equipment**
Those always-on items like computer monitors and printers can offer vast energy savings. ∎

steps are taken to minimize air loss. Also, consider having a "blower" test conducted by a third party on your finished home to find possible leaks before you sign off.

Air ducts: A typical home loses 20 to 30 percent of the air forced through its ventilation system. The culprit: ill-fitting ducts that allow air to escape, causing costly losses of heat and air conditioning. To optimize your system's efficiency, ensure that your builder has properly sealed and insulated all ducts and joints, especially those routed through attics and basements, where temperatures may vary widely from the home's living spaces.

Thermal insulation: The type and amount of insulation required in new homes varies by climate. Thermal insulation is assigned an "R-value" based upon its ability to resist heat; the higher the number, the greater the material's ability to keep your home warmer in the winter and cooler in the summer. Check with local utility companies and professional home-building associations to find your area's recommended R-value. Keep in mind that living spaces should be separated from attics, basements, and garages by insulated barriers.

Windows: When selecting windows for your new home, look for double-glazed or double-paned units that offer twice the insulation of single-paned models. Also, shop for windows with a transparent low-emissivity (low-e) coating on the glass that helps to reduce heat loss. Manufacturers have made the job easier by assigning windows a rating for purposes of comparison. The National Fenestration Rating Council assigns each encased window manufactured in the U.S. a "U-factor." In this case, the lower the U-factor, the better the insulating ability of the window. Once installed, your builder should weatherstrip all windows to eliminate air leaks.

Heating and Cooling Systems

Installing the correct-sized heating and cooling equipment in your home will guarantee comfort as well as savings. For maximum efficiency, forced-air furnace and air-condition-

ing units should be tailored to the square footage of your home. Once again, manufacturers have assigned ratings that meet industry standards for performance and efficiency. Look for furnaces with an Annual Fuel Utilization Efficiency (AFUE) rating of at least 80 percent and central air-conditioning units with a Seasonal Energy Efficiency Rating (SEER) of at least 12. Regardless of the system you choose, you'll want to make sure your builder installs an energy-saving programmable thermostat to regulate your indoor climate. One more tip: To keep your equipment running in top form, mark your calendar to change air filters at least twice a year once you've moved into your new home.

Water

Talk to your contractor about installing your hot-water heater off the kitchen or laundry room, rather than in an unheated basement. Not only will you minimize the distance that the water travels to point of use, but locating the tank in a warmer area of the home means it will take less energy to heat it. Also, by simply installing low-flow faucets, showerheads, and toilets, your household can easily save hundreds of gallons of water per year. In the near future, watch for instant hot-water heaters to make their way to the U.S. residential market. Already popular in Europe, these fuel-efficient systems eliminate holding tanks by instantly heating water as it travels through the pipes.

Appliances

To select the best appliances for your home, start by taking a look at your family's needs and matching those with the many models available. For example, buying a refrigerator that's too large can waste energy and money; on the other hand, one that's too small for your family adds up to extra trips to the market. Next, look for appliances that carry the Energy Star® label.

Everything from faucets to stove-tops offer possible energy savings in the long term.

This program, developed by the Environmental Protection Agency, is your best guide to selecting major appliances that use less energy and cost less to operate than similar models in the same category. How much can you save? A typical household that does approximately 400 loads of laundry per year would save 7,000 gallons of water, as well as the energy it takes to heat it, by choosing an Energy Star®-qualified washer.

Lighting

Use dimmer switches and motion-detector sensors on household lights to extend bulb life and automatically turn lights out when that area of the home is not in use. Use compact fluorescent light bulbs in place of traditional incandescent lights. Though these bulbs cost up to $15 apiece, you can expect an extended bulb life of up to 10 times longer than incandescent bulbs.

TEN MONEY-SAVING IDEAS

1. Look for a so-called "problem lot"—a hillside, narrow, or in-fill property. These might not sell as quickly or for as high of a price, but the right plan and a capable contractor can make them perfect for your new home.

2. Buy low-maintenance building materials like vinyl siding and metal roofing. Even if they are slightly more expensive at installation, they will pay for themselves in the long run.

3. Collect salvaged materials from demolition sites. Old barnwood, used bricks, and distinctive wood doors can add character to a home without exorbitant cost.

4. Splurge only on those things that you truly cannot live without. But don't skimp on structural components, or windows, since those will add to the safety and energy-efficiency of your home for years to come.

5. Don't overbuild for your neighborhood. A home that is bigger and better than any other in its area will not command a fair price at resale.

6. Monitor construction allowances as the home is being built to ensure that you are getting what you asked for (and are paying for).

7. Try to avoid site-preparation charges like hauling in-fill dirt, grading, clearing trees, or blasting rocks. Choose the best site you can afford and pick a plan that fits that site or can be modified to better suit it.

8. Avoid change orders—the changes in materials or blueprints that invariably occur in the midst of the building process. Not only do change orders cost more money, they add considerable time and frustration to the building process.

9. If you really want ceramic tile or hardwood flooring but it's beyond the budget, consider vinyl flooring. Vinyl makes a good underlayment, and the tile or wood can be installed right on top of it at a later date.

10. Do you really need a three-car garage? If you only have two vehicles but were counting on the extra bay for storage space, consider other areas of the home that will work just as well—attic space, space under a stairwell, or a spare bedroom. Or put up a garden shed, which is cheaper than building a huge garage and often more convenient.

YOUR FINAL INSPECTION

Once you've navigated the planning and building processes, there are a few more hurdles before you can move into your new home. Most important among those are the inspection and walk-through.

The local building department is required to complete a "final," meaning final inspection, for every new house that is built. The department will send an official to your new home to check the validity of previous inspections on the inspection card, and to ensure that building code provisions have been met. As the name implies, this will be the last time these inspections are made before you move in. It is a good idea to follow the inspector as he or she is making the rounds to ask any questions as they may arise.

The inspector will not be making any intrusive actions such as drilling or digging, so be prepared for a mainly visual inspection, focusing on mechanical, plumbing, and electrical systems, and flooring. He or she will also take a look at the design of staircases and handrails, ventilation systems, light fixtures, and other areas of the house that could potentially cause harm to an occupant if they are improperly designed. If there are missing components, such as vent registers and face plates for the ventilation system, they will have to be remedied and the inspector will be required to return at a later date to sign the card and effectively approve the house for occupancy.

Codes vs. Quality

A house that is compliant with building codes is not necessarily well-constructed. Remember that inspection is the process that ensures that minimum standards for health and safety have been met; it does not involve assessing quality or aesthetic standards of work. The inspector will have nothing to do with issues such as shoddy workmanship, unless it puts an occupant in danger. These issues will be taken up with your builder when the two of you take your 'walk-through' of your new home.

After the final inspection has been completed and the inspector has signed off on the card, the builder submits the card and any other required

SMART ADVICE

Learning how to identify items on your blueprints will help you stay involved in the process and plan for the space in your new home.

Your builder, or one of their sales reps, will accompany you on your final walk-through.

FINISHING
TOUCHES

As all homeowners know, your home is never "done." But with a new home, you can spend your time beautifying your property, rather than maintaining it. A few ideas for once you move in:

☑ **Green Thumb**
Professional landscape designs can add tremendous curb appeal and value to a home.

☑ **Hot Stuff**
Add a hot tub to your deck and you can have your own private spa.

☑ **Cash in Your Bonus**
Down the road you may want to finish off your bonus space, whether you need more room or just want to add to your home's resale value. ■

documents to the building department in order to secure a Certificate of Occupancy (C.O.). The building department, depending on their backlog, issues the C.O. to you, hopefully before your close of escrow. On occasion, they will issue a temporary Certificate of Occupancy, contingent on the actual one proceeding through its processes and reviews, to help you avoid issues with getting moved in or securing your interest rate or mortgage loan. The process of transferring title and handling the house begins when you receive the C.O.

YOUR WALK-THROUGH

The walk-through, completed after the final inspection and approval of the building department, is your opportunity to inspect the quality of workmanship, to review the operation and maintenance of systems and products, to point out any items that need touching up, and to ask your builder any questions about your new house.

Anticipating questions and concerns that you may have, some builders will conduct an internal inspection on their own a few days before they tour with you, and will compile a "punch list." The punch list is a roster of items that will need to be addressed either

before your move-in date, or fairly soon afterwards. It usually contains anything that may be considered imperfect or that could cause you surprise or confusion when you accompany him or her on your walk-through, such as details in the operation of various systems in your home.

Also included on the punch list are minor repairs, such as broken light bulbs, paint touch-ups, or loose tiles which will usually not take more than an hour or two of a general carpenter's time to fix. You are free to amend the list during your walk-through, and it is advisable to insist on a target repair date for these items. After close of escrow, you are the legal owner of your home. While you may choose a date that falls after the close, you have more leverage with your builder before that time.

The Timing

Ideally, the builder, or one of his or her sales representatives or superintendents, will schedule a date for the walk-through that falls before close of escrow and soon after the completion of the final inspection. You'll meet with the builder's representative to outline the purpose of the walk-through, your roles and responsibilities and those of the builder, and to discuss items on the punch list or any issues of concern to you.

HOW TO READ A BLUEPRINT

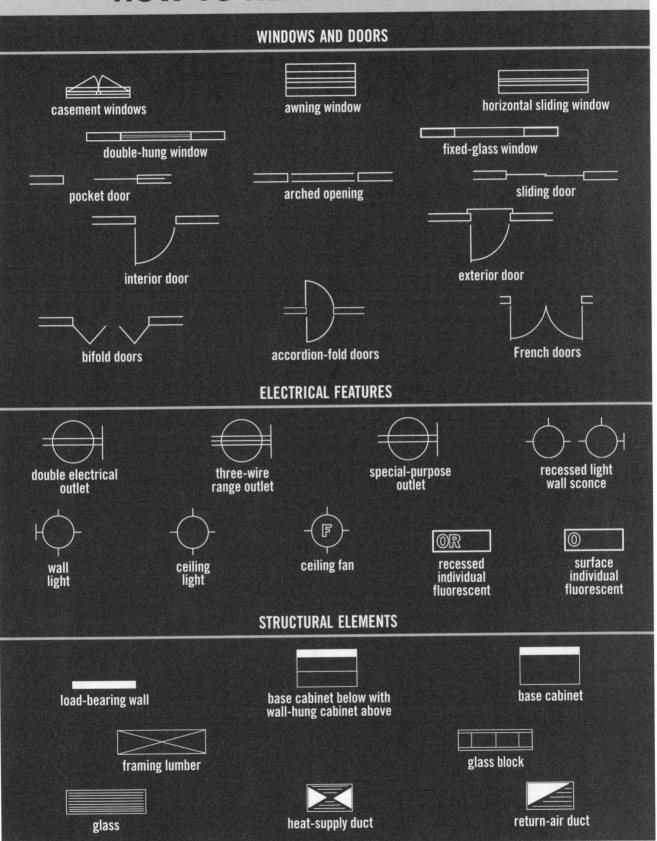

WINDOWS AND DOORS

casement windows

awning window

horizontal sliding window

double-hung window

fixed-glass window

pocket door

arched opening

sliding door

interior door

exterior door

bifold doors

accordion-fold doors

French doors

ELECTRICAL FEATURES

double electrical outlet

three-wire range outlet

special-purpose outlet

recessed light wall sconce

wall light

ceiling light

ceiling fan

recessed individual fluorescent

surface individual fluorescent

STRUCTURAL ELEMENTS

load-bearing wall

base cabinet below with wall-hung cabinet above

base cabinet

framing lumber

glass block

glass

heat-supply duct

return-air duct

By the end, everyone is eager to finish up the home-building process. But don't let that keep you from speaking up if you have questions or concerns during the walk-through.

SECOND-HOME CHECKLIST

Thinking of joining the growing second-home market? Here are some things to keep in mind:

☑ **Location**
You'll want your vacation get-away to be close enough to your year-round home so that you can realistically get away to it on a whim.

☑ **Finances**
Build a second home for the right reasons. They rarely make a great investment, since resale values of vacation homes often lag behind traditional homes, and rental income is often disappointing (and gets taxed).

☑ **The Future**
Planning to retire to your favorite vacation spot in the future? It makes sense to think ahead when you're building your vacation home to a time when you might live there year-round. ■

It is during this meeting where the builder may present you with a homeowner's handbook or binder that delineates a variety of information and instructions regarding the products and systems in your home, warranty details, contact procedures, and often a list of subcontractors and emergency services for your future use. Sometimes included in the binder are courtesy items, such as coupons for household items or a certificate for paint touch-ups after you move in. The representative will sometimes take this opportunity to explain the builder's referral system and include incentives for you if you recommend him or her to another potential home-builder.

Walk-throughs can take from one to four hours and average about 90 minutes, depending on the home and the scope established by the builder. Generally, walk-throughs will produce the best results if they are completed around midday when there are no shadows or glare to distort your view. Your builder may choose to use a checklist, or he or she may simply indicate punch-list items and advise you to take notes and write down any questions as they arise.

Either way, it is your responsibility to ask questions in order to understand the components of your new home. If you need to know how to program your new electronic thermostat or who to call for what issue, this is the time to document those questions.

Speak Up

Workmanship items such as gaps between finishes should be pointed out as well. Such issues may be subjective, but are worth noting on your punch list and can often be easily fixed to your standards. Also, be sure to seek out and document incomplete or missing items, anything that doesn't match the blueprints or specifications, any systems that aren't working properly, damaged fixtures, unclean conditions, etc.

When you are finished with the walk-through, you and the builder should sit and review the punch list again, this time including any items that were added along the way. During this meeting, or once the punch list is completed, the builder will ask you to sign off on the condition of the house indicating that its quality and workmanship are up to par.

You may feel intimidated to point out errors or problems to the builder during the walk-through, but remember: this will be your home, and this is the last chance—and best opportunity—to suggest improvements and ask questions. ■

Twin dormers and a front porch provide a welcoming exterior on Design HPK0400135 (see page 139 for details).

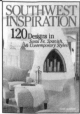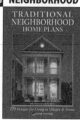

HomePlanners wants your building experience to be as pleasant and trouble-free as possible.
That's why we've expanded our library of do-it-yourself titles to help you along.

31 NATURAL LIGHT

223 Sunny home plans for all regions.
240 pgs. $8.95 NA

32 NOSTALGIA

100 Time-Honored designs updated with today's features.
224 pgs. $14.95 NOS

33 DREAM HOMES

50 luxury home plans. Over 300 illustrations.
256 pgs. $19.95 SOD2

34 NARROW-LOT

245 versatile designs up to 50 feet wide.
256 pgs. $9.95 NL2

35 SMALL HOUSES

Innovative plans for sensible lifestyles.
224 pgs. $8.95 SM2

36 OUTDOOR

74 easy-to-build designs, lets you create and build your own backyard oasis.
128 pgs. $9.95 YG2

37 GARAGES

145 exciting projects from 64 to 1,900 square feet.
160 pgs. $9.95 GG2

38 PLANNER

A Planner for Building or Remodeling your Home.
318 pgs. $17.95 SCDH

39 HOME BUILDING

Everything you need to know to work with contractors and subcontractors.
212 pgs. $14.95 HBP

40 RURAL BUILDING

Everything you need to know to build your home in the country.
232 pgs. $14.95 BYC

41 VACATION HOMES

Your complete guide to building your vacation home.
224 pgs. $14.95 BYV

42 DECKS

A brand new collection of 120 beautiful and practical decks.
144 pgs. $9.95 DP2

43 GARDENS & MORE

225 gardens, landscapes, decks and more to enhance every home.
320 pgs. $19.95 GLP

44 EASY-CARE

41 special landscapes designed for beauty and low maintenance.
160 pgs. $14.95 ECL

45 BACKYARDS

40 designs focused solely on creating your own specially themed backyard oasis.
160 pgs. $14.95 BYL

46 BEDS & BORDERS
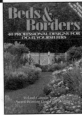
40 Professional designs for do-it-yourselfers
160 pgs. $14.95 BB

B O O K   O R D E R   F O R M

YES! PLEASE SEND ME THE BOOKS I'VE INDICATED:

To order your books, just check the box of the book numbered below and complete the coupon. We will process your order and ship it from our office within two business days. Send coupon and check (in U.S. funds).

❑ 1:IKI $12.95	❑ 17:WP2 ....$17.95	❑ 33:SOD2 ....$19.95
❑ 2:OS2 ....$9.95	❑ 18:650 ....$8.95	❑ 34:NL2 ....$9.95
❑ 3:MO2 ....$9.95	❑ 19:SI $14.95	❑ 35:SM2 ....$8.95
❑ 4:TS2 ....$9.95	❑ 20:DAG2 ....$17.95	❑ 36:YG2 ....$9.95
❑ 5:VS3 ....$9.95	❑ 21:COOL $10.95	❑ 37:GG2 ....$9.95
❑ 6:HH $9.95	❑ 22:CM2 ....$10.95	❑ 38:SCDH $17.95
❑ 7:FCP $10.95	❑ 23:PN $14.95	❑ 39:HBP $14.95
❑ 8:CN $9.95	❑ 24:SW $10.95	❑ 40:BYC $14.95
❑ 9:BS $8.95	❑ 25:SNG $12.95	❑ 41:BYV $14.95
❑ 10:UH $15.95	❑ 26:TND $12.95	❑ 42:DP2 ....$9.95
❑ 11:ENC3 ....$9.95	❑ 27:CC $12.95	❑ 43:GLP $19.95
❑ 12:SUN $9.95	❑ 28:GV $10.95	❑ 44:ECL $14.95
❑ 13:AH2 ....$9.95	❑ 29:MFH $17.95	❑ 45:BYL $14.95
❑ 14:VDH2 ....$15.95	❑ 30:WF $10.95	❑ 46:BB $14.95
❑ 15:EDH3 ....$16.95	❑ 31:NA $8.95	
❑ 16:LD3 ....$12.95	❑ 32:NOS $14.95	

Books Subtotal $ _____
ADD Postage and Handling (allow 4–6 weeks for delivery) $ 4.00
Sales Tax: (AZ & MI residents, add state and local sales tax.) $ _____
YOUR TOTAL (Subtotal, Postage/Handling, Tax) $ _____

YOUR ADDRESS (PLEASE PRINT)

Name _____

Street _____

City _____ State _____ Zip _____

Phone (_____) _____ — _____

YOUR PAYMENT

TeleCheck® Checks By Phone℠ available

Check one: ❑ Check ❑ Visa ❑ MasterCard ❑ American Express

Required credit card information:

Credit Card Number _____

Expiration Date (Month/Year) / _____

Signature Required _____

HomePlanners
3275 W. Ina Road, Suite 220, Dept. BK, Tucson, AZ 85741

[HPK04]

Canadian Customers Order Toll Free 1-877-223-6389

COPYRIGHT DOS & DON'TS

Blueprints for residential construction (or working drawings, as they are often called in the industry) are copyrighted intellectual property, protected under the terms of United States Copyright Law and, therefore, cannot be copied legally for use in building. However, we've made it easy for you to get what you need to build your home, without violating copyright law. Following are some guidelines to help you obtain the right number of copies for your chosen blueprint design.

COPYRIGHT DO

■ Do purchase enough copies of the blueprints to satisfy building requirements. As a rule for a home or project plan, you will need a set for yourself, two or three for your builder and subcontractors, two for the local building department, and one to three for your mortgage lender. You may want to check with your local building department or your builder to see how many they need before you purchase. You may need to buy eight to 10 sets; note that some areas of the country require purchase of vellums (also called reproducibles) instead of blueprints. Vellums can be written on and changed more easily than blueprints. Also, remember, plans are only good for one-time construction.

■ Do consider reverse blueprints if you want to flop the plan. Lettering and numbering will appear backward, but the reversed sets will help you and your builder better visualize the design.

■ Do take advantage of multiple-set discounts at the time you place your order. Usually, purchasing additional sets after you receive your initial order is not as cost-effective.

■ Do take advantage of vellums. Though they are a little more expensive, they can be changed, copied, and used for one-time construction of a home. You will receive a copyright release letter with your vellums that will allow you to have them copied.

■ Do talk with one of our professional service representatives before placing your order. They can give you great advice about what packages are available for your chosen design and what will work best for your particular situation.

COPYRIGHT DON'T

■ Don't think you should purchase only one set of blueprints for a building project. One is fine if you want to study the plan closely, but will not be enough for actual building.

■ Don't expect your builder or a copy center to make copies of standard blueprints. They cannot legally—most copy centers are aware of this.

■ Don't purchase standard blueprints if you know you'll want to make changes to the plans; vellums are a better value.

■ Don't use blueprints or vellums more than one time. Additional fees apply if you want to build more than one time from a set of drawings. ■

hanley ▲ wood
HomePlanners
ORDERING IS EASY

HANLEY WOOD HOMEPLANNERS HAS EVERYTHING YOU NEED TO BUILD THE home of your dreams, and with more than 50 years of experience in the industry, we make it as easy as possible for you to reach those goals. Just follow the steps on these pages and you'll receive a high-quality, ready-to-build set of home blueprints, plus everything else you need to make your home-building effort a success.

WHERE TO BEGIN?
1. CHOOSE YOUR PLAN

■ Browsing magazines, books, and eplans.com can be an exciting and rewarding part of the home-building process. As you search, make a list of the things you want in your dream home—everything from number of bedrooms and baths to details like fireplaces or a home office.

■ Take the time to consider your lot and your neighborhood, and how the home you choose will fit with both. And think about the future—how might your needs change if you plan to live in this house for five, 10, or 20 years?

■ With thousands of plans available, chances are that you'll have no trouble discovering your dream home. If you find something that's almost perfect, our Customization Program can help make it exactly what you want.

■ Most important, be sure to enjoy the process of picking out your new home!

WHAT YOU'LL GET WITH YOUR ORDER

Each designer's blueprint set is unique, but they all provide everything you'll need to build your home. Here are some standard elements you can expect to find in your plans:

1. FRONT PERSPECTIVE
This artist's sketch of the exterior of the house gives you an idea of how the house will look when built and landscaped.

2. FOUNDATION PLANS
This sheet shows the foundation layout including support walls, excavated and unexcavated areas, if any, and foundation notes. If your plan features slab construction rather than a basement, the plan shows footings and details for a monolithic slab. This page, or another in the set, may include a sample plot plan for locating your house on a building site.

3. DETAILED FLOOR PLANS
These plans show the layout of each floor of the house. Rooms and interior spaces are carefully dimensioned and keys are given for cross-section details provided later in the plans. The positions of electrical outlets and switches are shown.

4. HOUSE CROSS-SECTIONS
Large-scale views show sections or cutaways of the foundation, interior walls, exterior walls, floors, stairways, and roof details. Additional cross-sections may show important changes in floor, ceiling, or roof heights, or the relationship of one level to another. Extremely valuable during construction, these sections show exactly how the various parts of the house fit together.

5. INTERIOR ELEVATIONS
These elevations, or drawings, show the design and placement of kitchen and bathroom cabinets, laundry areas, fireplaces, bookcases, and other built-ins. Little extras, such as mantelpiece and wainscoting drawings, plus molding sections, provide details that give your home that custom touch.

6. EXTERIOR ELEVATIONS
Every blueprint set comes with drawings of the front exterior, and may include the rear and sides of your house as well. These drawings give necessary notes on exterior materials and finishes. Particular attention is given to cornice detail, brick, and stone accents or other finish items that make your home unique.

hanley▲wood
HomePlanners

ORDERING IS EASY

HANLEY WOOD
HOMEPLANNERS
ADVANTAGE
ORDER 24 HOURS!
1-800-521-6797

GETTING DOWN TO BUSINESS
2. PRICE YOUR PLAN

BLUEPRINT PRICE SCHEDULE

PRICE TIERS	I-SET STUDY PACKAGE	4-SET BUILDING PACKAGE	8-SET BUILDING PACKAGE	I-SET REPRODUCIBLE*
P1	$20	$50	$90	$140
P2	$40	$70	$110	$160
P3	$70	$100	$140	$190
P4	$100	$130	$170	$220
P5	$140	$170	$210	$270
P6	$180	$210	$250	$310
A1	$440	$490	$540	$660
A2	$480	$530	$580	$720
A3	$530	$590	$650	$800
A4	$575	$645	$705	$870
C1	$625	$695	$755	$935
C2	$670	$740	$800	$1000
C3	$715	$790	$855	$1075
C4	$765	$840	$905	$1150
L1	$870	$965	$1050	$1300
L2	$945	$1040	$1125	$1420
L3	$1050	$1150	$1240	$1575
L4	$1155	$1260	$1355	$1735
SQ1				.35/SQ. FT.

PRICES SUBJECT TO CHANGE

* REQUIRES A FAX NUMBER

plan (#)
READY TO ORDER

Once you've found your plan, get your plan number and turn to the following pages to find its price tier. Use the corresponding code and the Blueprint Price Schedule above to determine your price for a variety of blueprint packages.

Keep in mind that you'll need multiple sets to fulfill building requirements, and only reproducible sets may be altered or duplicated.

To the right you'll find prices for additional and reverse blueprint sets. Also note in the following pages whether your home has a corresponding Deck or Landscape Plan, and whether you can order our Quote One® cost-to-build information or a Materials List for your plan.

IT'S EASY TO ORDER
JUST VISIT
EPLANS.COM OR CALL
TOLL-FREE
1-800-521-6797

PRICE SCHEDULE FOR ADDITIONAL OPTIONS

OPTIONS FOR PLANS IN TIERS P1-P6	COSTS
ADDITIONAL IDENTICAL BLUEPRINTS FOR "P1-P6" PLANS	$10 PER SET
REVERSE BLUEPRINTS (MIRROR IMAGE) FOR "P1-P6" PLANS	$10 FEE PER ORDER
I SET OF DECK CONSTRUCTION DETAILS	$14.95 EACH
DECK CONSTRUCTION PACKAGE (INCLUDES I SET OF "P1-P6" PLANS, PLUS I SET STANDARD DECK CONSTRUCTION DETAILS)	ADD $10 TO BUILDING PACKAGE PRICE

OPTIONS FOR PLANS IN TIERS A1-SQ1	COSTS
ADDITIONAL IDENTICAL BLUEPRINTS IN SAME ORDER FOR "A1-L4" PLANS	$50 PER SET
REVERSE BLUEPRINTS (MIRROR IMAGE) WITH 4- OR 8-SET ORDER FOR "A1-L4" PLANS	$50 FEE PER ORDER
SPECIFICATION OUTLINES	$10 EACH
MATERIALS LISTS FOR "A1-SQ1" PLANS	$70 EACH

IMPORTANT EXTRAS	COSTS
ELECTRICAL, PLUMBING, CONSTRUCTION, AND MECHANICAL DETAIL SETS	$14.95 EACH; ANY TWO $22.95; ANY THREE $29.95; ALL FOUR $39.95
HOME FURNITURE PLANNER	$15.95 EACH
REAR ELEVATION	$10 EACH
QUOTE ONE® SUMMARY COST REPORT	$29.95
QUOTE ONE® DETAILED COST ESTIMATE (FOR MORE DETAILS ABOUT QUOTE ONE®, SEE STEP 3.)	$60

IMPORTANT NOTE   Source Key

■ THE I-SET STUDY PACKAGE IS MARKED "NOT FOR CONSTRUCTION."   HPK04

330

PLAN #	PRICE TIER	PAGE	MATERIALS LIST	QUOTE ONE®	DECK	DECK PRICE	LANDSCAPE	LANDSCAPE PRICE	REGIONS
HPK0400001	A4	5							
HPK0400002	A3	6	Y						
HPK0400003	A2	7	Y						
HPK0400004	C1	8							
HPK0400005	A3	9							
HPK0400006	C2	10	Y	Y					
HPK0400007	A3	11	Y						
HPK0400008	A2	12							
HPK0400009	C1	13							
HPK0400010	A4	14	Y						
HPK0400011	A4	15	Y						
HPK0400012	C2	16	Y	Y			OLA024	P4	123568
HPK0400013	A3	17	Y	Y			OLA091	P3	12345678
HPK0400014	A2	18	Y						
HPK0400015	A3	19	Y						
HPK0400016	A3	20	Y						
HPK0400017	A4	21	Y						
HPK0400018	A2	22	Y						
HPK0400019	A4	23							
HPK0400020	C2	24	Y						
HPK0400021	C2	25							
HPK0400022	A4	26	Y						
HPK0400023	A3	27	Y						
HPK0400024	C1	28	Y						
HPK0400025	C1	29	Y						
HPK0400026	A3	30	Y						
HPK0400027	A3	31							
HPK0400028	A2	32							
HPK0400029	A2	33							
HPK0400030	A2	34	Y						
HPK0400031	A4	35							
HPK0400032	A2	36	Y						
HPK0400033	A2	37							
HPK0400034	A4	38							
HPK0400035	A2	39	Y						
HPK0400036	A2	40							
HPK0400037	A3	41	Y						
HPK0400038	A1	42	Y						
HPK0400039	A2	43	Y						
HPK0400040	A2	44	Y						
HPK0400041	A4	45							
HPK0400042	A4	46							
HPK0400043	A4	47							
HPK0400044	A4	48							
HPK0400045	A4	49							
HPK0400046	A3	50	Y						
HPK0400047	A3	51	Y						
HPK0400048	A2	52							
HPK0400049	A3	53	Y						
HPK0400050	A2	54	Y						
HPK0400051	A4	55							
HPK0400052	A2	56							
HPK0400053	A3	57	Y						
HPK0400054	A2	58							
HPK0400055	A4	59							
HPK0400056	A3	60							
HPK0400057	A2	61	Y						
HPK0400058	A2	62	Y						
HPK0400059	A3	63							
HPK0400060	A4	64							
HPK0400061	A4	65							
HPK0400062	A2	66							
HPK0400063	A3	67							
HPK0400064	A2	68							
HPK0400065	A2	69							
HPK0400066	A2	70	Y						
HPK0400067	A3	71	Y						
HPK0400068	A2	72	Y						
HPK0400069	A3	73							
HPK0400070	A3	74	Y						
HPK0400071	C1	75	Y						
HPK0400072	A4	76	Y						
HPK0400073	A3	77							
HPK0400074	C1	78							
HPK0400075	C1	79							
HPK0400076	A3	80	Y						
HPK0400077	A3	81	Y						

PLAN #	PRICE TIER	PAGE	MATERIALS LIST	QUOTE ONE®	DECK	DECK PRICE	LANDSCAPE	LANDSCAPE PRICE	REGIONS
HPK0400078	C1	82							
HPK0400079	A3	83							
HPK0400080	A4	84	Y						
HPK0400081	A4	85	Y						
HPK0400082	A4	86	Y						
HPK0400083	A4	87	Y						
HPK0400084	A3	88							
HPK0400085	C1	89							
HPK0400086	A3	90	Y						
HPK0400087	A3	91	Y						
HPK0400088	C1	92							
HPK0400089	A4	93	Y						
HPK0400090	A4	94	Y						
HPK0400091	C1	95							
HPK0400092	A3	96	Y						
HPK0400093	A4	97							
HPK0400094	A3	98							
HPK0400095	C1	99	Y						
HPK0400096	A3	100	Y						
HPK0400097	A3	101	Y						
HPK0400098	A3	102	Y						
HPK0400099	A4	103	Y						
HPK0400100	A3	104							
HPK0400101	A3	105							
HPK0400102	A3	106							
HPK0400103	A4	107	Y	Y					
HPK0400104	A3	108	Y						
HPK0400105	C1	109	Y						
HPK0400106	A4	110	Y						
HPK0400107	A4	111	Y						
HPK0400108	A4	112	Y						
HPK0400109	A4	113	Y						
HPK0400110	A4	114	Y						
HPK0400111	A3	115	Y	Y					
HPK0400112	C1	116	Y	Y					
HPK0400113	A3	117							
HPK0400114	A3	118							
HPK0400115	A4	119							
HPK0400116	A4	120							
HPK0400117	A3	121							
HPK0400118	A3	122							
HPK0400119	A4	123							
HPK0400120	A4	124	Y						
HPK0400121	A4	125	Y						
HPK0400122	A4	126							
HPK0400123	C1	127							
HPK0400124	A3	128	Y				OLA004	P3	123568
HPK0400125	A3	129	Y						
HPK0400126	A3	130	Y						
HPK0400127	A3	131	Y						
HPK0400128	C1	132	Y						
HPK0400129	A3	133	Y						
HPK0400130	A4	134	Y						
HPK0400131	A4	135	Y						
HPK0400132	A4	136	Y						
HPK0400133	A4	137	Y	Y					
HPK0400134	A4	138	Y						
HPK0400135	A4	139	Y						
HPK0400136	A3	140	Y						
HPK0400137	A3	141	Y						
HPK0400138	A3	142	Y						
HPK0400139	C1	143	Y						
HPK0400140	A4	144	Y	Y					
HPK0400141	A4	145	Y	Y					
HPK0400142	A4	146	Y						
HPK0400143	C1	147							
HPK0400144	C1	148							
HPK0400145	A3	149	Y						
HPK0400146	A3	150	Y				OLA001	P3	123568
HPK0400147	C1	151							
HPK0400148	C1	152							
HPK0400149	C1	153							
HPK0400150	A3	154							
HPK0400151	C1	155							
HPK0400152	A3	156	Y						
HPK0400153	A4	157							
HPK0400154	C1	158							

PLAN #	PRICE TIER	PAGE	MATERIALS LIST	QUOTE ONE®	DECK	DECK PRICE	LANDSCAPE	LANDSCAPE PRICE	REGIONS
HPK0400155	A3	159	Y						
HPK0400156	A3	160	Y						
HPK0400157	A3	161							
HPK0400158	C1	162							
HPK0400159	A3	163							
HPK0400160	C1	164							
HPK0400161	C1	165							
HPK0400162	C1	166							
HPK0400163	C1	167							
HPK0400164	A3	168	Y						
HPK0400165	A3	169							
HPK0400166	C1	170							
HPK0400167	A4	171	Y						
HPK0400168	A3	172							
HPK0400169	A4	173							
HPK0400170	A3	174	Y						
HPK0400171	A3	175							
HPK0400172	A3	176							
HPK0400173	A4	177							
HPK0400174	C1	178							
HPK0400175	A3	179							
HPK0400176	A3	180							
HPK0400177	C1	181							
HPK0400178	A3	182							
HPK0400179	A4	183							
HPK0400180	C1	184	Y						
HPK0400181	A4	185							
HPK0400182	A4	186							
HPK0400183	A4	187	Y						
HPK0400184	A4	188	Y						
HPK0400185	C2	189	Y	Y					
HPK0400186	C2	190							
HPK0400187	A4	191							
HPK0400188	C2	192							
HPK0400189	C2	193							
HPK0400190	C1	194							
HPK0400191	C1	195							
HPK0400192	A4	196	Y						
HPK0400193	C2	197							
HPK0400194	C1	198							
HPK0400195	A4	199							
HPK0400196	C1	200	Y						
HPK0400197	C2	201	Y	Y					
HPK0400198	A4	202	Y						
HPK0400199	C2	203							
HPK0400200	C1	204	Y						
HPK0400201	C2	205	Y						
HPK0400202	C2	206							
HPK0400203	C3	207							
HPK0400204	C2	208	Y						
HPK0400205	A4	209	Y						
HPK0400206	C1	210	Y	Y	ODA006	P2	OLA021	P3	123568
HPK0400207	A4	211	Y						
HPK0400208	C1	212	Y						
HPK0400209	A4	213	Y	Y	ODA012	P3	OLA016	P4	1234568
HPK0400210	A4	214	Y						
HPK0400211	C1	215	Y						
HPK0400212	A4	216	Y						
HPK0400213	A4	217	Y						
HPK0400214	C1	218	Y						
HPK0400215	C2	219	Y						
HPK0400216	A4	220							
HPK0400217	C2	221							
HPK0400218	C1	222	Y						
HPK0400219	C1	223	Y						
HPK0400220	C1	224	Y						
HPK0400221	C1	225	Y						
HPK0400222	C2	226							
HPK0400223	A4	227							
HPK0400224	A4	228	Y		ODA006	P2	OLA004	P3	123568
HPK0400225	C2	229							
HPK0400226	C2	230							
HPK0400227	C1	231	Y						
HPK0400228	A4	232	Y						
HPK0400229	C1	233	Y	Y					
HPK0400230	C1	234							
HPK0400231	C1	235	Y						

PLAN #	PRICE TIER	PAGE	MATERIALS LIST	QUOTE ONE®	DECK	DECK PRICE	LANDSCAPE	LANDSCAPE PRICE	REGIONS
HPK0400232	A4	236							
HPK0400233	C1	237	Y						
HPK0400234	C1	238	Y		ODA012	P3	OLA010	P3	1234568
HPK0400235	C1	239	Y	Y					
HPK0400236	C1	240	Y	Y					
HPK0400237	A4	241	Y						
HPK0400238	A4	242	Y						
HPK0400239	A4	243	Y						
HPK0400240	A4	244							
HPK0400241	C2	245	Y						
HPK0400242	C2	246	Y						
HPK0400243	C1	247	Y						
HPK0400244	C1	248	Y						
HPK0400245	A4	249							
HPK0400246	C2	250							
HPK0400247	C2	251							
HPK0400248	C2	252							
HPK0400249	C2	253							
HPK0400250	C1	254	Y						
HPK0400251	C2	255							
HPK0400252	C2	256							
HPK0400253	C2	257							
HPK0400254	A4	258							
HPK0400255	A4	259	Y						
HPK0400256	A4	260							
HPK0400257	C1	261	Y				OLA001	P3	123568
HPK0400258	A4	262	Y						
HPK0400259	C2	263	Y	Y					
HPK0400260	C2	264							
HPK0400261	A4	265	Y						
HPK0400262	A4	266							
HPK0400263	C2	267							
HPK0400264	C2	268							
HPK0400265	A4	269							
HPK0400266	A4	270							
HPK0400267	A4	271							
HPK0400268	C2	272	Y						
HPK0400269	C2	273							
HPK0400270	A4	274							
HPK0400271	C2	275							
HPK0400272	C2	276							
HPK0400273	A4	277	Y						
HPK0400274	C2	278							
HPK0400275	C3	280							
HPK0400276	C3	281							
HPK0400277	C1	282					OLA012	P3	12345678
HPK0400278	C1	283							
HPK0400279	C3	284							
HPK0400280	C2	285							
HPK0400281	C1	286							
HPK0400282	C3	287	Y	Y					
HPK0400283	C1	288							
HPK0400284	C1	289							
HPK0400285	C1	290	Y						
HPK0400286	C1	291	Y						
HPK0400287	C1	292							
HPK0400288	C1	293							
HPK0400289	C1	294							
HPK0400290	C1	295	Y						
HPK0400291	C3	296							
HPK0400292	C3	297							
HPK0400293	C3	298							
HPK0400294	C3	299							
HPK0400295	C3	300							
HPK0400296	C1	301	Y						
HPK0400297	C3	302							
HPK0400298	C1	303	Y						
HPK0400299	C1	304							
HPK0400300	C3	305							
HPK0400301	C3	306							
HPK0400302	C1	307							
HPK0400303	C1	308	Y						
HPK0400305	C3	279							

ORDER ONLINE AT EPLANS.COM

WE OFFER A VARIETY OF USEFUL TOOLS THAT CAN HELP YOU THROUGH EVERY STEP OF THE home-building process. From our Materials List to our Customization Program, these items let you put our experience to work for you to ensure that you get exactly what you want out of your dream house.

MATERIALS LIST

For many of the designs in our portfolio, we offer a customized list of materials that helps you plan and estimate the cost of your new home. The Materials List outlines the quantity, type, and size of materials needed to build your house (with the exception of mechanical system items). Included are framing lumber, windows and doors, kitchen and bath cabinetry, rough and finished hardware, and much more. This handy list helps you or your builder cost out materials and serves as a reference sheet when you're compiling bids.

SPECIFICATION OUTLINE

This valuable 16-page document can play an important role in the construction of your house. Fill it in with your builder, and you'll have a step-by-step chronicle of 166 stages or items crucial to the building process. It provides a comprehensive review of the construction process and helps you choose materials.

QUOTE ONE®

The Quote One® system, which helps estimate the cost of building select designs in your zip code, is available in two parts: the Summary Cost Report and the Material Cost Report.

The Summary Cost Report, the first element in the package, breaks down the cost of your home into various categories based on building materials, labor, and installation, and includes three grades of construction: Budget, Standard, and Custom. Make even more informed decisions about your project with the second element of our package, the Material Cost Report. The material and installation cost is shown for each of more than 1,000 line items provided in the standard-grade Materials List, which is included with this tool. Additional space is included for estimates from contractors and subcontractors, such as for mechanical materials, which are not included in our packages.

If you are interested in a plan that does not indicate the availability of Quote One®, please call and ask our sales representatives, who can verify the status for you.

CUSTOMIZATION PROGRAM

If the plan you love needs something changed to make it perfect, our customization experts will ensure that you get nothing less than your dream home. Purchase a reproducible set of plans for the home you choose, and we'll send you our easy-to-use customization request form via e-mail or fax. For just $50, our customization experts will provide an estimate for your requested revisions, and once it's approved, that charge will be applied to your changes. You'll receive either five sets or a reproducible master of your modified design and any other options you select.

BUILDING BASICS

If you want to know more about building techniques—and deal more confidently with your subcontractors—we offer four useful detail sheets. These sheets provide non-plan-specific general information, but are excellent tools that will add to your understanding of Plumbing Details, Electrical Details, Construction Details, and Mechanical Details. These fact-filled sheets will help answer many of your building questions, and help you learn what questions to ask your builder and subcontractors.

HANDS-ON HOME FURNITURE PLANNER

Effectively plan the space in your home using our Hands-On Home Furniture Planner. It's fun and easy—no more moving heavy pieces of furniture to see how the room will go together. The kit includes reusable peel-and-stick furniture templates that fit on a 12"x18" laminated layout board—enough space to lay out every room in your house.

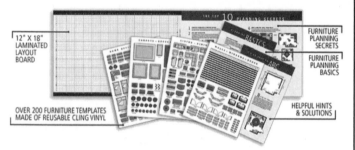

12" X 18" LAMINATED LAYOUT BOARD

THE TOP 10 PLANNING SECRETS

FURNITURE PLANNING SECRETS

FURNITURE PLANNING BASICS

HELPFUL HINTS & SOLUTIONS

OVER 200 FURNITURE TEMPLATES MADE OF REUSABLE CLING VINYL

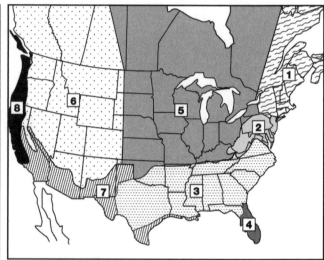

DECK BLUEPRINT PACKAGE

Many of the homes in this book can be enhanced with a professionally designed Home Planners Deck Plan. Those plans marked with a **D** have a corresponding deck plan, sold separately, which includes a Deck Plan Frontal Sheet, Deck Framing and Floor Plans, Deck Elevations, and a Deck Materials List. A Standard Deck Details Package, also available, provides all the how-to information necessary for building any deck. Get both the Deck Plan and the Standard Deck Details Package for one low price in our Complete Deck Building Package.

LANDSCAPE BLUEPRINT PACKAGE

Homes marked with an **L** in this book have a front-yard Landscape Plan that is complementary in design to the house plan. These comprehensive Landscape Blueprint Packages include a Frontal Sheet, Plan View, Regionalized Plant & Materials List, a sheet on Planting and Maintaining Your Landscape, Zone Maps, and a Plant Size and Description Guide. Each set of blueprints is a full 18" x 24" with clear, complete instructions in easy-to-read type.

Our Landscape Plans are available with a Plant & Materials List adapted by horticultural experts to eight regions of the country. Please specify from the following regions when ordering your plan:

Region 1: Northeast
Region 2: Mid-Atlantic
Region 3: Deep South
Region 4: Florida & Gulf Coast
Region 5: Midwest
Region 6: Rocky Mountains
Region 7: Southern California & Desert Southwest
Region 8: Northern California & Pacific Northwest

OUR EXCHANGE POLICY

With the exception of reproducible plan orders, we will exchange your entire first order for an equal or greater number of blueprints within our plan collection within **60 days** of the original order. The entire content of your original order must be returned before an exchange will be processed. Please call our customer service department at 1-888-690-1116 for your return authorization number and shipping instructions. If the returned blueprints look used, redlined, or copied, we will not honor your exchange. Fees for exchanging your blueprints are as follows: 20% of the amount of the original order, plus the difference in cost if exchanging for a design in a higher price bracket or less the difference in cost if exchanging for a design in a lower price bracket. (Reproducible blueprints are not exchangeable or refundable.) Please call for current postage and handling prices. Shipping and handling charges are not refundable.

ABOUT REPRODUCIBLES

Reproducibles (often called "vellums") are the most convenient way to order your blueprints. In any building process, you will need multiple copies of your blueprints for your builder, subcontractors, lenders, and the local building department. In addition, you may want or need to make changes to the original design. Such changes should be made only by a licensed architect or engineer. When you purchase reproducibles, you will receive a copyright release letter that allows you to have them altered and copied. You will want to purchase a reproducible plan if you plan to make any changes, whether by using our convenient Customization Program or going to a local architect.

ABOUT REVERSE BLUEPRINTS

Although lettering and dimensions will appear backward, reverses will be a useful aid if you decide to flop the plan. See Price Schedule and Plans Index for pricing.

ARCHITECTURAL AND ENGINEERING SEALS

Some cities and states now require that a licensed architect or engineer review and "seal" a blueprint, or officially approve it, prior to construction. Prior to application for a building permit or the start of actual construction, we strongly advise that you consult your local building official who can tell you if such a review is required.

ABOUT THE DESIGNS

The architects and designers whose work appears in this publication are among America's leading residential designers. Each plan was designed to meet the requirements of a nationally recognized model building code in effect at the time and place the plan was drawn. Because national building codes change from time to time, plans may not fully comply with any such code at the time they are sold to a customer. In addition, building officials may not accept these plans as final construction documents of record as the plans may need to be modified and additional drawings and details added to suit local conditions and requirements. Purchasers should consult a licensed architect or engineer, and their local building official, before starting any construction related to these plans.

LOCAL BUILDING CODES AND ZONING REQUIREMENTS

At the time of creation, these plans are drawn to specifications published by the Building Officials and Code Administrators (BOCA) International, Inc.; the Southern Building Code Congress International, (SBCCI) Inc.; the International Conference of Building Officials (ICBO); or the Council of American Building Officials (CABO). These plans are designed to meet or exceed national building standards. Because of the great differences in geography and climate throughout the United States and Canada, each state, county, and municipality has its own building codes, zone requirements, ordinances, and building regulations. Your plan may need to be modified to comply with local requirements. In addition, you may need to obtain permits or inspections from local governments before and in the course of construction. We authorize the use of the blueprints on the express condition that you consult a local licensed architect or engineer of your choice prior to beginning construction and strictly comply with all local building codes, zoning requirements, and other applicable laws, regulations, ordinances, and requirements. Notice: Plans for homes to be built in Nevada must be redrawn by a Nevada-registered professional. Consult your building official for more information on this subject.

TERMS AND CONDITIONS

These designs are protected under the terms of United States Copyright Law and may not be copied or reproduced in any way, by any means, unless you have purchased reproducibles which clearly indicate your right to copy or reproduce. We authorize the use of your chosen design as an aid in the construction of one single- or multi-family home only. You may not use this design to build a second or multiple dwellings without purchasing another blueprint or blueprints or paying additional design fees.

HOW MANY BLUEPRINTS DO YOU NEED?

Although a four-set building package may satisfy many states, cities, and counties, some plans may require certain changes. For your convenience, we have developed a reproducible plan, which allows you to take advantage of our Customization Program, or to have a local professional modify and make up to 10 copies of your revised plan. As our plans are all copyright protected, with your purchase of the reproducible, we will supply you with a copyright release letter. The number of copies you may need: 1 for owner, 3 for builder, 2 for local building department, and 1-3 sets for your mortgage lender.

DISCLAIMER

The designers we work with have put substantial care and effort into the creation of their blueprints. However, because we cannot provide on-site consultation, supervision, and control over actual construction, and because of the great variance in local building requirements, building practices, and soil, seismic, weather, and other conditions, **WE MAKE NO WARRANTY OF ANY KIND, EXPRESS OR IMPLIED, WITH RESPECT TO THE CONTENT OR USE OF THE BLUEPRINTS, INCLUDING BUT NOT LIMITED TO ANY WARRANTY OF MERCHANTABILITY OR OF FITNESS FOR A PARTICULAR PURPOSE. ITEMS, PRICES, TERMS, AND CONDITIONS ARE SUBJECT TO CHANGE WITHOUT NOTICE.**

IT'S EASY TO ORDER JUST VISIT EPLANS.COM OR CALL TOLL-FREE 1-800-521-6797

OPEN 24 HOURS, 7 DAYS A WEEK
If we receive your order by 3:00 p.m. EST, Monday-Friday, we'll process it and ship within two business days. When ordering by phone, please have your credit card or check information ready.

CANADIAN CUSTOMERS
Order Toll Free 1-877-223-6389

ONLINE ORDERING
Go to: www.eplans.com

After you have received your order, call our customer service experts at 1-888-690-1116 if you have any questions.

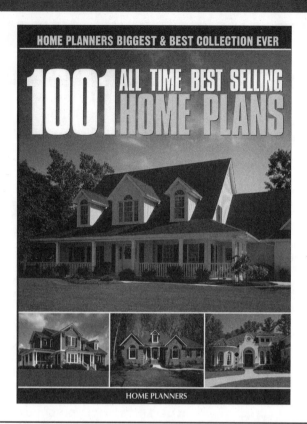
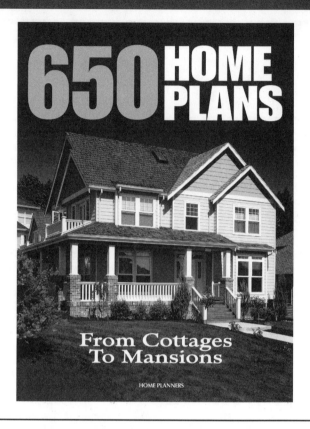
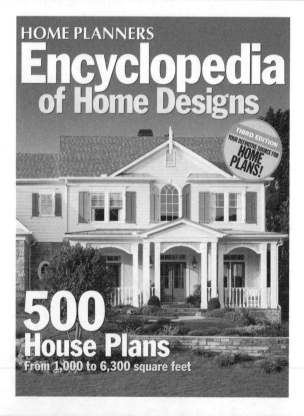